THE THIRD WORLD WAR SCARE IN BRITAIN

The Third World War Scare in Britain

A Critical Analysis

Philip A. G. Sabin
Lecturer in War Studies, King's College, London
Research Associate, International Institute for Strategic Studies, London

Foreword by Lawrence Freedman
Professor of War Studies, King's College, London

MACMILLAN

First published 1986

Published by
THE MACMILLAN PRESS LTD
Houndmills, Basingstoke, Hampshire RG21 2XS
and London
Companies and representatives
throughout the world

Typeset by Vine & Gorfin Ltd, Exmouth, Devon

Printed and bound in Great Britain by
Anchor Brendon Limited, Tiptree, Essex

British Library Cataloguing in Publication Data
Sabin, Philip A. G.
The Third World War scare in Britain : a
critical analysis.
1. World War III
I. Title
303.4'9   U313
ISBN 0-333-40778-4

To my parents

Alexander asked the Celtic envoys what they were most afraid of in this world, hoping that the power of his own name had got as far as their country, or even further, and that they would answer, 'You, my lord.' However, he was disappointed, for the Celts, who lived a long way off in country not easy to penetrate, and who could see that Alexander's expedition was directed elsewhere, replied that their worst fear was that the sky might fall on their heads . . .

Arrian, The Campaigns of Alexander (trans. 1971) p. 49.

Contents

Foreword

The horrific consequences of a nuclear war naturally come to mind whenever we begin to contemplate a superpower confrontation or a conflict of any sort in which one or more of the great powers appear to have an interest. We may recognise that most disputes most of the time can be managed without great violence and that the prospect of fighting on any scale, let alone of getting involved in nuclear exchanges, exercises a sobering influence on the practice of international affairs. Nevertheless the risk of something going terribly wrong cannot be excluded and the thought of what 'going terribly wrong' might involve crowds out consideration of less horrendous if more likely possibilities. This colours the public debate on security matters and encourages writing and speeches of the 'mankind at the crossroads' variety. The choice is always stark – 'suicide or survival', 'sanity or madness' – and the decision is urgent: we are on the 'edge of an abyss' with the 'sword of Damocles hanging above on a thin thread'.

This sense of a fundamental decision with the wrong choice leading almost inexorably to an utter catastrophe is a familiar feature of discussion on these matters. It adds a sense of drama and intensity, but at the cost of conveying little of the complexity of the issues, or the extent to which proposed courses of action may have consequences far different from those intended or the degree to which the future might be much more messy and confused than the stark alternatives would suggest. We have avoided becoming either 'red' or 'dead' up to now; why should this not continue? If war does come, would it necessarily take the form of an immediate conflagration or something more restrained and uncertain.

In the 1970s, for example, a number of politicians and pundits suggested that a war could start with a 'standing start' attack by the Warsaw Pact. Soviet advantages in ready forces, especially the 'crack' divisions based in East Germany, and available reserves would mean that they could sweep through to the Channel with NATO unable to mobilise in time to resist. Scenarios such as this were offered with little consideration of the political circumstances in which such a war could come about, as well as the factors that might well make for caution in Soviet military calculations.

The same tendency was apparent in analyses of the prospect of nuclear war. Improbable scenarios, involving, for example, a Soviet attack confined to US land-based missiles that assumed that the US President would respond only with shocked submission and not with the many remaining weapons of retaliation in the US arsenal, were offered as real possibilities. Such scenarios then began to exercise an inordinate degree of influence on US policy. Not surprisingly, the more US policy-makers began to talk of nuclear planning in terms of actual scenarios rather than remote, uncertain and improbable contingencies, the more this encouraged consternation among the populations of the West.

This sense of immediacy, along with the difficulty of discussing nuclear issues in anything other than absolute terms, was fully illustrated during the lively public debate on nuclear policy that was such a prominent feature of British (and more generally European) political life during the first half of this decade. In the course of this debate the wisdom of established policies of nuclear deterrence was challenged as was the proposed introduction of new weapons to support deterrence and the improvement of civil defence preparations in case, by some mischance, deterrence should fail. Although the debate has now subsided, the underlying issues of policy remain. Also left unresolved are the conflicting understandings of Britain's current security position that were brought to bear on this debate and which naturally involved conflicting policy prescriptions.

One stimulus to a revived debate could be a similar deterioration in the international situation of the sort that led to so much anxiety at the start of this decade. In the presence of weapons of such enormous destructive power, many ready for immediate use, it can never be asserted that the risk of disaster is zero, so it is always a matter of judgement as to just how high that risk actually is. In the highly charged atmosphere of the early 1980s it was widely believed that the risk was getting unusually – and dangerously – high. The Soviet invasion of Afghanistan and the stirring of *Solidarity* in Poland, the hostage crisis in Iran, the failure to ratify the 1979 Strategic Arms Limitation Treaty, the hawkish mood in the United States and Ronald Reagan's election to the US Presidency all contributed to this sense of what was described as a 'new cold war'. The fact that a series of decisions on nuclear weapons and civil defence were made, to some extent coincidentally, at the time added a nuclear dimension to the sense of deep international crisis. The absolutist language of nuclear protest (from the hawks as well as the doves) gained credibility in a developing East–West confrontation.

The interpretation of all these events dominated much of the debate at both the popular and specialist level. Were events moving towards the grand and cataclysmic confrontation that had been so feared since the start of the first cold war and the awareness of the power of thermonuclear weapons? Or were we just being provided with indications of how things might start to get out of hand in an even more unsettled and reckless time? Or was this no more than a fine demonstration of how the international system could cope with a higher-than-usual degree of turbulence? To some the answers to these questions were less relevant than the reappearance of the haunting spectre of a nuclear holocaust that had been out of sight and out of mind during the calmer years of *détente* when it had been possible to assume a steady progression to a more orderly world.

In this context deep fears and anxieties can soon get aroused and to some extent manipulated, especially in the context of an intensive political debate in which all involved believed themselves to be playing for the highest stakes. Anyone caught up with this debate could not but be aware of the degree and extent of this fear and anxiety. This could come out in anything from comments over dinner at a friend's house or questions at a public meeting or academic seminars. One vivid memory is of a television interview in April 1980 just after the failure of the US mission to rescue the diplomatic hostages held in Teheran. 'Is this the start of the Third World War?' I thought the question was ridiculous but it turned out to be one that many people were asking. In conversations the next day I discovered that my answer 'Of course, not' had somehow been found to be reassuring.

It is difficult to keep a sense of perspective when events are moving fast and the political argument is getting heated, especially when for their own reasons the various protagonists stress the great dangers that will follow should the policies of their opponents be pursued. It is also difficult to keep a sense of the complexity of the situation, for a heated debate encourages simplification. In this context a failure to convey a frantic alarmism can easily appear as a smug complacency, and an analytical approach as an ivory-tower detachment.

For any participant in this debate, to read Philip Sabin's book is a salutary experience. Philip Sabin has read the major – and a good number of the minor – contributions to this debate and has subjected them to a critical analysis that illuminates the issues at its heart as well as identifying the sources of distortion and exaggeration. He takes us through the vivid portrayals of a future conventional battle in Europe that were designed to encourage remedial action by Western governments as well as the equally vivid and much more horrific portrayals of nuclear war. He is able to make comparisons with the late 1930s when the 'scare' had rather more basis in reality as well as trace the concept of the Third World War in the professional literature of strategic studies. Instead of making assertions about what public opinion 'really thinks', he has mined a rich seam of opinion poll data to back up his argument. However, this is more than a critique of a certain set of ideas that gained currency and popular attention during the early 1980s, or an analysis of the way that this country handles the difficult issues of war and peace in the nuclear age, it is also an important contribution to the continuing debate, with its own distinctive perspective.

The Third World War Scare in Britain reminds us that our dread of nuclear war is no excuse for the suspension of critical faculties nor should it be exploited by lobbyists and protest groups in an attempt to panic us into policies that might not survive a more careful examination. With this lucid and forceful argument Philip Sabin shows how a future debate might avoid the excesses of the past.

King's College, London   LAWRENCE FREEDMAN

Preface

This book had its origins in my anti-nuclear activism as a Cambridge undergraduate in 1979–81. Like many other idealistic students of the time, I felt impelled to cry out against the nuclear arms race and to campaign energetically to 'save the world' from what seemed to be an accelerating slide towards an apocalyptic Third World War. However, the more I learned about the political and historical background to the frightening hardware and rhetoric, the more I came to share the opinion of most defence experts that there is actually very little risk of a major East/West conflict in the foreseeable future. This change of perspective encouraged me to try to analyse in my PhD thesis the outburst of alarm and controversy in which I myself had been caught up. The resulting analysis is presented here, with the aim of providing a comprehensive overview of the recent upsurge of anxiety from the distinctive standpoint of one whose own initial alarm has been tempered by a growing scepticism about the risk of war.

My thanks are due to the members of the War Studies Department at King's College, London, and especially to Professor Lawrence Freedman and Dr Barrie Paskins, for their invaluable advice and encouragement. Professor Michael Howard of Oxford University also provided many useful comments. I am grateful to the polling organisations (Gallup, Marplan, NOP Market Research, Market & Opinion Research International, and the British Broadcasting Corporation) for their help with this study and for permission to quote from their unpublished poll data. Particular thanks are due to Bob Wybrow of Gallup for his considerable hospitality and advice. Finally, I should like to express my gratitude to The Macmillan Press, and to the many other individuals and groups who have helped in the production of this book. Although responsibility for any errors remains mine alone, without the wide-ranging assistance I have received this book could not have become a reality.

King's College, London   PHILIP A. G. SABIN

List of Abbreviations

ADIU	Armaments and Disarmament Information Unit (University of Sussex)
BAOR	British Army of the Rhine
BBC	British Broadcasting Corporation
BOAS	Bulletin of Atomic Scientists
CND	Campaign for Nuclear Disarmament
EEC	European Economic Community
END	European Nuclear Disarmament
FCO	Foreign and Commonwealth Office
HCJ	House of Commons Journal (Fifth Series up to March 1981, Sixth Series thereafter)
HLJ	House of Lords Journal (Fifth Series)
HMSO	Her Majesty's Stationery Office
ICBM	Intercontinental Ballistic Missile
IISS	International Institute for Strategic Studies (formerly the Institute for Strategic Studies)
INF	Intermediate Nuclear Forces
IRA	Irish Republican Army
MAD	Mutual Assured Destruction
MOD	Ministry of Defence
MORI	Market & Opinion Research International
MP	Member of Parliament
NATO	North Atlantic Treaty Organisation
RIIA	Royal Institute of International Affairs (Chatham House)
RUSI	Royal United Services Institute for defence studies
SALT	Strategic Arms Limitation Talks
SDP	Social Democratic Party
SIOP	Single Integrated Operational Plan
SIPRI	Stockholm International Peace Research Institute

1 Introduction

Ten years ago, in the mid-1970s, one could have been forgiven for thinking that the spectre of a devastating Third World War, after haunting the world for three decades, had finally lost its force.[1] There had been flurries of concern about a superpower collision during the conflicts in Vietnam and the Middle East, but nothing to match the sustained anxiety of the original Cold War.[2] H-Bomb tests, 'Ban-the-Bomb' marches and 'eyeball-to-eyeball' confrontations across the Iron Curtain had become little more than disturbing memories, and attention had shifted to the more pressing and down-to-earth concerns of economic stagnation, environmental pollution and the manifold problems of the Third World. Professionals still tended the arsenals and the war plans of the opposed blocs, but they did so against a background of profound ignorance and indifference among the public at large. This indifference was understandable given the prevailing climate of *détente* between East and West, with the signing in 1975 of the Helsinki Accords on European Security and Co-operation seeming to set the seal on the determination of both blocs to avoid a catastrophic war.

The feeling of security was not, however, destined to last. Far from ushering in a new era of peaceful relations between the blocs, the Helsinki conference of 1975 (like the Geneva Summit twenty years earlier) proved to be only the calm before the storm. Over the ensuing decade East/West tension revived, and the spectre of World War Three, which had once appeared almost out of date, returned with fresh force. Some individuals were so worried by the strategic situation that they bought nuclear fallout shelters as a 'hedge against the holocaust', while others took a different view of the action required and gave up their careers to campaign for disarmament.[3] The revival of anxiety about war was intimately associated with a revival of the defence debate which had taken place in the West twenty years earlier, and there were bitter disagreements, both at the popular level and within the defence community itself, about which strategic posture would best reduce the risk of superpower conflict. Although very many individuals remained satisfied with NATO policy and complacent about the continued avoidance of war, the alarm which did develop was so widespread that it approached the level of a true war scare.

Why this upsurge of controversy and concern about the possibility of a Third World War occurred is a highly contentious question, but one

1

which has nevertheless received very little detailed analysis. Those who themselves see a real danger of superpower conflict have regarded the wave of anxiety as a natural consequence of the issue being brought to public attention, while more optimistic observers have tended to see the outburst of concern as an artificial product of frightening news reports and confusion within the defence establishment.[4] The present study, written from a standpoint of scepticism about the real danger of World War Three, will attempt a deeper and more comprehensive analysis of the recent war scare, of how and why it arose, of its relationship to the renewed controversy about defence policy, and of how it is likely to develop in the future.

The British dimension

The anxiety which has grown up over the past decade about the possibility of a devastating Third World War has not been confined to any one particular country or region, but has spread to embrace the globe. Peace movements have flourished in many Western nations, developing countries have expressed their concern, and there have even been a few unofficial protests within the Eastern bloc against the sterile self-righteousness of official 'peace' propaganda.[5] Because the recent war scare has been so widespread, the only way in which it can be examined in any depth is by artificially restricting the scope of the enquiry to a specific geographical area. The present study will concentrate on the anxiety which has developed in Great Britain, the country with which the author is most familiar, and one whose unique blend of strategic characteristics make it an especially useful subject for a case-study of the recent outburst of alarm in the West as a whole.

Britain was not the first nation to be affected by the recent revival of concern about World War Three. *Détente* had been under serious attack by hard-liners in the United States for some years before British hawks began to capture the headlines in the mid-1970s, while the initial flurry of anti-nuclear protest provoked by the neutron bomb episode of 1977–8 aroused more support in Holland and other continental nations than it did in the United Kingdom.[6] However, Britain cannot be claimed to have been dragged into the recent war scare by the bandwagon effect of alarmist warnings from overseas. On the contrary, she herself served in many ways to set the pace for the truly international anxiety which developed from 1980 onwards. General Sir John Hackett's 1978 book *The Third World War* sold over three million copies in ten languages, and the 1984 BBC television film *Threads* about a nuclear holocaust attracted a similarly widespread audience.[7] British academic E. P. Thompson was one of the main driving-forces behind the formation of the European Nuclear Disarmament Movement, and the even more ambitious World Disarmament Campaign was also a largely British initiative.[8] It is therefore reasonable to take Britain as a test case for an analysis of the recent war scare.

For reasons which will be discussed at length in Chapter 3, it is difficult to judge how the depth of the recent British anxiety about World War Three has compared with that in other Western nations. An opinion poll in 1983 found that war fears in Britain matched those in the United States and considerably exceeded those in other European countries, but survey results alone may not give a true picture of overall concern.[9] Peace demonstrations on the Continent have consistently been larger than those in the United Kingdom, and West Germans in particular have displayed considerable *Angst* about the possibility of a Third World War.[10] The reasons for this apparent dissonance between different nations' opinions and reactions will be discussed in due course, but, for the present, it is enough to suggest that British anxiety about World War Three has at least equalled that in the West as a whole.

British thinking about a possible Third World War has naturally been moulded by specific national influences such as Britain's geographical situation and her strategic role within the Western Alliance. Other factors which have almost certainly affected the way in which East/West conflict is perceived are Britain's particular historical experience and political ethos. However, the fact that the recent war scare has become global in extent means that British anxiety cannot be accounted for in narrowly national terms. This contrasts somewhat with the experience of the 1950s, when the British CND movement was a fairly singular pheno-menon which, although focused on a profoundly international issue, seems to have had its roots in social and political factors at the national level.[11] Parochial explanations are insufficient to account for the British dimension of the more recent war scare, and it will instead be argued that this scare was caused by circumstances which, although particularly evident in Britain, extended also to the many other nations in which anxiety has appeared.

In view of the international nature of the recent concern about World War Three, it is impossible to confine the present enquiry strictly to the fears expressed by Britons themselves. Alarmist or reassuring statements by world figures have naturally had some influence upon British perceptions, as have certain foreign books and articles about the defence issue.[12] Britain's membership of the NATO alliance has meant that her defence community has been particularly receptive to foreign (primarily American) intelligence material and strategic analysis. More populist American works seem also to have had some influence upon British thinking about East/West conflict, with Richard Nixon's hawkish tract *The Real War* and Jonathan Schell's apocalyptic book *The Fate of the Earth* both selling widely, and a substantial proportion of the British public seeing the 1983 US television film *The Day After* about the outbreak and effects of a nuclear holocaust.[13] Foreign arguments and imagery do not seem to have played a dominant part at any stage of the recent war scare in Britain, but they will be mentioned where necessary, alongside the much more influential factor of international events themselves.

The domestic context

It is very difficult to analyse how British thinking about defence varies within society as a whole, because so many different variables need to be taken into account. Besides the question of optimism or pessimism about war, which forms the subject of the present enquiry, it is necessary to consider the 'hawkishness' or 'dovishness' of an individual's views, how much interest he displays in the defence issue, how knowledgeable he is about it, and finally, how much influence he has upon the policy process. Although the correlation between certain of these variables is often quite strong, it is by no means sufficient to permit the analysis of British thinking about defence according to a single linear scale. To make matters worse, most of the variables are not themselves linear – an individual may be a hawk on some issues but a dove on others, may be an expert on the technical minutiae of defence but ignorant of the political context, or may have great influence upon the views of the general public but very little upon actual decision-making. A broad overview of the complex pattern of British thinking about defence will now be attempted, using as a basis the criterion of how much time each person devotes to the issues concerned.

The full-time defence community in Britain is far smaller than that in the United States, and is more sharply split between insiders and outsiders. In the former class falls the actual defence establishment of ministers, civil servants and senior serving officers, exercising a virtual monopoly upon security policy formation within the constraints imposed by the Cabinet as a whole. The defence establishment is notably introspective, and its contacts with outsiders tend to be highly formalised and entirely on its own terms. Official government statements and White Papers, and service recruitment campaigns, are the main forms of contact initiated by the defence establishment itself; other contacts occur largely as a reaction to informed discussions and enquiries, parliamentary challenges, and public concern. Conservative administrations are usually more open about defence than Labour ones (which have to tread carefully because of the anti-defence bias of many of their activist supporters), and the rise of parliamentary committees and knowledgeable independent commentators does appear to have eroded the traditional isolation of the defence establishment, but neither political party has in the past encouraged major outside participation in the decision-making process itself, nor allowed insiders to express opinions or anxieties radically at variance with the official line.[14] The result has been that the professional defence establishment, for all its power and expertise, has tended to play a somewhat subdued and stilted role in the public defence debate.

Outside the official hierarchy, the number of people who concern themselves with strategic issues on a full-time basis has increased markedly in recent decades, but is still probably little over 100 in Britain as a whole.[15] These individuals work as university academics, media commentators, or staff members of the various institutes and campaigning organisations associated with the defence field. All are well informed about the strategic situation, with many tending to specialise in one particular area: Michael Howard in military history, Lawrence Freedman in nuclear strategy, Peter Vigor in Soviet studies, David Greenwood in defence economics, and so on.[16] As to policy views, there is a broad spectrum ranging all the way from the hawkish attitudes of Brian Crozier and the Institute for the Study of Conflict to the dovish outlook of Paul Rogers and the School of Peace Studies at Bradford University.[17] The influence of the full-time defence commentators is hard to judge – they have many contacts within the policy-making establishment and dominate the 'expert' side of the public debate, but one cannot help feeling that they are sometimes talking mainly to their own colleagues and to the small minority of outsiders who take a detailed interest in the strategic situation.[18]

Among those who concern themselves with defence on a part-time basis, two groups may usefully be distinguished – those whose interest is enduring, and those who are impelled to take an active role only when they feel that something is wrong. In the former category fall those ex-ministers, retired officers and civil servants who make up for the constraints placed upon them during their term of office by contributing frequently to the public defence debate thereafter.[19] Other regular participants in defence discussions are those few Members of Parliament (from both Lords and Commons) whose interest in strategic issues encourages them to take every opportunity to press their views within their party, the House and the country at large.[20] Backbenchers often enter the defence debate because they have an axe to grind, but there is usually a more even balance between dissatisfaction and support for the status quo among Front Bench spokesmen and one-time members of the defence establishment. As part of the 'official' side of the defence policy process, politicians and ex-practitioners tend to command at least as much influence as do those who base their claims to attention purely upon specialist knowledge.

The revival of international tension and strategic controversy which has taken place over the past decade has encouraged many individuals not normally involved in the defence debate to campaign actively for the adoption of their own preferred policies. Some have championed military strength or civil defence, but the majority have demanded a halt to the arms race and a radical revision of Western security policy. The anti-nuclear case has been backed up by a large quantity of detailed (if contentious) strategic analysis, often produced by professional people such as journalists, academics and doctors with no previous experience of the defence field.[21] Attempts by the disarmers to win the support of various unions, churches and professional institutions have called forth a reaction from members opposed to their ideas, with the result that the defence debate previously monopolised by politicians and strategic experts has spread to embrace a much wider range of participants.[22] However, those taking an active part in discussions on defence remain no more than a tiny minority of the population as a whole.

Only two numerically significant groups of the British public spend more than a small fraction of their time thinking about issues of war and peace. The first group is made up of those hundreds of thousands of individuals who have come to take part in protest movements such as the Campaign for Nuclear Disarmament.[23] The second group, larger and more enduring than the first, consists of those who concern themselves with the practical side of modern warfare, either through participation in the regular or Territorial armed forces or through that vicarious fascination with war and slaughter which is evidenced by the vast number of popular books and magazines about conflict and military hardware.[24] Both anti- and pro-military individuals tend to be more interested in the technical than the political dimension of the defence issue, a characteristic which seems to have played a large part in the development of the recent war scare, and which will be discussed further in due course.

The vast majority of Britons, at all levels of society, have almost no abiding interest in defence or foreign affairs.[25] Events such as the Falklands war or the Russian invasion of Afghanistan do provoke brief flurries of popular interest, but attention soon drifts away when more immediate domestic concerns supervene. Public knowledge about defence is generally very poor – opinion polls in 1980 found that less than two-thirds of respondents knew that there were any nuclear weapons in Britain, while less than one-third knew that 'NATO' stood for the North Atlantic Treaty Organisation.[26] Popular ignorance and indifference about defence issues seem to have been eroded somewhat in recent years by anxiety about World War Three, the sharpened competition for national resources and the revival of debate about the fundamental basis of security policy, but these influences appear for the most part to have done no more than to produce shallow and simplistic opinions where previously there were no real opinions at all.[27]

No mention has yet been made of the central issue of how views about the likelihood and probable nature of a Third World War have fitted in to the pattern of societal variation; this will be discussed at length in Chapters 2 and 3. The purpose of the current section has been to provide a broad overview of the domestic context of British thinking about defence, so that shorthand terms such as 'hawks', 'doves' and 'the general public' will be recognised as very imprecise labels for groups which differ as much internally as they do from society as a whole. Such labels do have to be used if any sense is to be made of the complex pattern of the British defence debate, but their limitations should always be borne in mind, since what is really being considered is the interaction of a large number of heterogeneous individuals who defy simple categorisation, and the most prominent of whom are almost by definition exceptions to the general rule.[28]

Source material and technique

The principal analytical technique employed in the present study will be to try to set the recent war scare in its historical perspective. The evidence on which the enquiry is based has therefore been drawn not only from the past decade and the preceding era of *détente*, but also from British thinking about future warfare in earlier periods, especially that of the original Cold War. There are many similarities between the current wave of controversy and concern about the strategic situation and that which developed in the late 1950s and early 1960s. Simplistic historical analogies may, however, be misleading, and a conscious effort will therefore be made to discern the differences as well as the parallels between the current war scare and those which have taken place in the past.

The character of the source material used for the present enquiry is extremely diverse. This stems partly from the breadth of the subject involved, but mainly from the fact that the investigation has had to cover opinions from all sections of British society. Analyses of defence policy formation usually concentrate their attention upon the influential elite at the apex of the defence community,[29] but the present study, concerned not with the decision-making process but with fears of World War Three, has had to include a whole variety of individuals ranging from politicians and defence experts to disarmament campaigners and the man in the street. This has made it impossible to examine every scrap of the voluminous source material, but a sufficiently large sample has been studied to yield a reliable overview of the evidence as a whole.

Secondary sources have been of only limited and indirect assistance in the present enquiry. Their principal utility has been in providing information on the historical background to the recent war scare, and even in this field recourse has been made to large quantities of primary evidence in order to get the true 'feel' of the periods involved. As to the recent war scare itself, little analysis has yet been produced. The few academic studies which have already appeared about the revived defence debate have been nothing like as comprehensive as earlier works dealing with British thinking about defence in the 1950s and 1960s, and have concentrated more upon people's views about security policy than upon their fears of a Third World War.[30] Secondary sources have been of help with regard to fringe issues such as the strengths and limitations of the opinion poll technique, but on the central issue of the character and causes of the recent war scare it has been necessary to rely almost entirely upon primary source material.

The largest single class of primary evidence is made up of the hundreds of books and pamphlets which Britons have produced about the defence issue in recent years, ranging from thoughtful and informed works such as Neville Brown's *The Future Global Challenge* to alarmist tracts like Michael Pentz's *Towards the Final Abyss*.[31] Journals on defence are the second major class of primary source material, and include professional publications such as *Survival* and *International Affairs* as well as more polemical works like the CND magazine *Sanity* and the short-lived civil defence journal *Protect and Survive Monthly*. Attention has not been confined to those books and journals produced in the United Kingdom – a search has also been made for British contributions in overseas publications, whether volumes of collected essays, or journals such as *Foreign Affairs* or the *Bulletin of the Atomic Scientists*. The third class of primary evidence consists of governmental literature, ranging from official documents and White Papers to the reports of parliamentary committees and the records of parliamentary proceedings themselves.

Media articles make up the fourth major class of primary source material. *The Times* and the *Daily Telegraph* (together with their Sunday equivalents) have been used both as an additional source of information about individual perceptions and as a day-to-day record of the impact of international events upon British thinking about the risk of war. Weekly newspapers such as the *New Statesman*, and popular dailies such as *The Sun*, have also been examined to obtain a different perspective upon media coverage of the defence issue. Radio and television programmes about defence, and films such as *The War Game* shown privately by pressure-groups like CND, have been studied both directly and through reviews and articles in publications such as *The Listener*. The final class of primary evidence has been provided by the results of over a thousand opinion poll questions about defence which have been asked in Britain over the past four decades. This material has been studied through the unpublished files of the polling organisations themselves rather than through the scattered and incomplete news reports of survey findings; full percentage results will be quoted for every poll referred to, but for those who wish to pursue the matter further, the addresses of the pollsters will be given in the Bibliography.

It is the survey data which presents the most specific problems of interpretation, and these problems will be discussed at length in the Appendix. The main difficulties associated with the remainder of the source material are those which always dog contemporary historiography – the problem of attaining a detached perspective, and the fact that all the data is not yet in. No strict cut-off date has been imposed upon the collection of source material because of the continuing appearance of important evidence about the development of the recent war scare, but it should be pointed out that coverage of the period after 1982 has been less complete than that of preceding years. This is a regrettable deficiency, but its implications for the integrity of the forthcoming analysis may not in fact be unduly grave, since the war scare seems to have reached its height in Britain long before the end of 1982, with the ensuing period seeing little more than the institutionalisation and gradual decay of the anxiety involved.

One source-related problem which will not be resolved except by a considerable passage of time is the incomplete and potentially misleading nature of current evidence about the perceptions of many individuals within the defence community. Cabinet records and political memoirs from the 1950s and 1960s reveal how British leaders then were often more anxious about the prospect of war than their public statements at the time revealed,[32] and modern British statesmen may similarly be imagined to have put on a brave face in order to reduce popular concern, or to have masked their doubts about NATO's resolve to use nuclear weapons against a Soviet conventional attack in order to avoid undermining the credibility of the West's deterrent posture. The opposite process may equally well be envisaged, with certain commentators indulging in alarmist exaggeration of the danger of war in order to scare people into adopting their preferred policies. In the absence of more objective evidence, the author's own personal experience leads him to suspect that alarmist or complacent rhetoric is usually not deliberately insincere but stems rather from a concentration upon advocating the preferred policy, to the almost complete exclusion of detached speculation about the risk of war. This important question of advocacy will be discussed further in Chapters 4 and 6.

The approach adopted in the present study will be to systematically analyse various component aspects of the recent wave of anxiety about World War Three. Chapter 2 will consider the different images which people have of a Third World War; Chapter 3 will assess who has been most alarmed and how deep their alarm has been; Chapter 4 will ask why the concern has developed; Chapter 5 will discuss why people have been so fascinated by the idea of a convulsive all-out conflict, and Chapter 6 will examine the impact which the war scare and the World War Three notion itself have had upon the wider defence debate. There will be no attempt to hide the author's own profound scepticism about the likelihood of conflict and about the validity of the whole Third World War concept, but the thrust of the study will be less to directly contradict recent alarmist claims than to try to explain why such a sizeable outburst of concern should ever have taken place if the danger of conflict is actually exceedingly remote.[33] In the conclusion, the various strands will be drawn together in a chronological analysis of the processes behind the recent upsurge of alarm, and some suggestions will be made as to how controversy and concern on the defence issue might in future be channelled into more realistic paths.

2 Images of World War Three

'What will the next war be like?' 'Will it be anything like the last?' These are questions that, in the present state of apprehension or resigned curiosity, are almost daily hurled at anyone who is a student of the grim branch of knowledge which is sometimes called the science of war.[1]

Those words, written by the strategist Liddell Hart in 1937, show that conjecture about future conflict has long aroused widespread interest. Such conjecture has, of course, always been important to professional defence planners, and current official 'scenarios' for World War Three are the latest in a long line of hotly debated and frequently mistaken governmental planning assumptions about 'the next war'.[2] What makes current scenarios different is firstly that they are constructed less from the perspective of individual nations and more from that of the NATO alliance as a whole, and secondly that they are focused less upon the kind of conflict which is most likely to happen and more upon the kind of conflict which it is most important to deter. These two changes have introduced political and strategic distortions into official predictions of future warfare which seem to have played a considerable part in the development of the recent war scare, and which will be discussed further in due course.

Speculation about future conflict has rarely been confined to politicians and military men. Over the last century, especially, concrete images of possible wars have also come to fascinate the British public as a whole. This has led to a proliferation of predictive novels, which have often had great influence upon public opinion. In the Victorian and Edwardian eras, for example, invasion stories such as *The Battle of Dorking* led to popular pressure for improved defence, while in the 1930s, apocalyptic visions like *The Gas War of 1940* served to reinforce public horror of war.[3] In the initial decades of the atomic era, nuclear anxiety seems largely to have been sublimated in tales of science fiction or natural catastrophe.[4] 'Thinking about the unthinkable' was left to sinister American strategists such as Herman Kahn, and when a BBC producer did make a film in 1965 about the effects of nuclear war, it was banned by his superiors as being too horrific (and partisan) to show.[5]

11

Recently, however, images of future conflict have begun to reappear in popular films and literature. One of the principal characteristics of the recent war scare has been the erosion of the taboo which had developed about conflict speculation outside the defence community, and the proliferation of detailed representations (often just as propagandist as their pre-1945 counterparts) of what a Third World War might actually be like.

There is thus a considerable body of evidence available by which to judge both popular and informed images of World War Three. Opinion poll data gives an additional check on public perceptions, and provides some indication of just how detailed the average layman's image of potential conflict actually is. In this chapter, the characteristics of the various images of World War Three will be discussed, and an assessment will be made of how influential each particular image has been among different sections of the British population.

I THE POLITICAL CONTEXT

The antagonists

In historical terms, confidence about the identity and alignment of the combatants in any future war has been the exception rather than the rule. Both popular novels and official war plans have in the past envisaged a wide range of possible antagonists.[6] Something of this uncertainty resurfaced in the era of East/West *détente*, when Sino–Soviet or Sino–American conflict seemed as plausible as a direct superpower collision. The recent war scare, however, has been based firmly upon the military and political confrontation which has dominated the post-war world – that between the Western bloc (including Britain) led by the United States, and the Eastern bloc headed by the Soviet Union. A senior British officer put the matter plainly:

> Who will be the enemy should World War III come? Surely there need be no hypocrisy or beating about the bush. The enemy would be Soviet Russia, presumably supported to greater or lesser extent by other countries forming the Warsaw Pact. The lines of battle have been drawn up for more than thirty years, although as yet there has been no battle. The war has remained cold.[7]

Just as important in producing this certitude as the revival of East/West tension has been the rapprochement between China and the West. The

Chief of the British Defence Staff told a Peking audience in 1978 that 'we both have an enemy at our door whose capital is Moscow', and, two years later, Britain's Minister of Defence remarked of China that 'those who are not against me are for me'.[8] This new outlook has not lessened fears of a Sino–Soviet conflict, but it has strengthened the idea that such a conflict might set off a true 'world war' between Russia and the West.[9] China's likely role in a superpower conflict in which she is not initially involved is rarely considered, and the usual expectation seems to be that it would be predominantly opportunistic.[10]

World War Three is thus seen almost exclusively in terms of a contest between the Warsaw Pact and the Western Alliance. The wartime cohesion of these blocs, and the participation of non-aligned nations in the struggle, is not often considered. In part this is due to the long-standing tendency of conflict predictions to concentrate upon the tangible technical characteristics of future warfare rather than upon the uncertain political context, a tendency which has been reinforced by the decreased relevance of detailed 'balance of power' calculations in the present thermonuclear age. In part, however, the low level of speculation about which nations would be involved in a Third World War seems to stem from the political sensitivity of this topic within the Western Alliance.

Official NATO scenarios for World War Three tend to assume the full participation of all Alliance nations, with only France being a legitimate subject for doubt on account of her absence from the integrated command structure. In order to make this ideal of collective defence credible, NATO planning focuses upon the specific threat which the Alliance exists to deter – that of a direct Soviet attack upon Western Europe. Very little is said by NATO governments in Europe about East/West conflicts stemming from other causes such as an invasion of a European neutral or an out-of-area confrontation between the two superpowers. The result is that strategic discussion is channelled away from political questions of national participation and towards the technical aspects of the great battle in Central Europe, the prevention of which provides the unifying purpose of the NATO organisation.

The question of greatest importance to Britons is naturally the likely role of their own nation in any East/West conflict, and it does seem to be generally agreed that, if a Third World War did break out, the United Kingdom itself would be fully involved. Government spokesmen have repeatedly emphasised that Britain's strategic importance makes such involvement inevitable in the context of a European war.[11] Some members of the peace movement have suggested that Britain might escape a superpower nuclear exchange sparked by a confrontation outside Europe if she expelled American bases, but they see little hope of such evasion while the present situation prevails. The general public probably takes participation in World War Three for granted, given the United Kingdom's central role in World Wars One and Two. It is noteworthy that British involvement in a Third World War is usually seen as a matter of inevitability rather than of conscious choice.

This outlook seems also to affect predictions about the involvement of other nations, and many countries are thought likely to be dragged into war, either by invasion or nuclear bombardment, whether they like it or not.[12] The Warsaw Pact states are expected to be dragooned into participation by Soviet pressure, although their enthusiasm is widely questioned and at least one writer has suggested the alternative extreme of a concerted East European revolt.[13] As for the cohesion of NATO, predictions range from Sir John Hackett's fairy tale scenario in which even neutral nations such as Ireland and Sweden join the Western cause, to Shelford Bidwell's nightmare vision of blunder and confusion in which West Germany is initially deserted by all her NATO allies.[14]

Opinion polls reveal that, in alliance terms, the British public has most trust in the United States, and least in France and the Mediterranean members of NATO.[15] However, the general level of trust is far from high, and a 1983 survey found that over half the British population had little or no confidence that America would defend them if this risked a direct attack upon the United States itself.[16] Similar distrust of allies has occasionally been expressed by outspoken politicians, and it is possible that memories of Britain's isolated stand in 1940 have more resonance within the defence establishment than is generally admitted.[17] Nevertheless, it is the politically anodyne official scenario for World War Three which has acted as the basis for most current anxiety, and considerations of national participation have tended to be overshadowed by the dreadful spectre of the fighting itself.

War aims

Clausewitz, famous for his doctrine that war is 'a continuation of political activity by other means', refused to make any predictions about a given military confrontation unless he knew the political aims of the states involved.[18] Liberal thinkers, on the other hand, have traditionally regarded 'war' as a distinct and abstract entity, somehow independent of practical political objectives.[19] This tendency has reached its apotheosis in the notion of 'World War Three', with military hardware shaping the image of hostilities and political causes then being sought to fit. As one commentator wrote (after a lengthy examination of the technical side of East/West conflict):

> The missing ingredient in our picture of the Third World War is morale. At the moment it is hard to conceive of any cause worth fighting for, so it is hard to imagine anyone willing to fight. And this squares with the facts, for as far as I know there is no cause worth going to war about and therefore no imminent prospect of the war happening. When a cause appears we shall see whether people are prepared to run the risk for it.[20]

The reasons for this disjunction between military and political analysis, which seems to lie at the heart of the recent war scare, will be discussed at length in Chapter 5. For the moment, it will simply be suggested that the principal cause of the widespread reluctance to speculate about what objectives the antagonists might have in any future hostilities has been the unprecedented destructiveness of modern weapons. As many writers have observed, it is difficult to conceive of any political aim which would justify unleashing (or even risking) such terrible devastation.[21] Some commentators have suggested that warring states might still be driven by traditionally acquisitive motives such as competition for dwindling natural resources,[22] but most observers now seem to see the only war aim which could impel East or West to resort to direct military force as being to counter threats posed by the opposing bloc.

The crucial question is, of course, how broadly such threats are defined. NATO has adopted a very narrow definition by pledging to use force only if actually attacked, and its strategy of 'flexible response' is wholly geared to resisting aggression and inducing the enemy to withdraw.[23] There has, however, been something of a resurgence of the 'roll-back' idea of the 1950s among Western hard-liners arguing that there is 'no substitute for victory' in the Cold War,[24] and although such individuals have explicitly disavowed direct military action, the confrontational posture adopted by the United States in recent years has led many Britons to fear that force might be applied actively in a tangled collision with the Soviet Union outside the NATO area.[25] Others have suggested that, if conflict ever did break out, democratic emotion might impel some Western nations to go beyond their purely defensive posture and to press for a more assertive war aim such as the liberation of Eastern Europe.[26] Only a few left-wingers, however, continue to believe in the image of imperialist aggression against a peace-loving socialist camp;[27] the vast majority of Britons see the West's strategic objectives in essentially passive and defensive terms.

There are many who believe that the Soviet Union, also, has basically defensive aims, and that NATO's military posture acts less to restrain than to provoke Russian enmity. Members of the peace movement argue frequently that the behaviour of both blocs is essentially reactive, with fear of enemy attack being the most likely motive for initiating hostilities. As Edward Thompson succinctly put it, 'What is the Cold War now about? It is about itself.'[28] Other commentators are less convinced that Soviet hostility towards the West is an artificial product of the Cold War confrontation (if only because the liberal democracies pose an ideological threat to Russia quite independent of their military posture), but there is nevertheless a widespread feeling that in present strategic circumstances NATO is more likely to be attacked through fear than through ambition. In Michael Howard's words:

> We are not a prey to be devoured. We are a potential threat which might have to be neutralised, reluctantly and in extremis, in full consciousness of all the social, political, as well as military costs involved, and only if all else fails. The Soviet Union would undertake the invasion and occupation of Western Europe without enthusiasm, simply to destroy our military power and ensure our continued debellation.[29]

Not all Britons share this reactive interpretation of Soviet motives. A number of individuals, especially over the past decade, have suggested that Russia's principal political aim is to subjugate the West and achieve world domination.[30] This view has been encouraged both by Marxist dogma and by Soviet planning for an all-out offensive should war with the West ever appear inevitable.[31] Official *Western* scenarios for East/West conflict also tend to support the idea of implacable Soviet aggression, since the passivity of NATO's own strategy requires that the worst construction be placed upon Warsaw Pact capabilities if a politically acceptable scenario is to be produced.[32] This in-built artificiality, and its effect on the recent war scare, will be discussed further in Chapters 4 and 5.

There is very little correlation between perceptions of Soviet aggressiveness and predictions of how intense the fighting in World War Three might be. This appears to be because limited war is seen as more likely to result from fear of mutual devastation than from limited political aims. Hawks who believe in a Russian drive for world domination often envisage the Third World War as a very low-intensity conflict, while doves who remain unconvinced of a Soviet threat nevertheless fear that accident or miscalculation could spark off an all-out nuclear exchange.[33] Nothing could better illustrate the low value placed upon political criteria in most British thinking about World War Three.

There seems thus to be little evidence of coherent predictions about the objectives which East and West might have in any future hostilities. Although British images of a Third World War often do suggest the adoption of particular war aims, this owes less to considered political judgement than to the fact that any conflict scenario is bound to suggest *something* about the motives of the antagonists. It is unusual for politics to come before technology in conflict speculation, especially at the popular level. Even defence experts tend to make a virtue for deterrent purposes of disregarding Soviet intentions and basing their analyses solely upon military capabilities.[34] Attention will now therefore be turned to examining the kind of conflict which modern weapons are expected to entail.

II CHARACTER OF THE FIGHTING

One striking difference between the current war scare and that of twenty-five years ago is that there is now much less agreement about what East/West conflict might actually involve. The term 'World War Three' has recently been applied to various images besides the traditional spectre of an all-out nuclear exchange.[35] Other visions of East/West conflict have existed for a long time, but they have tended hitherto to be divided into neat conceptual compartments such as 'total war', 'limited war' and 'cold war'.[36] What is new is the blurring of these boundaries by concepts such as 'escalation' and 'Finlandisation', and the consequent amalgamation of several different but interlinked images within the overall notion of a 'Third World War'. How important this confusion of imagery has been in sparking the recent alarm will be discussed in due course. First, however, the different images will be examined to reveal exactly what the alarm has been about.

A prolonged confrontation
The most low-intensity concept of East/West conflict is radically different from other British images of World War Three, primarily because it envisages the war as *already taking place*. This notion is not altogether new. The bitter confrontation which actually occurred between the blocs from the late 1940s to the early 1960s was known at

the time as the 'Cold War', and is sometimes even accorded a place alongside World Wars One and Two in modern historical writing.[37] Despite this experience, however, it has been very difficult for Britons to fully adjust to such an unfamiliar image of war. Major-General J. L. Moulton put the problem very well:

> For a century and a half a vision, derived from the Napoleonic period, of armed conflict as a decisive, violent but comparatively short convulsion dominated political and military thought . . . This concept of warfare as a convulsion, disastrous but soon over, continues to dominate political and military attitudes towards conflict to the detriment of our handling of the real problem of today, conflict less violent but indefinitely prolonged.[38]

It was in order to overcome this conceptual barrier (as well as to avoid the pejorative label of 'cold warriors') that certain hawkish writers in the mid-1970s began to describe the East/West confrontation itself as the 'Third World War'.[39] Although this tactic had been conceived much earlier, it became prominent only when the Soviet dissident Alexander Solzhenitsyn used it to try to shock the West out of the complacency of *détente*.[40] The new terminology appealed most to hawkish experts on guerilla warfare and subversion, as illustrated in the following passage by Brian Crozier:

> For more than twenty-five years the countries of the Western Alliance have been preparing themselves against the dread possibility of a nuclear war with the Soviet Union. This war, which the strategists have called . . . the Third World War, has never come, and may never come. Meanwhile, the real Third World War has been fought and is being fought under our noses, and few people have noticed what was going on.[41]

The historical Cold War was said to have been only one phase of this continuing conflict, which some writers claimed had begun before the end of World War Two itself. Although Solzhenitsyn sometimes took the despairing line that the Third World War had already ended in a Western defeat, a more common view was that hope still remained, if the West would only recognise the danger and take immediate action. As to the actual form of the conflict, Brian Crozier gave a useful definition when he described World War Three as:

. . . a war unlike previous ones, without armed hostilities between the superpowers or rival alliances, with fighting mainly in peripheral areas, such as Korea or Vietnam; a unilateral war of expansion and aggression from the Soviet land mass; an ideological war by a counter-church militant; 'fought' mainly with non-military or para-military techniques, such as subversion, disinformation, psychological war, espionage, diplomatic negotiations, military and economic aid programmes, terrorism, guerilla war.[42]

There seem to have been three main differences between this 1970s image of a continuing Third World War and the 'Cold War' concept which had prevailed two decades earlier. The first such difference was that (despite the particular interest displayed by experts on subversion) the conflict was seen as based less upon ideology and more upon geopolitics and the balance of power. Fears of a sinister 'world communist conspiracy' were replaced by anxiety about the policies of the Soviet Union itself, particularly its military build-up and its direct or proxy interventions in the Third World.[43] Even when massive popular peace movements sprang up to oppose Western military programmes, they were regarded as composed more of sincere but misguided liberals than of fellow travellers or 'reds under the bed'.

The second (and somewhat contradictory) change in perceptions of the East/West confrontation was that Soviet strategy in 'World War Three' was regarded as more devious and underhand than in the original Cold War. Instead of engaging in a straightforward contest of rhetoric and brinkmanship, Russia was feared to have lulled the West into a false sense of security by adopting a strategy of indirect approach.[44] Intimidatory 'rocket rattling' had been replaced by the quiet but inexorable pursuit of military predominance. The cultivation of *détente* in Europe was accompanied by continual Soviet attempts to acquire greater influence in the Third World. This *global* dimension of Soviet expansionism was repeatedly stressed by hawkish commentators, who made great play of the threat allegedly posed to the West's oil and mineral resources in Africa and the Middle East.[45]

The third major difference between perceptions of the East/West confrontation in the 1950s and the 1970s was that 'World War Three' was regarded as potentially more decisive than the head-on nuclear stalemate of the Cold War. The combination of Western irresolution with growing Soviet power and influence made many fear that the West could be 'Finlandised' or even conquered without a shot being fired.[46]

Some thought that this could occur gradually, without Russia needing to make any overt challenge, while others believed that the Soviet Union might one day lay aside pretence and present the West with the stark choice of 'surrender or suicide'.[47] The thermonuclear paradox of a 'war without winners' was thus complemented by the inverse notion of a 'victory without war'.

Hawkish support for the idea that the Third World War was already in progress seems to have reached a peak in the later 1970s. Margaret Thatcher adopted this notion in some of her defence speeches, and many other right-wing commentators (including former US President Richard Nixon) also asserted that the real war with Russia was already under way.[48] However, the new terminology never really caught on except as an alarmist gimmick, coming nowhere near to displacing the traditional convulsive image of major conflict, and being almost entirely overshadowed in the 1980s by fears of a 'true' Third World War. Shelford Bidwell probably spoke for many when he wrote that:

> . . . the condition of the world may be seen not as an existent, continuing 'World War 3' but as a *world-wide state of warfare*, first in one locality and then in another, encouraged and damped down according to the advantage likely to be gained or the danger incurred by the two superpowers.[49]

What seems to have made commentators such as Bidwell sceptical of the notion of an ongoing Third World War is not so much a disbelief in the whole *concept* of a low intensity contest between the opposed blocs as an unwillingness to portray it in such all-pervasive and Manichean terms. Although many hard-liners have insisted that Russia's policy is to assail the West by all means short of nuclear war, Britons have been more chary than Americans of seeing the hand of the Soviet Union behind every outburst of conflict in the Third World. There have certainly been many British hawks who have seen an organised campaign of Soviet proxy activity aimed at seizing the West's oil and mineral resourses, but the general view of the global situation has been more equivocal, as illustrated by the following extract from Britain's 1981 Defence White Paper:

> The global challenge to Western interests has loomed large in discussions on security during the past year. It would be wrong to let it either overshadow the threat in NATO's own area, or project an over-simplified pattern of East-West antagonism on the wider

world. Disturbance anywhere, of any origin, offers the Soviet Union fresh opportunities to exploit. But the causes of instability in different states and regions are complex, often owing more to long-standing local rivalries and racial, religious and political tensions than to any outside stimulus.[50]

More influential among the defence community as a whole than the idea of a concerted Soviet proxy campaign outside the NATO area has been an increasing tendency to see the role of Russia's own military power as one of passive intimidation rather than active coercion. The 'age of peace' in the early 1970s prompted a number of academics to re-examine the place of force in international relations, and to argue that latent threats could be just as effective as actual military operations in the achievement of political objectives.[51] British Defence White Papers in the mid-1970s began to stress that Soviet preponderance in Europe was less likely to encourage an actual attack than to enable Russia to overawe and pressurise individual Western states in time of peace.[52] Fears of a shooting war revived in the crisis of 1980, but by 1981, the Ministry of Defence was likening the East/West contest to a chess game in which judicious force deployments could bloodlessly forestall political bullying by the opposing bloc.[53]

Some commentators embraced this concept of 'force without war' with scant reservations, but others pointed out that military preponderance would only have a political effect if it could clearly be translated into a meaningful advantage in an actual conflict.[54] This latter criterion was the main rationale behind the various World War Three 'scenarios' suggested by hawks in the later 1970s. Many such scenarios ended by asserting that the terrible events described would probably never happen, but that the very possibility would intimidate the West in any future crisis, in exactly the same way that Finland was deterred by her palpable vulnerability to military coercion from provoking the wrath of her mighty Soviet neighbour.[55]

This concept of Finlandisation was more subtle than the crude ideas of brinkmanship and nuclear blackmail which had prevailed in the 1950s. Superpower acceptance of Mutual Assured Destruction was felt to have transferred competition from a political contest over which side was most prepared to risk total war to a technical struggle for a preponderance in limited war capabilities which would place the onus of catastrophic escalation upon the opponent. The types of limited war which British thinkers considered most feasible will be discussed later in this chapter. Suffice to say here that, although the alleged Soviet capability for naval blockade of Western Europe or for a counterforce strike against American ICBMs aroused some fears of political intimidation,[56] British anxiety was concentrated upon the disheartening implications of Russia's supposed ability to quickly defeat NATO in a full-scale conventional war. If the West, as was widely thought, would be unwilling to cross the nuclear threshold even amidst the destruction and passion of actual hostilities, how much more would anticipation of this reticence hamstring Western actions in time of peace, when the destruction and passion were merely theoretical.

Such subtle reasoning was common within the defence community, but cut very little ice with outsiders. The general public only barely grasped or trusted even the crudely catastrophic model of nuclear deterrence, let alone the arcane and deceptive logic of the modern strategists.[57] Dovish commentators almost completely neglected the possibility of political intimidation, seeing the renewed Cold War merely as the potential trigger for a nuclear holocaust, and depicting new weapons and strategies as sinister and perilous departures from the straight road of traditional nuclear deterrence.[58] There was thus a wide conceptual gulf between the public at large, who saw the threat of East/West hostilities as very real, and the defence community, which tended to concentrate on the political implications of various artificial conflict scenarios. This dissonance appears to have been of profound importance in the development of the recent war scare, and will be discussed further in Chapter 4.

Limited conventional war

The possibility of an East/West war confined wholly to conventional fighting in a limited area has not been one of the primary causes of anxiety in the recent war scare. Although many have suggested that World War Three need not involve nuclear weapons (as will be discussed in the following section), surprisingly little attention has been paid to the possibility that a direct military clash between the blocs could be subject to further fundamental limitations of intensity and geographical extent. Limited conventional war has usually been seen less as a threat in its own right than as a possible starting point for escalation into a true Third World War.

There are generally thought to be two basic ways in which a direct but limited military clash between East and West could come about. The first involves competitive superpower intervention in a neutral country or region, leading to a conflict confined to that region (just as hostilities between America and China were confined to the Korean peninsula in the 1950s). As was pointed out earlier in this chapter, the NATO defence establishment has been reluctant to speculate about such a conflict outside Alliance borders because of the strain that it would place upon NATO's political cohesion. Independent commentators, however, have been less inhibited, and the possibility of a messy regional collision between East and West has been a major source of anxiety over the past decade. Doves, especially, have laid great stress upon the risk that a superpower conflict might start outside rather than within the territories of the blocs themselves (although their worry has tended to be less that this would provoke a limited contest than that it would quickly lead to catastrophic escalation). As disarmament campaigner Brigadier Michael Harbottle put it:

> The obsession with the European theatre of war and the insistence that this is where the Third World War will be fought and won influences the whole thinking that, so long as mutual balance in nuclear weapons is maintained and control of the battlefield is secured, there will be no Third World War. The flaw in this philosophy lies in the fact that Europe is not the world and the East–West confrontation is not confined within the perimeters of that continent. There are just as serious threats to peace elsewhere in the world . . .
>
> These 'small wars' are the reality of contemporary conflict and should not be ignored; for if they are they can easily escalate to proportions where international efforts are powerless to control them, nor able to prevent the nuclear World War Three which could follow.[59]

Many world trouble-spots outside the Eastern and Western blocs have been seen in recent years as capable of sparking a superpower confrontation, but few such flashpoints have been associated with the idea of a direct local conflict between opposing intervention forces. The two neutral regions in which limited superpower conflict has appeared most likely over the past decade are Yugoslavia and the Persian Gulf. Before Tito's death in May 1980, the Soviet invasion of Yugoslavia which some feared might follow the ruler's demise was one of the standard scenarios for embroiling NATO and the Warsaw Pact in a shooting war.[60] The bloody turmoil in the Gulf, and America's formation of a 'Rapid Deployment Force' to protect Western interests there, has recently aroused even greater anxiety about a regional superpower collision, especially with Iran in the hands of a yet more charismatic but infirm leader than President Tito.[61]

The second possible route to limited war is seen as a restrained attack by one bloc upon the territory or military forces of the other. Because of NATO's clear commitment to a defensive strategy, this attack is usually expected to come from the Warsaw Pact. Doves have been sceptical of the likelihood of cold-blooded Soviet aggression, but some other commentators have argued that specific local objectives might indeed prompt a limited Russian assault. Two suggested motives have been the suppression of an Eastern European rebellion which somehow 'spills over' across the Iron Curtain, or the forestalling of West German acquisition of nuclear weapons by a pre-emptive strike such as that launched by Israel against Iraq's nuclear plant in 1981.[62] A senior British general said in 1967 that:

> I have always felt that ... if I were on the other side on Christmas Eve or Easter Saturday and there was something like a university in a forward area and I knew it to be working on a nuclear weapon, I as a Russian would probably feel that it could not be borne and that I would have to stop it, and then I would pinch it off with a quick conventional attack.[63]

Most scenarios for limited Soviet attacks have been conceived by hawks, who tend to see such attacks as deliberate tactical ploys to test NATO resolve or to face down the West, without running too great a risk of nuclear war.[64] (Hard-line sceptics of the likelihood of Russian probing operations argue that they would forewarn NATO, and thus forfeit the advantage of surprise in a later invasion.)[65] Berlin is still seen as the most likely pressure point on NATO's Central Front (although a more enterprising strike such as the 'Hamburg grab' has not been entirely dismissed, and certain politicians have even suggested the possibility of an independent Soviet airborne attack upon Britain herself.)[66] What has caused more anxiety, however, is the threat of a Russian strike on NATO's Northern or Southern flanks, where political and military circumstances are thought to make it easier for the Soviet Union to stage an independent trial of will.[67]

Hawkish scenarios for limited East/West conflict have not been confined to operations on land. The great flexibility of maritime forces has led British thinkers to suggest a wide range of naval scenarios, from gunboat diplomacy in a prolonged confrontation, through harassment and sinkings to test NATO's resolve, to a full-scale Soviet blockade of the West's oil or reinforcement routes.[68] A few commentators have claimed that a war between East and West might be confined almost entirely to the sea, although this idea has been dismissed by many other observers.[69] In a different field, new developments in satellite technology have occasionally given rise to sensationalist claims that World War Three might be fought entirely in space, with President Reagan's Strategic Defense Initiative of 1983 being widely associated with the science-fiction film *Star Wars* which has achieved great popularity over the past decade.[70] However, the 'High Frontier' programme has little credibility within the British defence community, and even its advocates tend to see space as just an additional (though important) dimension in the overall East/West contest, whether that contest is pursued by peaceful force deployments or by overt hostilities.[71] Other radically new forms of warfare remain confined as yet to the realms of science fiction and speculative futurology.[72]

The domination of limited wars by political rather than technical criteria makes their course especially difficult to predict. This helps to explain why few suggested scenarios for a limited war between East and West have gone beyond the actual commencement of the conflict, except by envisaging escalation to a supposedly less arbitrary level of hostilities. Despite the adoption by the United States of a strategy of 'horizontal escalation' whereby attacks in one region might be met by ripostes in another, British commentator Neville Brown's image of a 'limited World War' carried on by tit-for-tat attacks in various parts of the globe has been less influential in the United Kingdom than has the idea that limited conventional conflict might be the deliberate or unintentional prelude to a true Third World War fought in the old convulsive style.[73]

Full-scale conventional war

For reasons which will be discussed at some length in Chapter 5, Britons have always tended to draw a particularly sharp distinction between nuclear and conventional warfare. This has had two important consequences for their images of World War Three. In the first place, since crossing the nuclear threshold has generally been regarded as the most drastic escalatory step beyond actually going to war, it has been possible to envisage full-scale conventional hostilities between East and West as a distinct level of warfare, only partially and coarsely influenced by the overhanging nuclear threat. In the second place, despite frequent acknowlegements of the destructiveness of modern conventional war, non-nuclear conflict has tended to be seen as a traditional military contest, far removed from the purposeless devastation associated with the nuclear arsenals.

It is the prospect of full-scale conventional hostilities between East and West which overwhelmingly preoccupies the NATO defence establishment. In stark contrast to the tendency of outside observers to focus upon the nuclear dimension of the East/West confrontation, defence professionals (certainly outside the United States) tend in normal circumstances to ignore the nuclear arsenals and to concentrate their attention upon more traditional weapons such as tanks, aircraft and warships. There was a period during the 1950s and 1960s when the British Army and the Royal Air Force (though never the Royal Navy) embraced the use of nuclear weapons in any major conflict, but this acceptance was soon reversed as NATO moved towards a strategy of flexible response, and all three services now base their plans and exercises upon the notion of all-out conventional hostilities with the Soviet bloc. The concept of a full-scale conventional war thus has its detailed roots in the day-to-day activities of the professional defence establishment.

Despite the continuing preoccupation of outside observers with the nuclear threat, the past decade does seem to have witnessed increasing interest in Parliament and among the public at large in the prospect of World War Three being fought at the conventional level, either as one phase of an ultimately nuclear conflict or as a wholly non-nuclear war. In 1977, the publishers Sidgwick & Jackson persuaded retired general Sir John Hackett to write an elaborate 'future history' of a largely conventional Third World War.[74] The book sold remarkably well, as did a similar 'military projection' edited by Brigadier Shelford Bidwell.[75] Both books seem to have had the ulterior motive of frightening the public into demanding an enhanced NATO defence effort, and their effect on the recent war scare will be examined further in Chapter 4.

These books, and the many less elaborate scenarios produced both by officials and by independent commentators over the past decade, reveal a striking measure of agreement about the likely form of a full-scale conventional conflict between East and West. One common feature of almost all British predictions has been that Europe itself is seen as the most likely focus of the war. Many reasons may be adduced for this concentration on Europe, but, for the present, it is sufficient to note that the high levels of weaponry in the region have provided the most common rationale for such an approach.[76] A further common feature of most British predictions about a conventional Third World War is that the Warsaw Pact is expected to launch an immediate, full-scale attack upon NATO forces. This perception is based not only upon NATO's widely accepted conventional inferiority and the avowedly defensive character of the West's own strategic posture, but also upon Russia's oft-expressed belief that, whatever the situation which sparks the conflict, the best form of defence is attack. Britain's 1981 Defence White Paper set out the resulting NATO nightmare very well:

> Soviet military doctrine stresses offensive action as the key to success. In a war with NATO the Warsaw Pact would plan to launch a rapid offensive under cover of surprise and deception, backed by massive fire-power. The tank armies would play a key role, using their mobility and fire-power to exploit weaknesses exposed by the initial attack. They would try to break quickly through NATO's lines, by-passing defences and helping to destroy centres of political and economic power in the rear areas. Attacks would then be developed from the side and rear.[77]

Almost every technical detail of the fighting which such an invasion would produce, as well as of the sea and air hostilities which are expected to accompany the ground war in Europe, has been minutely analysed in classified and unclassified defence literature. Elaborate official war games and exercises have been staged to test NATO strategy, and detailed simulation games about 'the Next War' have even been produced by private firms for sale to the general public.[78] Despite all this detailed analysis, however, British predictions about a conventional Third World War have remained ambivalent on three specific issues, which will now be discussed in turn.

The first such issue is whether the Warsaw Pact is more likely to attack NATO after prolonged mobilisation or in a surprise assault by the forces already stationed along the Iron Curtain. Official British planning in the 1970's, with its heavy reliance on advance warning of Russian aggression, inclined strongly towards the former alternative.[79] The recent war scare, however, has seen an upsurge of alarm among a number of hawks about the possibility of a surprise Soviet blitzkrieg, launched from a standing start.[80] What has complicated the issue is that, although Russian military doctrine lays great stress upon the importance of tactical surprise (a factor demonstrated by the operations in Eastern Europe over the past three decades), a sudden attack would have political problems and military disadvantages which have led other hard-liners in Britain to suggest that a Soviet assault would probably take a more deliberate and well-prepared form.[81] The sudden attack scare has declined in the 1980s thanks to the overall increase in NATO preparedness, but financial pressures in the future may re-open controversy about how best to strike the balance between a strong mobilisation base and resilience to a 'bolt from the blue'.[82]

The second ambivalent aspect of British predictions about a conventional Third World War concerns the use of chemical and biological weapons. Britain has long maintained a high level of anti-gas precautions among her armed forces, but before 1980 there was almost no debate about her lack both of a chemical retaliatory capability and of any form of protection for her civilian population. Such a debate did develop to a limited extent in the early 1980s, but never acquired anything like the momentum of the controversy over nuclear weapons and fallout shelters.[83] This seems to have been less because of reasoned scepticism about the possibility of gas attack than because of an almost wilful neglect of the whole horrific prospect – alarmist warnings about nerve gas stockpiles or Warsaw Pact preparations for chemical warfare have fallen flat not because they have been contradicted but because many people refuse to think about such a 'dirty' and insidious form of conflict.[84] As for biological warfare, this is considered to be entirely beyond the pale, and even predictions of an all-out nuclear holocaust take little specific account of poisons other than radioactive fallout.

A similar (but more surprising) ambivalence dominates the third contentious aspect of World War Three imagery, namely how far Britain herself would be placed at risk in a non-nuclear conflict. Britons have often tended to feel a comfortable detachment from conventional warfare, and Home Defence in the 1970s was seen almost exclusively in nuclear terms.[85] Hawkish agitation about the threat of conventional bombing has recently led to an increased UK air defence effort, and warnings by other hard-liners about the possibility of hostilities on the British mainland (ranging from sabotage and raids to a full-scale airborne and seaborne invasion) have prompted the formation of a volunteer Home Defence force, but anxiety on these issues is on nothing like the scale of the pre-nuclear age.[86] The subjugation of Britain herself by invasion or naval blockade is generally regarded as unlikely to come into question until after the conclusion of the battle in Central Europe which dominates the conventional image of World War Three.

Most informed Britons appear to believe that, whatever the preliminaries, a Third World War would at least temporarily take the form of the full-scale conventional conflict anticipated in NATO planning. It is this scenario which has provided the basis for almost all the recent anxiety about the threat of military defeat. Although there have been suggestions by both hawks and doves that nuclear weapons might be used from the outset of an East/West conflict, such suggestions have been nothing like as prominent as in the original Cold War, when belief in a conventional phase tended to be the exception rather than the rule.[87] Even Sovietologists, who were at first extremely sceptical about the possibility of a non-nuclear attack by the Soviet Union, have reported increasing Russian preparations for an initially conventional assault.[88] As to the outlook of the public at large, little evidence is available, but an opinion poll in 1980 found that almost half of respondents considered that conventional forces would play an important part in World War 3.[89]

There have been endless abstruse debates within the defence community about the state of the conventional military balance between East and West.[90] Major political uncertainties about the coherence of the two bloc structures in the event of conflict lessen the validity of detailed technical comparisons of the opposing forces, but there has nevertheless developed a widespread view that the military balance can be measured, and that it is inclined strongly in favour of the Warsaw Pact.[91] Dovish observers have long tried to challenge this impression of Western military inferiority, and they have been joined in recent years by other commentators arguing that with only a little extra effort, the Alliance could build a robust conventional defence.[92] However, the idea of Soviet preponderance has become deeply ingrained in British thinking, with poll respondents in 1980 asserting by a four-to-one majority that Warsaw Pact forces were stronger than those of NATO.[93]

The result of this perception of Soviet military superiority has been that most informed observers have tended to treat the initial result of full-scale conventional hostilities in Europe as a foregone conclusion. The question, it is said, is not *whether* but *when* the West would lose.[94] Hawkish writers have generally been the most pessimistic on this score, and their nightmare scenarios of a Soviet triumph after only a few days of fighting have been condemned by some for encouraging defeatism and despair. In Sir John Hackett's words, 'a cautionary tale that makes children pee in their beds, instead of frightening them into a sense of doing better, fails in its object'.[95] Many commentators (including Hackett) have adopted a more positive approach by suggesting that successful conventional resistance is possible, but their arguments have usually been based upon major improvements or amendments to NATO's existing force structure.[96] In the present situation, a Soviet blitzkrieg is widely expected to take two weeks or less to occupy large tracts of West Germany and to bring NATO forces to the brink of defeat.

What would happen next is a far more controversial issue. Official NATO doctrine is that the West would use tactical nuclear weapons in a limited strike to persuade the aggressor to withdraw.[97] This view, as well as the belief of some observers that nuclear weapons might already have been used (either by Russia or the West) to pre-empt an enemy nuclear strike, will be examined in the following section. Attention will now be concentrated upon the outlook of those who doubt that either side would have the resolve to cross the nuclear threshold at all.

Dovish observers have generally expressed little scepticism about the idea that conventional fighting between East and West would quickly escalate into nuclear exchanges. Certain other individuals, however, have been less willing to dismiss the possibility that hostilities would remain confined to the conventional level, if not for their entire duration then at least for a longer interval than allowed for in NATO planning.[98] As one commentator put it, 'The stress and strain of war within the European theatre, when public and political opinion alike would be preoccupied with attempts to avoid the terrible disaster of a Soviet nuclear attack upon West European cities, would surely effectively inhibit any question of a NATO nuclear response at any level even to an overwhelming Soviet conventional attack.'[99] It seems likely that many other defence experts share this view, but do not express it for fear of undermining deterrence. As for the general public, opinion polls reveal that approximately one-third of respondents (less among Labour supporters) believe that nuclear weapons would not be employed at any stage in World War Three.[100]

The past decade has witnessed an increasing divergence of opinion about what a wholly non-nuclear Third World War would involve. Sceptics of nuclear escalation have traditionally argued that such a conflict might last months or even years, and have therefore emphasised the need for improvements in war stocks, reserves, and convoy protection.[101] In the words of one politician, 'The last two wars were supposed to be over by Christmas, but they lasted for years. The same will happen again.'[102] Many adherents of this view believe that Soviet restraint or the arrival of American reinforcements would halt the Warsaw Pact blitzkrieg, stabilise the fighting in Europe, and produce a long-running battle of attrition like that in the Iran/Iraq war.[103] Others, however, foresee a continuing global contest between the superpowers after the fall of continental Europe, with Britain subjected to air attack and blockade while fulfilling its traditional role as a forward base for freedom.[104] There have even been calls, reminiscent of Air Chief Marshal Dowding's recommendations in 1940, for Britain not to 'place its best equipment on the sacrificial altar of Germany' at the expense of its capability for subsequent defence of the UK.[105]

A radically different view, which acquired especial prominence with the scare about a surprise Soviet blitzkrieg, is that a conventional conflict in Europe would not be long drawn-out, but as short and shocking as the Arab/Israeli war of 1967. Britain's Minister of Defence in 1981 felt able to justify naval cuts by asserting that convoy protection would be of secondary importance in the 'nasty, brutish and short conventional war' which constituted the most pressing threat.[106] This view has found favour with several defence commentators, who suggest that the most likely pattern of East/West conflict is a swift and sharp conventional battle followed by a peace settlement negotiated under the shadow of nuclear escalation.[107]

Who would win such a war is far from clear. NATO's best hope has long been that stern Western resistance coupled with the threat of nuclear escalation would induce Russia to change her mind and withdraw her forces, after intensive negotiations during the conventional 'pause'.[108] This scenario, however, appears to carry little conviction outside official rhetoric, and critics of the short war assumption have claimed that if NATO fought such a war, she would be bound to lose.[109] A few commentators have argued that with expanded forces NATO could seize territory in Eastern Europe to trade away for Soviet gains in the West, but most observers tend to see Russian occupation of part or all of West Germany as the likeliest outcome of a short conventional war.[110]

This threat of military defeat has played a prominent part in hawkish anxiety over the past decade, but, just as very few dovish alarmists have made any personal preparations for the nuclear holocaust which they claim to be imminent, so very few hard-liners seem to have considered the practical implications of a victorious Russian offensive. Only a handful of commentators have given any detailed thought to how Britain might actually come to terms with a Soviet victor,[111] and less has been written about the prospect of Russian occupation than about the now purely hypothetical question of what would have happened if Britain had fallen to the Nazis in World War Two.[112] Opinion polls suggest that the public at large, in the face of ambivalent pronouncements from the defence community, have little clear idea of who (if anyone) would actually win an East/West war.[113]

This ambivalence seems to be only one aspect of the striking lack of logical coherence behind much British thinking about full-scale conventional hostilities. The tactical aspects of the opening campaign are analysed in incredible detail, but the wider context of nuclear threats and political negotiations tends to be almost entirely ignored, or else introduced in the role of a *deux ex machina* to get over uncomfortable problems such as Soviet preponderance or the depletion of Western ammunition and reserves. This tendency to see conventional fighting between the blocs as a traditional all-out military contest is of highly dubious validity, since (as Garnett has observed), 'The rules of the game have been changed in a very significant way. No matter how violently a limited conventional war is being conducted . . . the combatants will probably be spending at least as much time worrying about the violence held in reserve as they are with the battle in hand'.[114] The contradictions of the concept of full-scale conventional warfare seem to lie at the heart of the recent war scare, and will be discussed further in Chapters 4 and 5.

Limited nuclear war

The prominence which the notion of 'limited nuclear war' has achieved in Britain over the past decade appears to have sprung primarily from sceptical alarm. Many commentators have asserted that 'any use of nuclear weapons is almost bound to escalate to the holocaust', and even Laurence Martin, the leading British proponent of limited nuclear options, has expressed grave reservations about the practical feasibility of the restraints which he suggests.[115] Opinion poll data on personal survival makes clear that nuclear war is seen in a similarly apocalyptic light by the public at large.[116] Despite this overwhelming scepticism, however, certain forms of limited nuclear war do appear to have gained some tentative credibility in recent years, and will now be examined in detail.

British views on which side is the more likely to use nuclear weapons first in an East/West war seem to be profoundly ambivalent. Official doctrine is that NATO itself would probably have to initiate nuclear strikes due to its conventional weakness, but this aspect of Western strategy is rarely stressed because it is so prone to misinterpretation.[117] A wide range of commentators stress the alternative possibility of *Soviet* first-use, with hawks pointing to the chilling precepts of Russian strategic writing, and doves emphasising the pressures towards pre-emption which operate upon both blocs alike.[118] In view of this ambivalence, it is hardly surprising that surveys reveal no clear consensus within the public at large about which side would be the first to cross the nuclear threshold in World War Three.[119]

British opinions differ also about the likely size and character of the initial nuclear strike. Few observers believe that either side would be mad enough to deliberately provoke an all-out nuclear exchange by means of an unrestrained initial attack. Instead, the notion of 'escalation' has become central to British thinking about nuclear war, with the conflict seen as advancing through several sets of possible limits until it finally becomes the holocaust. Doves tend to argue that pressures towards pre-emption would make progress up the escalatory ladder extremely swift, while hard-liners often assert that the Soviet emphasis on shock and surprise might lead to the skipping of several rungs.[120] However, British scepticism about limited nuclear war seems to stem less from the belief that it would never occur than that, once in progress, it could not be contained.

The kind of nuclear strike considered by informed Britons to have the best chance of avoiding escalation involves the use of a handful of weapons in a primarily political role. The small number of detonations is considered to be more important than the nature of the targets, and several commentators have hypothesised one or more Hiroshima-style attacks against selected cities.[121] However, the implausibility of such controlled nuclear coercion to the majority of Britons is illustrated by the furore which was aroused when American Secretary of State Alexander Haig revealed that NATO might fire a demonstrative nuclear shot to induce Russia to cease a conventional attack.[122] In the words of one Labour MP, 'Would it not be useful if people were enabled to express an opinion whether General Haig should be given the opportunity to start a demonstrative Third World War by firing one of those missiles from British soil?'[123]

It is ironic that condemnation of the demonstrative shot concept should fall upon the United States, since the idea of using nuclear weapons as a signal of resolve has traditionally found more favour in Britain herself. Labour party defence experts have long argued that NATO's initial nuclear strikes should occur 'in the air over the Mediterranean' or 'in an unpopulated non-military area of the Soviet Union as a warning that the nuclear threshold was about to be crossed',[124] and although the United States has remained convinced that nuclear weapons are best employed to create catastrophic military effects, the British Defence White Paper of 1980 argued that 'their underlying purpose lies not in those effects themselves but in seeking to convince an aggressor that he must halt his attack and withdraw or risk devastating consequences.'[125] Many Britons have admittedly expressed grave doubts that a 'warning shot' would influence the Soviet Union after it had made the decision to attack, but (officially at least) the British government remains sanguine.[126] The Minister for Defence Procurement made the following statement in 1981:

> We do not believe that . . . it necessarily follows that the first use of a nuclear weapon by defenders of freedom and democracy would automatically result in nuclear retaliation. The aggressor would

take stock from his bunkers as to whether his prize was attainable at an acceptable cost . . . I therefore regard the term 'nuclear exchange' as misleading.[127]

This idea that one side might accept an enemy nuclear strike without retaliation has found less favour among British commentators than has the idea that both blocs might recoil in horror after an initial nuclear exchange. Even such staunch sceptics of limited nuclear war as Lord Zuckerman and Sir John Hackett have admitted a possibility that attacks might end after a single nuclear strike by each side, and other writers have suggested that a tactical exchange in Germany might produce a bloody stalemate with neither side prepared to escalate further.[128] If the war did continue, several commentators believe that it would take the form of a series of limited strikes, punctuated by frantic negotiations.[129]

Although most British sceptics of the holocaust see limited nuclear war in primarily political terms, some have suggested that nuclear attacks might be restricted to military targets in a European conflict. This has not represented a vote of confidence in battlefield nuclear weapons, and even hard-liners in Britain seem to have little faith that 'mini-nukes' such as the neutron bomb could safely be used to stop a Russian tank offensive.[130] In the words of one senior British officer, 'I am absolutely certain and I will go to my grave being certain that if you let off a neutron bomb anywhere in Europe you have gone 90 per cent of the way to triggering a strategic nuclear exchange.'[131] It is the increasingly accurate *Soviet* theatre nuclear arsenal which some hawks fear might be used in a discriminate strike against NATO military targets throughout Western Europe, leaving the Alliance no choice but to accept defeat or to intitiate suicidal escalation.[132] However, even this scenario does not carry great conviction, and the menace of the Russian SS-20 missile is more usually portrayed in terms of the protective nuclear umbrella which it could extend over a Soviet *conventional* attack.

The possibility that the superpowers would refrain from striking each other's homelands in a nuclear war has been suggested by a handful of British politicians.[133] Surprisingly, however, there appears to be a distinct dissonance between those who consider such restraint to be practicable, and those who most fervently oppose 'theatre nuclear war' strategies in Europe or elsewhere. This latter group has always tended to argue that a nuclear war started in a particular region would escalate to destroy the superpowers themselves. Dan Smith, for instance, wrote that, 'Horrible as a limited nuclear war would be, there is the yet more ugly prospect of an American government sailing gaily into a limited war and ending up with the holocaust.'[134] The idea that Britain and France might become 'nuclear sanctuaries' by virtue of possessing independent deterrents seems to have very little credibility in Britain even among those who foresee a similar sanctuarisation of superpower territory, although Lawrence Freedman has suggested that the United Kingdom might at least *attempt* to opt out of the nuclear battle by threatening genocidal retaliation.[135]

An opinion poll in 1983 found a surprisingly high level of popular agreement with the idea that a nuclear war in Europe would not necessarily lead to a nuclear attack on the United States.[136] This result may, however, be somewhat artificial. A less formal opinion survey in 1981 found that many people had never heard of limited nuclear war until it was mentioned by the investigator, and were quite taken aback to find that such a concept existed.[137] The questions which this raises about the reliability of the normal opinion poll technique will be addressed in the Appendix. Here, it will simply be suggested that, although the standard public image of nuclear war is confined to the holocaust facing Britain herself, peace movement propaganda or official gaffes about 'theatre' nuclear war do have the potential to arouse substantial popular alarm.[138]

The kind of limited nuclear war which seems to have least credibility in British circles is that of counterforce exchanges between the opposing nuclear arsenals. Only a handful of hawks have shown any sympathy with American alarm about a Soviet 'surgical strike' against US ICBMs.[139] A more usual reaction has been that scenarios of 'escalation dominance' at the strategic nuclear level are sheer fantasy, given the massive devastation which the various 'warfighting' options would cause.[140] Missile accuracy and counterforce doctrines have indeed caused widespread anxiety in Britain, but they have not encouraged belief in the feasibility of a limited nuclear war. In the words of science writer Nigel Calder:

> . . . the most probable nuclear war in the era of counterforce weapons is one in which both sides simply smash each other as rapidly as they can, while their missiles survive . . . The sophistication about 'limited war', 'counterforce options' and the like leads back to exchanges just as bloody-minded but more deadly and less controllable than 'mutually assured destruction' at its most facile.[141]

British commentators have thus tended to see limited nuclear war as an extremely problematic concept, which is only conceivable at the lowest levels of nuclear exchange. This concentration on extremely restricted nuclear strikes has not, however, made nuclear war appear more akin to a conventional military contest than to a catastrophic holocaust. Two former Chiefs of the Defence Staff have recently stressed that 'wars cannot be fought with nuclear weapons', and Britain's Minister of Defence stated bluntly in 1981 that, 'A localised tactical nuclear war would be absurd. Any nuclear exchange would be madness.'[142] Observers from all sides of the political spectrum have agreed that the local effects of a limited nuclear war would be virtually indistinguishable from those of the holocaust, and that almost any scale of nuclear exchange would devastate the continent of Europe, whether or not it led to the ultimate catastrophe of all-out nuclear war.[143]

A catastrophic holocaust
The dominant image of a Third World War, especially among dovish observers and the public at large, remains that of an unrestricted nuclear exchange. East and West are envisaged as flinging their entire nuclear stockpiles at each other as quickly as possible, in a mindless orgy of mutual destruction. This horrific prospect is hardly seen as a 'war' at all. Neither side is expected to be capable of further aggressive action after 'pushing the button' for the initial spasm exchange. Notions of a drawn-out campaign of atomic bombardment have long since given place (both in popular and official imagery) to the idea of a rain of thermonuclear warheads lasting a few hours at most, and the 1950s concept of 'broken-backed warfare' continuing after a nuclear exchange was described by Britain's Minister of Defence almost twenty years ago as 'a blasphemous mockery'.[144]

The idea of a war without winners is far from new. Neville Chamberlain said in 1938 that, 'In war, whichever side may call itself the victor, there are no winners, but all are losers.'[145] Only in the nuclear age, however, has this aphorism acquired near-universal acceptance. It is a long time since British military leaders constructed scenarios of Western 'victory' in an all-out thermonuclear campaign.[146] Recent American talk of 'prevailing' in a nuclear war has aroused only ridicule and alarm on this side of the Atlantic.[147] The idea that *Russia* might possess a war-winning capability has gained slightly more credence in hawkish circles, but the main motive for studying Soviet nuclear strategy has remained the negative one of attempting to predict where the bombs might fall.[148]

To the public at large, 'the holocaust' appears less as a military contest than as a devastating, impersonal catastrophe. This attitude is reflected in the recent wave of books and films about nuclear war. Although events leading up to the attack are sometimes portrayed from a global perspective, the war itself is shown through the eyes of individual citizens on the receiving end of the rain of bombs.[149] The 'self-help' policy set out in civil defence literature reinforces this individualist viewpoint, and popular disbelief in any idea of a communal war effort is demonstrated by the fact that most Britons do not think Britain as a nation would survive a nuclear attack.[150] Lord Mountbatten gave a graphic description of the collapse of organised society expected to result from a nuclear holocaust:

> Our fine great buildings, our homes, will exist no more. The thousands of years it took to develop our civilisation will have been in vain. Our works of art will be lost. Radio, television, newspapers, will disappear. There will be no means of transport. There will be no hospitals. No help can be expected for the few mutilated survivors in any town to be sent from a neighbouring town – there will be no neighbouring towns left, no neighbours; there will be no help; there will be no hope.[151]

Official predictions of a Russian nuclear attack (which have been remorselessly 'exposed' by journalist Duncan Campbell for the edification of the anti-nuclear movement) envisage that Britain would be struck by a hundred or more Soviet bombs and warheads, with a total explosive yield of some two hundred megatons. This attack is expected to kill roughly half of the British population, or even more if fallout, starvation and disease take a greater toll than the actual explosions.[152] To try to prevent this latter eventuality, the government maintains a minimal framework of civil defence precautions designed to alleviate the situation in the aftermath of the attack itself.[153]

It is only recently that non-professionals have come to examine the holocaust in any detail. Nuclear imagery in the 1950s and 1960s was dominated by wilful ignorance and apocalyptic exaggeration. The few novels and films which did appear (notably *On the Beach* and *Dr Strangelove*) shared the twin motifs of a detached perspective and a fascination with universal death.[154] Although this kind of imagery remains common, the recent war scare has been characterised by the appearance of many more detailed and 'realistic' portrayals of the effects of nuclear attack.[155] Peace movement supporters, especially, have produced an unprecedented flood of academic studies and predictive imagery about the holocaust, and although Peter Watkins' 1965 film *The War Game* remains confined to private showings in village halls and the like, its less overtly propagandist counterparts *Threads* and the American film *The Day After* have recently been seen on television by a substantial part of the British population.[156]

This new readiness to 'think about the unthinkable' appears to have been prompted partly by a belief that nuclear war was being contemplated as a serious policy option within the professional defence community. Much peace movement literature has been devoted to condemning or satirising government civil defence precautions, especially those recommended in the public information booklet *Protect and Survive*.[157] Perhaps the most biting attack has been in Raymond Briggs' story *When the Wind Blows*, with an old couple exchanging lines like, 'Do you have to dig a hole, like the old Andersons in the War?' 'Oh no dear. That's all old fashioned. With modern scientific methods you just use doors with cushions and books on top'.[158] On the more academic side, many pages of detailed analysis, and even a computer simulation, have been employed to challenge the official assertion that simple fallout precautions could enable thirty million Britons to survive a nuclear holocaust.[159] The object of all these grisly images and calculations appears to have been to foil what is seen as a sinister government plot to condition the British public into accepting the possibility of a nuclear war.[160]

If such a plot exists, it has been remarkably unsuccessful. Opinion polls provide no grounds whatsoever for the belief that popular images of the holocaust are excessively optimistic. A 1983 survey found that no fewer than 60 per cent of Britons considered themselves to have no chance at all of living through a nuclear attack.[161] Individual preparations for the holocaust are on nothing like the scale of the 'survivalist' movement in the United States, and civil defence is generally regarded with considerable scepticism.[162] It seems likely that the impact of films such as *The War Game* stems less from removing hope of survival than from replacing comfortingly vague images of a quick, clean 'flash in the sky' with a horrific picture of injury, sickness and privation. Some of those living near the Polaris submarine base at Faslane are known to draw comfort from the idea that they would die quickly in a nuclear war, and many others have expressed a similar preference for instant death should war come.[163] In the words of radio commentator Neil Hepburn:

> I shall be driving like hell to the centre of the expected blast and a quick fry-up: better a shadow on the pavement than an

irradiated, maddened and irresistible target for the ones with guns who cannot stand looting.[164]

Not all Britons share this sentiment, and the majority probably retain the will to survive even such a terrible holocaust. However, this should not be taken to mean that nuclear war is regarded in anything other than utterly catastrophic terms. Scientific analysis may have cast doubt on the apocalyptic idea of universal death, but is has also made nuclear war appear more vividly horrific, particularly as regards long-term consequences such as radiation sickness, starvation and disease.[165] Newly realised effects like ozone depletion and the recently discovered 'nuclear winter' phenomenon, although at first reviving the spectre of human extinction, have come to be regarded as additional horrors facing the survivors of a nuclear exchange.[166] Zealous advocacy of civil defence tends to do little more than bring the horror home, and the tentative efforts made by the British government in this area have probably been the best present the peace movement ever had.[167] What makes this even more ironic is the fact that most of the recent anxiety within the defence community itself has sprung from the idea that the Third World War might not take the form of a mutually suicidal nuclear holocaust after all.

3 The Nature of the Scare

In the early 1970s, little seems to have been further from people's minds than the possibility of a Third World War. The few opinion polls which were taken on the subject reveal a lower level of anxiety than at any time since 1945.[1] This complacency was understandable. The Vietnam conflict was drawing to a close, and President Nixon went so far as to say that, 'I seriously doubt if we will ever have another war. This is probably the very last one.'[2] Negotiations between East and West flourished, producing major deals such as the 1972 Strategic Arms Limitation Agreement and the 1975 Helsinki Accords on European Security. Britain's Prime Minister spoke of a halcyon era in overseas relations, and strategic commentator Alastair Buchan drew parallels with 'la belle epoque' and with the Peace of Westphalia.[3] The prevailing optimism was well expressed in the following passage by Michael Howard:

> Today we are living in an age of peace which is quite unprecedented, first in the length of time it has lasted – some 20 years or more – and secondly in intensity; in the degree to which people feel that there will not be another major war. The existence of nuclear weapons, the perception that any major conflict will be nuclear and therefore inconceivable and intolerable, and the determination not to conceive of it or tolerate it – this is something almost totally new in intellectual history.[4]

Not everyone was pleased with the prevailing complacency about the avoidance of war. Members of the defence establishment repeatedly lamented the anti-militarism which feelings of security produced, arguing that force or the threat of force remained central to international relations.[5] Britain's Minister of Defence complained in 1970 of the paradox that, 'Because NATO has been so successful as a deterrent, people are inclined to say that its forces are never required to fight; that they have no useful job to do; and that there is not going to be a war.'[6] The armed services themselves were not immune from problems of recruitment and motivation caused by this lack of a sense of threat. As one Army officer wrote:

> The deterrent philosophy is already in existence, in that most thinking members of the Army realise that their role is now

40

dissuasive, rather than involved with the possibility of actually fighting a war. However, it is doubtful whether this philosophy is clearly enough understood at all levels. Indeed, it is very difficult to explain: anyone can grasp the idea when being given a lecture in barracks on, say, the importance of BAOR in preserving the peace in Europe, but it makes less sense in terms of real motivation when passing the same tree during an attack exercise on a well-known bit of German heath for the third time in two training seasons. The temptation to treat it as a bit of a bore becomes strong.[7]

It was not only the defence establishment which felt uncomfortable during the 'age of peace'. The widespread complacency about the avoidance of war was also criticised by some dovish observers, on the grounds that it removed the pressure for continued efforts to curb the arms race and the military confrontation between East and West.[8] In David Owen's words, 'the smell of burning is not just confined to the dramatic headline-catching situation. It hangs threateningly but inscrutably over every military strategy and incident.'[9] There was thus an undercurrent of tension beneath the complacency of the early 1970s, with individuals on both sides of the political spectrum wishing to cultivate a livelier sense of threat in order to win support for their own particular policy ideas. This chapter will discuss how the concern about war spread as the decade progressed, and will assess who became most alarmed and how deep their alarm actually was.

I THE DEVELOPMENT AND DISTRIBUTION OF ANXIETY

Britain awake!

Anxiety about World War Three began to revive in Britain long before East/West relations themselves slid into the 'New Cold War' of the early 1980s. Even at the time of the Helsinki conference in 1975, concern was growing among certain informed observers of the international scene about what they saw as dangerous trends in the underlying strategic situation. For hawks, the danger was twofold – first, that continued Soviet proxy advances in the Third World would jeopardise the West's vital resources, and second, that Russia's unchallenged military build-up would provide her with a 'window of opportunity' to attack or coerce NATO in the early 1980s, before remedial Western force increases could take effect.[10] Doves saw a different peril, namely that the accuracy of new nuclear missiles, and the associated 'counterforce' strategies, would undermine deterrence and make nuclear war much more likely.[11] For a war scare thus to be sparked by reasoned anticipation and intellectual analysis was nothing new. Michael Howard wrote that:

> . . . in general men have fought during the past two hundred years neither because they are aggressive nor because they are acquisitive animals, but because they are reasoning ones; because they discern, or believe that they can discern, dangers before they become immediate, the possibility of threats before they are made.[12]

Hawkish doubts about *détente* had been building up for a long time. As early as 1968, the Labour government's defence cuts had prompted a flurry of alarm and protest both among the Tory opposition and among senior serving officers.[13] Sir John Hackett (then commanding NATO's Northern Army Group) jeopardised his career by writing to *The Times* to argue that if the West's conventional defences were weakened further, the Russians might be tempted to advance to the Rhine just as the Israelis had pushed to the Jordan and the Suez Canal in the previous year.[14] This wave of anxiety died away with the fall of the Labour administration and the continuing improvement of the international climate. In the mid-1970s, however, concern re-emerged with fresh force. The Labour Party was back in office, and there was no sign of any halt in Russia's military build-up. The climate was thus ripe for a fully-fledged hard-line campaign to awaken Britons to the Soviet threat.

Three individuals dominated the initial stage of this alarm. The first was the exiled Russian dissident Alexander Solzhenitsyn, who toured the West, warning of impending doom in the manner of an Old Testament prophet. As he told British television viewers in 1976, 'The situation at the moment is such, the Soviet Union's economy is on such a war footing, that even if it were the unanimous opinion of all the members of the Politburo not to start a war, this would no longer be in their power.'[15] The second prominent hawk was the new Conservative leader Margaret Thatcher, who deliberately cultivated an image as an 'Iron Lady' by repeated and urgent warnings of the threat posed by Soviet expansionism.[16] In her words, 'The Russians are bent on world dominance and they are rapidly acquiring the means to become the most powerful imperial nation the world has ever seen.'[17]

The third prominent hard-liner was Lord Chalfont, a former Minister of Disarmament who had once concentrated his attention upon the dangers posed by the nuclear arms race.[18] As late as 1974 he wrote that,

'In the current political climate, armed aggression by the Soviet Union or its allies is what strategic analysts would call a scenario of zero probability – in other words it is not going to happen.'[19] However, Soviet policies soon caused Chalfont to change his outlook, and from 1976 onwards his articles in *The Times* became focused almost entirely upon the manifold aspects of the Russian threat to the free world.[20]

An increasing number of commentators, politicians and military men came to share the anxiety which Solzhenitsyn, Thatcher and Chalfont expressed. The activities of Soviet proxy forces (especially Cubans) in Africa aroused widespread concern, and similar fears were prompted by the state of the military balance, with the sheer size of the Soviet armed forces (particularly the Red Navy) being taken as evidence that Russia's intentions were far from defensive.[21] Even the remedial measures instituted by Western governments in 1978 failed to defuse hawkish anxiety, since it was feared that Russia might be encouraged to strike while she still had the advantage.[22]

The deteriorating international climate and the drawn-out general election campaign increased the fervour of the right-wing war scare in Britain as the end of the decade approached.[23] Senior politicians and military leaders joined more traditional alarmists in proclaiming that the early 1980s would be a period of grave peril.[24] The media was full of articles and features about East/West conflict, and there even appeared two full-length books about a possible Third World War only a few years in the future.[25] Any possibility that this anxiety would die away after the Conservative election victory of 1979 (as it had nine years earlier) was precluded by the depth of the concern and by the pattern of subsequent events. Furthermore, alarm about World War Three was no longer a monopoly of the hawks.

Dovish commentators came late to the recent war scare. Although several writers in the 1970s did express growing concern about the dangers of the nuclear arms race, this was nothing to the anxiety which developed after 1979.[26] Most earlier alarmists had been making prophecies of doom for years, regardless of the international situation, and the 'doomsday clock' of the *Bulletin of Atomic Scientists* remained stationary from the Indian nuclear explosion in 1974 until the end of the decade.[27] Doves in the 1970s supported defence cuts more by stressing the stability than by proclaiming the instability of East/West relations, and Britain's Minister of Defence in March 1979 agreed with West German Chancellor Helmut Schmidt that Europe was the second safest continent after Australasia.[28]

When dovish anxiety did arise in the later 1970s, it tended to be largely reactive. The hawks themselves were blamed for increasing the risk of war by 'sabre-rattling' and imperilling *détente*. In the words of one MP, 'I say to those so anxious to dance on the grave of detente, "Beware. You may be dancing on the grave of civilisation at the same time".'[29] Prime Minister James Callaghan warned in 1978 that to encourage competitive superpower intervention in Africa was to risk a world war, and other commentators laid stress on the dangers which might result simply from creating a war psychosis in the West.[30] Such recrimination between doves and hawks came to play an even greater part in the later stages of the recent war scare, and its role in fuelling British anxiety about an East/West conflict will be discussed in Chapter 4.

Lack of evidence makes it difficult to gauge the effect which the predominantly right-wing alarm of the later 1970s had upon the public at large. Hawks continually complained of public apathy and of a 'conspiracy of silence',[31] but the few opinion polls which were conducted do seem to show an increase in popular anxiety. A survey in late 1977 found that almost one in four respondents considered there to be at least a 50–50 chance of a Third World War in the next ten years, and another poll in July 1979 revealed that 40 per cent of adults thought that Britain was likely to be involved in a major war before the end of the century (although only 11 per cent agreed with the hawkish contention that the danger lay in the early 1980s).[32] Perhaps the most interesting feature of these findings was that, although CND recruitment had not yet taken off, alarm was greater among Labour supporters than among Conservatives. The war scare which the hawks had whipped up was about to backfire.

The year of crisis

Even the gloomiest prophet could hardly have predicted the combination of crises which assailed the world in 1980. Russia's invasion of Afghanistan was described by President Carter as 'the gravest threat to peace since the Second World War', and the continuing crisis in neighbouring Iran aroused similar fears when the Americans tried to rescue their hostages from Tehran.[33] The year 1980 also saw two events in Europe which had long been cited as possible preludes to World War Three – the death of Yugoslavian president Tito, and the outbreak of workers' dissent in Poland.[34] As if this were not enough, the year also witnessed the start of the Iran/Iraq war, and the prelude to a renewed bloodbath in the Lebanon. Although many saw these events only as regional problems which did not forebode the collapse of central deterrence, many others feared that the apocalyptic scenarios put forward in the late 1970s for a slide into East/West conflict through a combination of local crises were coming horribly true.

This notion was strengthened by the reactive measures which the West had finally begun to take to remedy its supposed military unpreparedness. The holding of large-scale exercises and the hasty improvisation of defence hardware gave an alarming impression of impending conflict.[35] At the nuclear level, decisions to modernise NATO's theatre arsenal and Britain's independent deterrent were accompanied by disturbing reports of American nuclear accidents, and by a less than reassuring revival of official interest in civil defence.[36] East/West *détente* collapsed, with the downfall of the SALT process, the partial boycott of the Moscow Olympics, and the election of the notorious hawk Ronald Reagan as US President. The atmosphere of the period was perhaps best captured by former Chief of the Defence Staff, Sir Neil Cameron, who remarked in April 1980, 'There is a whiff of war in the air.'[37] As another observer later noted, 'For many people throughout the world, in high office, in military commands, in their simple homes, the whiff of war was very real.'[38]

The sheer variety of the year's developments in defence and international affairs meant that almost everyone could see his own particular nightmare coming true. Hawkish commentators certainly saw no reason to mitigate their alarmism after the invasion of Afghanistan. The 1980s were repeatedly described as a 'decade of danger' and there were frequent scares about a Soviet attack on Yugoslavia, Poland, or the Gulf.[39] Although hawkish anxiety was concentrated upon the threat of *conventional* conflict (as was discussed in Chapter 2), repeated calls were made for improvements in civil defence, in order to strengthen the credibility of Britain's deterrent posture and to protect the population against limited attack.[40] This pressure, and the response which it evoked from the Conservative government, served to fuel the anxiety developing on the opposite wing of the political spectrum about the risk of a nuclear holocaust.

The leading dovish alarmist was undoubtedly the Marxist historian E. P. Thompson, whose polemical pamphlet *Protest and Survive* became the bible of the revived anti-nuclear movement. In Thompson's words, 'I have come to the view that a general nuclear war is not only possible but probable, and that its probability is increasing. We may indeed be approaching a point of no return when the existing tendency or disposition towards this outcome becomes irreversible.'[41] Thompson's work heralded a flood of books, articles and pamphlets whose common theme was that militarism and the arms race were hurling mankind headlong towards a thermonuclear World War Three, and that the only way to avert such a catastrophe was to move towards disarmament.[42] Apocalyptic scare tactics thus came for a brief period to dominate both sides of the renewed defence debate.

Perhaps more striking than the rhetoric of either hawks or doves was the growth of anxiety among those who had no simplistic prescriptions for averting an East/West collision. The media in 1980 was flooded with non-polemical references to the possibility of a Third World War. A common theme was that the world was in danger of sliding into war as it had in 1914, and that there was no easy or obvious way to reverse the trend.[43] As one commentator wrote (after cataloguing the many conflicting perils of the strategic situation), 'my feelings are those of a busybody who has shouted "Fire!" in the theatre and now cannot point to the safe way out.'[44] When the war scare reached its height, in the first half of 1980, it was dominated by feelings of powerless anxiety, even among many informed observers of the international scene. Sometimes the only remedy people could suggest was to improve civil defence in the hope of saving as much as possible if the holocaust should occur.[45]

There is no doubt that the crisis year of 1980 brought a marked increase in anxiety among the public at large. Newspapers received thousands of letters from individuals ranging from housewives to university professors, calling for disarmament or (more rarely) for an increase in civil defence.[46] There were hundreds of enquiries about domestic nuclear shelters, and tens of thousands of recruits for the various peace groups which sprang up as the year progressed.[47] The many opinion polls which were taken reveal an unprecedented level of pessimism (irrespective of age, sex, or political allegiance) about the danger of a Third World War.[48] This contrasts somewhat with the experience of continental European countries, where *Angst* has been concentrated among the younger generation.[49] In Britain, although young people have been the most active in opposing established security policy, war fears seem to have been more evenly distributed across the population as a whole.

So widespread was British anxiety about World War Three in 1980 that it is reasonable to ask which groups (if any) were *not* alarmed. There were a few government statements to the effect that war was not even probable, let alone imminent or inevitable, but the Tory administration was precluded by its own rhetoric from adopting a wholly reassuring tone. What does seem to have been the case is that the anxieties of the professional defence establishment were based less upon an actual convulsive conflict than upon political pressure or regional entanglement.[50] In other words, disagreement lay not over whether danger existed, but over what form that danger took. This subject will be discussed at greater length in Chapter 5, but first, an assessment will be made of how the recent war scare has developed in the years since 1980.

Alarm becomes institutionalised

There have been few dramatic shifts in the international situation, either for good or for ill, since the upheavals of 1980. East/West relations have remained frosty, suspended in a kind of limbo between *détente* and a true cold war. Arms control talks have been resumed, broken off, and resumed once more, without much visible sign of progress. The crises in Iran, Afghanistan, Poland and the Lebanon have dragged incon-clusively on, occasionally flaring back into prominence with events such as the imposition of martial law in Poland or attacks on oil tankers in the Gulf. There have also been new flashpoints such as the Soviet shooting down of a Korean airliner in 1983, as well as totally independent events such as the Falklands conflict between Britain and Argentina. Only since 1984, with the marked softening of President Reagan's bellicose rhetoric, and with the advent of a younger and more dynamic Soviet leader in Mikhail Gorbachev, has there been any real sign of improvement in the East/West climate.[51]

The result of this ambivalent pattern of events has been the institutionalisation of British anxiety about a Third World War. The spontaneous alarm of 1980 has gradually declined, but the extension of the crisis in East/West relations over a period of years has encouraged the full reflection of this alarm in the media and in political debate. Films and literature on every aspect of the World War Three issue have continued to pour out at an undiminished rate, even reaching such extremes as a television comedy series and civil defence advice on the protection of pets![52] More importantly, anxiety about war has fuelled a far-reaching defence debate, involving massive street demonstrations and a sharp split between the major political parties over what security posture Britain should adopt. As in the 1970s, the risk of war has become a central item of controversy in this debate, with supporters of existing policy stressing the stability of the current situation, while those pressing for radical reform highlight the many ways in which conflict might break out.

Unlike in the 1970s, it is the doves who have recently been most alarmist. The dominance of hard-line security policies (especially in the United States) has prompted a flood of peace-movement literature, packed with emphatic assertions that this is the most dangerous period in human history and that the risk of a nuclear holocaust is increasing year by year.[53] The 'doomsday clock' of the *Bulletin of Atomic Scientists* was kept at four minutes to midnight in 1982 and 1983, and was moved even closer to the fateful hour in 1984 and 1985.[54] This sustained alarmism was at first accompanied by increased political support – the Labour Party embraced the cause of unilateral nuclear disarmament, and CND membership increased seven-fold between 1980 and 1983.[55] However, since the Tory election landslide and the successful introduction of INF, the peace movement seems to have lost its momentum; debate has shifted from new nuclear deployments to the more esoteric issues of conventional deterrence and 'Star Wars' defences, prompting the less committed activists to drift away to demonstrate and pass resolutions about other things.[56] The dovish challenge to British security policy has thus developed from an upsurge of popular outrage into an increasingly sophisticated but narrowly-based intellectual critique.

Hard-line observers have been quicker to de-emphasise the threat of East/West conflict, despite the fact that the supposed 'window of vulnerability' if anything reached its height in the early 1980s. There have been a few alarmist warnings from the most hawkish officers and politicians, but official spokesmen have laid more and more stress upon the stability of deterrence and the improbability of conflict.[57] Most moderate observers and defence academics have been sceptical all along of the spectres of calculated Soviet aggression or of a self-generating nuclear holocaust, arguing that the technical dangers of the military balance have been greatly exaggerated and that the *political* differences between East and West are quite insufficient to cause a war.[58] In the words of one commentator, 'We are living in the most stable European environment since the beginning of this century – perhaps even since Metternich.'[59] The British defence establishment has thus eschewed the scare tactics of the 1970s and united behind the assertion that there is actually very little risk of any form of Third World War.

Public fears have subsided much more gradually since the anxious months of early 1980. Differences in the wording of questions make it hard to directly compare successive opinion poll statistics, but it is only in 1984 that more people came to question than to accept the likelihood of a Third World War within the next few decades.[60] This stubbornly persistent pessimism about the long-term avoidance of East/West conflict contrasts sharply with the wildly fluctuating hopes and fears of the 1950s and 1960s, a contrast which will be discussed at length later in this chapter. Breakdowns of poll results across different societal groups show concern gradually becoming more prominent among Labour supporters, women and the young, which is what one would expect given the growing identification of alarmism with dovish opponents of existing security policy.[61]

The recent war scare has thus passed through several different phases since its inception in the mid-1970s. Starting among hard-line defence experts, alarm gradually spread through society as a whole, before becoming localised among dovish observers and disarmament campaigners. It is tempting to conclude that the scare has now run its course and that anxiety will slowly subside back to the low levels of the era of *détente*. However, neither the state of East/West relations nor the current levels of political debate, media coverage and poll responses on the defence issue as yet indicate any immediate prospect of a cessation of concern. How anxiety might develop over the next few years will be discussed towards the end of the present study. First, however, an assessment will be made of just how acute the recent war scare has actually been.

II THE DEPTH OF ANXIETY

It is hard to judge the depth of the recent British anxiety about a Third World War, because of a fundamental contradiction within the available evidence. On the one hand, direct statements about the risk of war have often tended to be extremely pessimistic, with no fewer than one in three survey respondents in 1980 stating that Britain was likely to be involved in a nuclear war within the next ten years.[62] On the other hand, indirect expressions of concern in terms of practical reactive measures have been strikingly lacking. Only a handful of Britons have made any attempt to protect themselves against nuclear attack, and even the hundreds of thousands of individuals who have joined marches for peace constitute only a tiny minority of the population as a whole. Of the one third of poll respondents who stated in 1980 that there was likely to be a nuclear war in the next decade, only half admitted to ever worrying about the prospect.[63] To judge from people's behaviour rather than from their expressed opinions, there has hardly been a war scare at all.

Most of the attempts which have so far been made to account for this contradiction between opinions about and reactions to the threat of war have stemmed from dovish observers, infuriated by the lack of public outcry at what they see as a very real peril. The American writer

Jonathan Schell addressed the issue in his apocalyptic work *The Fate of the Earth*, and British scientist Nick Humphrey gave a television lecture on the subject in 1981, in which he claimed that, 'we behave as though we have been hexed by the Bomb – put under a spell'.[64] Both these individuals put forward a plethora of psychological explanations for 'why we do not scream', but they tended to take for granted that the anxiety itself was both real and justified. The present study will examine the disjunction between fears and reactions in the recent war scare from a more sceptical perspective, first by analysing how the danger of conflict is currently perceived, and then by comparing this with the experience of the past.

Risk and reaction
One central characteristic of the threat of a Third World War is that no one is capable of assessing the risk of such a conflict in even a remotely scientific way. Analytical methods such as the 'fault-tree' system used in the nuclear power industry are quite useless because of the incredible complexity of political interactions, not to mention the fundamental controversy about what actually causes wars. The alternative 'empirical' technique of estimating risks from the known frequency of earlier events of a similar kind is ruled out by the unique political and technological characteristics of the current strategic situation.[65] It is, indeed, arguable that for such a singular phenomenon as World War Three the whole statistical concept of 'risk' becomes invalid, with the only meaningful question being whether and when a given individual, on the basis of his own subjective interpretation both of the contemporary situation and of historical precedent, expects conflict to occur.

This has not, however, prevented the majority of observers from speaking in terms of the 'likelihood' or 'probability' of war, as if it were as susceptible to statistical analysis as a car accident or an airline crash. Some individuals (including opinion pollsters) have even employed actual numbers – the Secretary General of the Pugwash organisation claimed in 1974 that, 'the odds are around one in three that a nuclear weapon will be used in a conflict situation before the year 1984, and . . . even or worse for nuclear war to occur in the twenty-six years remaining in this century.'[66] Most questionable of all were President Kennedy's remarks that the risk of war in the Berlin crisis of 1961 was one in five, and in the Cuba confrontation of the following year between one in three and evens, for what happened in these crises depended heavily upon Kennedy's own decisions.[67]

What appears to have prompted this spuriously statistical approach to the threat of East/West conflict has been an extreme reluctance to accept the more straightforward view (asserted frequently by the Chinese) that World War Three is positively inevitable and that the only question is how long it can be postponed.[68] Even the most alarmist British observers have eschewed such a despairing line, and have argued that there is a great risk of conflict, which can only be reduced if the proper policies are pursued.[69] Doves have frequently asserted that the odds of war and peace are almost evenly balanced, with catastrophe being at least as probable as the success of the peace campaign.[70] As Lord Brockway commented in early 1980:

> Today the scene is dark. I used to say that the chances of a nuclear world war were about 50–50. I must honestly say now that I believe the chances are 60–40. We will prevent the present situation developing into world war only if there is restraint on both sides.[71]

Opinion polls suggest that this reluctance to believe that East/West conflict is completely unavoidable is shared by the public at large. Although 80 per cent of survey respondents in 1981 said that there was some chance of a nuclear war in their lifetimes, and 38 per cent considered such a catastrophe to be likely, only 3 per cent believed that it was absolutely certain to occur.[72] This retention of hope seems to lie at the heart of the failure of the recent anxiety about World War Three to evoke substantial reactive measures. It cannot, however, account for the contradiction in strictly logical terms. In Bernard Brodie's words, 'even if we estimate the probability of a general war within any given time span as very low, say one per cent, the implications for policy may be very great'.[73] The attitude of the British government, sceptical about the threat of war but nevertheless maintaining minimal civil defence precautions as 'an "insurance premium" against the remote risk that NATO's continuing deterrent policy might fail' may conceivably be seen as logically consistent,[74] but the outlook of those who do nothing about the threat of conflict despite professing to consider it a possible or even probable occurrence requires a less rationalistic explanation. Such an explanation will now be sought in the experience of the past.

A historical yardstick

There have been many war scares in modern British history, but the jingoistic fears of invasion which characterised popular anxiety before 1914 bear very little resemblance to the current dread of a mutually devastating conflict between Russia and the West.[75] The recent war scare may profitably be compared only to its two most immediate predecessors – the original Cold War, and the anxious years of the 1930s. The similarity with the Cold War is obvious, but the parallel between British war fears in the 1980s and in the period prior to World War Two may require some explanation.

British horror of war in the 1930s seems to have been almost as great as that which has arisen in modern times. This stemmed partly from the searing experience of trench warfare in 1914–18, but also from an exaggerated fear of aerial bombardment. Just as the atomic bombing of Hiroshima and Nagasaki at the end of World War Two has today helped to fuel apocalyptic fears of an all-out thermonuclear holocaust, so the Zeppelin raids and poison gas attacks of World War One led to widespread fears that improved military technology would permit inconceivable slaughter to be inflicted upon the populations of the belligerent countries if conflict should ever again occur.[76] Even official estimates foresaw millions of civilian casualties, while popular imagery equated war with Armageddon and the end of civilised society.[77] Just as today, there were those who predicted that war would begin in a more 'conventional' fashion, but many others thought that death itself would be preferable to the apocalypse in store, and even contemplated killing their children if war broke out.[78] As one observer asserted (in a passage which, although written in 1932, would not have sounded out of place fifty years later):

> The collapse of civilization, under circumstances of unimaginable horror – that, and nothing less, is what a future war, on the grand scale, has in store for us and ours. So far as there can be any certainty in human affairs, this thing is certain.[79]

The parallel with the 1930s will be examined in due course, but first, attention will be turned to how the recent anxiety about World War Three compares with that which existed at the time of the original Cold War. Modern views on which was the more dangerous period are ambivalent. Those who today see little danger of a Third World War tend to argue that the current situation is far less perilous than that of twenty-five years ago.[80] Alarmists, however, assert that the new threat is on a par with earlier perils such as the Cuban missile crisis, or (more usually) that the risk of war is now greater than at any time since the 1930s.[81] One concerned scientist commemorated the twenty-fifth anniversary of the Russell-Einstein manifesto of 1955 with the pessimistic observation that:

... if, after congratulating ourselves on surviving so far, we take a sombre look at the world today, we must come to the conclusion that the peril has not been averted. Indeed, the world situation is far more perilous than it was 25 years ago; the probability of a nuclear war during this century is very high.[82]

Such claims may perhaps be ascribed partly to rhetorical exaggeration, but other evidence does seem to suggest that, whatever the actual relative danger of the 1950s and 1980s, the war scares themselves reached a comparable pitch of anxiety. Recent opinion polls, in particular, appear to indicate almost unprecedented levels of pessimism and concern. In 1980, a higher proportion of survey respondents said that there was much danger of world war than at any other time since the height of the Korean conflict in 1951, and a 1983 poll found just as much worry about nuclear war as had existed in 1958.[83] Other indicators such as media coverage, literature output, and the size of CND demonstrations also seem to suggest broad comparability between the recent war scare and that of twenty-five years ago.[84] However, there is a definite artificiality to the recent concern compared to the days when (in Khrushchev's evocative phrase) 'the smell of burning hung in the air'.[85] Only 4 per cent of British poll respondents in 1980 said that international affairs was the most important problem facing the country, compared to no less than 46 per cent who had placed defence or foreign affairs first twenty-five years earlier.[86] This contrast will now be explored further, with reference to the even sharper anxiety which existed in the late 1930s.

Although there is obviously no question of the actual risk of war being greater now than it was in 1939, several observers have suggested that the Russian threat is even graver than that posed by Hitler's Germany, or that nuclear weapons have made the early 1980s the most dangerous years in human history.[87] As one MP asserted, 'Never, since the great Barbarian invasions and the fall of the Roman Empire, have the people of the West been in such peril as they are today'.[88] Opinion poll evidence, peace demonstrations and the like all seem on the surface to suggest a broad comparability between the war scare of the 1930s and that of recent years. In this case, however, the underlying difference of atmosphere is too striking to be ignored. Many modern commentators, especially those with personal experience of the pre-war period, have poured scorn on the idea that either the danger or the anxiety of the 1980s is as great as that which existed before 1939.[89] In Enoch Powell's words:

> Those of us of a certain age lived through the 1930s when there was
> a real and growing fear of war . . . We shall always know the smell –
> the acrid, perceptible, unmistakable smell – of the rising threat of
> force . . . It is absurd to suppose that this is the state of mind among
> the nations of Europe and here in this country.[90]

The difference of atmosphere between the pre-war period and the
modern era seems to have been most tangibly manifested in the striking
contrast between the apathetic pessimism of the 1980s and the panic
which occurred fifty years before. The Munich crisis of 1938 prompted a
flood of hasty marriages, a boom in the sales of wills, the hoarding of
sugar and petrol, and widespread thoughts of evacuation.[91] A year later,
private refugees from the cities at least equalled the hundreds of
thousands of official evacuees dispersed before the outbreak of war.[92]
When set against such a precedent, the recent flurry of interest in civil
defence, and the installation of a handful of private fallout shelters
(numbered by one newspaper in 1983 at less than three dozen) pale
almost into insignificance.[93] Part of the explanation for the contrast is
undoubtedly that many people today think survival measures pointless
in the face of a nuclear holocaust.[94] However, the main implications of
the behavioural dissonance between the 1930s and the 1980s seem to be
intimately tied up with the contradiction between opinions and
reactions which was discussed at the start of this section.

If there is any single piece of evidence which provides the key to
understanding the paradox of modern reactions to the threat of World
War Three, it lies in a series of social surveys carried out by a group
called 'Mass Observation' in 1938 and 1939.[95] These surveys provide
what is probably the best available insight into how people react to the
prospect of total war. The methods used in the surveys did include the
opinion poll technique which has now become so universal, but they
also involved passive observation and the verbatim recording of
individual views. The results obtained appear rather subjective and
unscientific to modern eyes, but they also feel far fuller and truer to life
than the cold statistics of more recent opinion surveys.

The adequacy of the opinion poll technique itself will be discussed in
the Appendix. Here, attention will be confined to the specific
implications of the Mass Observation studies for assessing the depth of
the recent anxiety about World War Three. The 1930s evidence seems to
suggest that people's reactions to the threat of war pass through three
broad stages as the danger becomes graver and more immediate. At
times of peace or low tension, opinions about the risk of war tend to

involve fairly stable judgements (often based upon the flimsiest of criteria) about the long-term prospects for avoiding conflict. Such judgements, even if profoundly pessimistic, seem to have very little impact upon behaviour, either because it is assumed that (despite the danger) war will be averted, or because the expected catastrophe is too far in the future to worry about. It is this refusal to accept that war might actually come that has made civil defence precautions so emotional an issue in every war scare from Munich to the present day.[96] These responses which Mass Observation collected in March 1938 convey the flavour of popular opinions at a time of no immediate crisis:

Man of 17:	'Reckon we're in for a war.'
Man of 35:	'I think we shall have another war sooner or later, not yet.'
Man of 50:	'There's trouble brewing. These armaments are not for nothing.'
Woman of 40:	'Don't think there'll be a war for another three years.'
Man of 25:	'Not yet. If Czechoslovakia is invaded there will be a war.'
Man of 45:	'I can't think. I hope it comes to nothing.'
Woman of 40:	'If your name's on the bomb, it's all up with you. That's that. I don't read the newspapers.'
Man of 25:	'Think we'll muddle through.'
Woman of 45:	'No possibility of a war.'
Man of 55:	'There won't be a war. Chamberlain is seeing to that.'[97]

When a crisis occurs, the threat of war becomes more immediate, and so triggers a whole battery of psychological defences. The Mass Observation studies report many classic instances of the avoidance of disturbing information and the search for reassurance, but more important for the present purpose is the operation of wishful thinking. The closer war appears, the more compelled people feel to deny that it will occur. An opinion poll at the height of the Munich crisis found that public fears had apparently decreased since earlier in the year, and on the very eve of war in 1939, the approach of conflict was denied by a two to one majority of survey respondents.[98] Popular anxiety at times of crisis seems thus to be characterised less by unprecedented pessimism than by a striking intensity and volatility in the opinions held, as illustrated by the following Mass Observation report from 1939:

A working-class wife in Worktown said on August 26th that she thought war would not come. 'It is just a bluff; and have you seen the paragraph in the Evening News which says that Hitler is already climbing down?' She said she was worried by the situation, but was trying not to think about it. 'I haven't made any preparations; haven't bought blind or anything; haven't even bought food – couldn't have afforded it, really.' Two days later, the same woman said, 'I feel very depressed today. Yesterday's news on the radio really got me down. I don't know what to do. I still haven't made any preparations. I think the danger of war today is more serious than I thought on Saturday, though the Stars say there will be no war. My husband follows Lyndoe in the *People*, and he says that there will be no war.'[99]

The principal cause of volatility in public opinion during a grave crisis appears to be that, when the confrontation passes a certain point, wishful thinking collapses, and opinions swing suddenly towards a panic acceptance of the imminence of war. This happened after the German invasion of Poland in 1939, but it had also occurred a year earlier during the final stages of the Munich crisis. There was nothing calm or philosophical about the resignation involved – many individuals were roused to extreme belligerence, others experienced physical symptoms of sickness and nausea, and active preparations such as hoarding and evacuation began in earnest.[100] Such signs of panic thus seem to mark the radical difference between abstract pessimism about the likelihood of war and true acceptance that it will actually come.

The three-stage progression which the Mass Observation evidence reveals in public reactions to the threat of total war allows a better understanding of the difference between the anxiety of the 1980s and the 1950s. In neither case did concern reach the stage of resignation and panic on a mass scale as happened in 1938, but popular fears during the crises of the 1950s and 1960s do indeed appear to have been more intense and volatile than in recent years, suggesting that the threat of war impinged more upon the public consciousness. Wishful thinking seems to have prevented this from being reflected in greater reactive measures or overt pessimism, but there appears to have been a stronger sense of repressed tension, as illustrated by the following extract from an insurance salesman's recollections of the Cuban missile crisis:

I have over 700 families on my books, and the thing that struck me most about the Cuban affair was the fact that when the crisis was at its height, nobody dared mention it. My policy-holders, normally talkative, looked worried out of their lives, but paid their premiums like automatons, and studiously avoided any mention of the thing that was obviously uppermost in their minds.[101]

The recent war scare is comparable less with British reactions to the Munich, Berlin and Cuba crises than with less anxious periods such as the early 1930s and the mid-1950s, when no immediate great power confrontation was in train. In both these cases, the destructiveness of new military technology prompted apocalyptic visions such as *The Shape of Things to Come*, despite the lack of an obvious political cause for such a devastating conflict.[102] In both cases, many individuals called for disarmament and world government as the only alternative to the suicide of civilisation.[103] However, both these earlier periods of anxiety proved only a foretaste of the concern which would arise as true great power confrontations developed, whereas the more recent war scare, in the absence of such head-on confrontations, has remained at the level of abstract worry and fatalism about mankind's future in the long-term.

It is sometimes suggested that fear of war is actually a greater motivation in the CND movement today than it was twenty-five years ago, when the protest was allegedly driven largely by moral outrage.[104] However, this is an extremely questionable assertion. The undoubted moral outrage of the early CND was accompanied by an urgently felt need to head off an impending nuclear war, an impulsion which led to the disastrously divisive direct action of the Committee of 100.[105] The present situation seems to be rather different. Fear certainly plays a dominant role in current activism, but it has not prevented the disarmament campaign from adopting a long-haul strategy of public education and political pressure with little impact upon more immediate international developments. One need only compare the current rhetoric of E. P. Thompson about a degenerative process of exterminism with Bertrand Russell's urgent warnings during the original Cold War of the risk of a nuclear holocaust in the next few weeks or months to see that today's disarmers tend to take a markedly more long-term view of the perils concerned.[106]

Historical experience thus appears to suggest that the current war scare, for all its peace marches and pessimistic rhetoric, is actually rather less acute than either of its immediate predecessors. The greater seriousness of the earlier scares seems to have been somewhat masked, because psychological factors impelled people to resist the notion that war was imminent by ignoring or denying the threat until the last possible moment. A similar process appears to have operated in West Germany in early 1980, with opinion polls showing an apparent lack of concern despite the obvious presence of considerable anxiety.[107] Indeed, one study in 1983 revealed that there was very little reflection in survey data alone even of such wide differences as those between Holland, with its powerful protest movements, and France, with its pervasive popular acquiescence on the defence issue.[108] Both historical precedent and international comparisons thus indicate the need to rely on other evidence besides opinion poll results for a proper assessment of public anxiety about World War Three.

The experience of the 1930s and 1950s does not itself provide all the answers required. Serious questions remain, such as why, if the recent war scare was actually rather less acute than either of its predecessors, it gave rise to a comparably-sized peace movement and popular defence debate. This problem will be discussed in Chapter 6. In the remainder of the present chapter, attention will be turned to the wider issue of whether there have been any secular changes either in the alarm itself or in the societal context which make it invalid to infer simply from the lack of overt panic that the recent war scare has been less serious than those which have gone before.

The changing atmosphere

There appear to be four main factors other than a lower sense of threat which can help to account for the fact that gut anxiety in the recent war scare has been less than that in the 1950s, or at least than that in the years before 1939. In the first place, television has brought live images of world events into British homes, without eroding the tendency to leave the actual running of societal affairs (particularly those in the defence field) to professionals and to 'the government'. The vast majority of citizens have thus been cast even more strongly in the role of inactive spectators, bombarded by a continuous flood of vicarious imagery, but unused to reacting without a clear official lead. In this situation, the possibility of a Third World War seems for many to have become just another remote and abstract 'issue' on which an opinion is required. How this state of affairs is interpreted depends on one's views about the actual danger of war; Nick Humphrey lamented that, 'we have become passive, fascinated spectators of the slowly unfolding nuclear tragedy', but the present study will later argue that it is the pessimism rather than the inaction which is artificial, and that the widespread dissemination of often sensationalist imagery via the modern media has itself been responsible for much of the recent anxiety about World War Three.[109]

The second possible reason for the absence of overt panic is that the nuclear threat and the possibility of annihilation have existed long enough for people to become habituated to the risks involved. Anxiety and panic cannot be maintained indefinitely no matter how certain an ultimate disaster appears, and prolonged periods of danger tend to evoke much less reaction than do crises which develop over a fairly short period of time. The CND movement has always drawn most of its followers from the young generation only just discovering the nuclear threat, despite the fact that pessimism about World War Three does not seem to have been drastically less among older age-groups. It appears to have been the *novelty* as much as the frightfulness of the threat of aerial bombardment which sparked off popular anxiety in the 1930s, and it is noteworthy that today's disarmament campaigners have had to stress new dangers such as cruise missiles and counterforce strategies, rather than renewing Bertrand Russell's frontal assault upon the whole concept of nuclear terror. As early as 1964, Christopher Driver remarked that 'We have lived long enough on the brink to have become rather blasé about it.'[100]

The third reason for the peculiar mixture of pessimism and passivity in the recent war scare appears to lie in the nature of Third World War imagery itself. Britons in the 1930s may have had an exaggeratedly apocalyptic image of future warfare, but it was still easier for them to come to terms with impending conflict than it is for people nowadays to truly accept the prospect of whole cities being vaporised in a nuclear holocaust. Nuclear devastation is impossible to comprehend in terms of everyday experience, and (as Humphrey put it), 'The so-called facts pass clean through us and away, like radio emissions from the stars.'[111] After a certain point, terrifying threats tend to deaden rather than stimulate practical reactions, and this point seems certainly to have been reached in the case of Britain's palpable vulnerability to nuclear attack. In the words of Harold Macmillan, 'when one lives on Vesuvius, one takes little account of the risk of eruptions.'[112] Even during the Cuban missile crisis, resistance to the idea that war might actually come was so strong that no civil defence preparations were made, and only a handful of people fled the assumed target area.[113] Nuclear war is such an appalling prospect that its imminence would probably not be truly accepted until hostilities between East and West had actually begun.[114]

If the nuclear holocaust fails to engage popular anxiety because it so unthinkably horrific, conventional warfare, on the other hand, seems now to appear *insufficiently* terrifying for the prospect to induce alarm and panic among the public at large. This profound shift from the situation in the 1930s seems to stem less from greater popular sang-froid than from a greater feeling of detachment from conventional hostilities. Aerial bombardment is now associated almost exclusively with nuclear weapons, while the threat of enemy occupation still touches no historical chords. Even the rigours of rationing and conscription have seemingly been banished by the short war assumption and the professionalisation of the armed forces. The threat of military defeat still provokes considerable anxiety (especially among hawks), but the idea of a conventional Third World War seems to cause nothing like the same horror in Britain that it does in West Germany, where war fears have been far less abstract and offhand.[115]

The fourth (and probably the most important) reason why British pessimism about World War Three has been rather blasé appears to be that war has not usually been expected to come in the immediate future. Only in early 1980, when growing superpower entanglement in the Persian Gulf seemed a real possibility, did the danger seem as close as in the many successive crises of the original Cold War (let alone as close as in pre-war crises such as Munich, when over half of survey respondents at one point asserted that war would come 'on Saturday, if not before').[116] Hawkish warnings have recently been the most urgent, but even they have usually envisaged a time scale of some two to five years.[117] A few hard-liners did emphasise that a Soviet attack might come at any time, but it is noteworthy that hawkish alarm tended to decline when the predicted 'window of opportunity' actually arrived.[118] Dovish observers have generally suggested an even longer time scale than hawks for the danger of World War Three, talking mostly in terms of one to three decades. As one writer asserted:

> Unless the nuclear arms race is stopped and reversed, the occurrence of nuclear war, or wars, is probably just a matter of time. Quite possibily it will occur within the lives of our children or grandchildren.[119]

The general public appears likewise to take a far longer-term view of the danger of conflict than it did in previous war scares. This is illustrated by a comparison of three opinion polls, from March 1938, August 1950 and May 1980. In all these surveys, roughly two-thirds of respondents said they thought war would one day come. However, whereas 37 per cent of respondents in 1939, and 32 per cent in 1950, said that war would break out within two years, only 11 per cent of the 1980 poll sample thought that conflict would occur that soon.[120] By 1983, concern had become even less urgent, and only one in ten of those who said that there would one day be a Third World War suggested it would come before 1988.[121]

The prevailing disbelief in the idea that World War Three will occur in the immediate future seems to be indirectly reflected in the fact that alarmists on both sides of the political spectrum have been forced to rely on more subtle tactics than simply shouting 'Do this, or the heavens will fall!.' Hawks have often admitted that an actual Soviet attack is unlikely even if Western 'weakness' continues, but they have laid great stress upon the less tangible peril of the gradual 'Finlandisation' of Europe by Soviet military predominance. As one writer claimed in 1976:

> The danger is not that Russia's overwhelming military might will be unleashed suddenly against us. It is that fear of provoking this power, hope of softer living, and lack of confidence in our own values – which are all the time under psychological assault – may incline us to make our own position indefensible on any terms on which we should be prepared to defend it.[122]

Doves have been less ready to dismiss the risk of an actual war, but have tried to overcome popular scepticism about the likelihood of conflict in the immediate future by concentrating their alarmism upon the longer term. In order to motivate people to active protest in the short run, E. P. Thompson has constructed the notion of 'exterminism', an inexorable historical process which (he claims) is bound *eventually* to lead to nuclear war, if the slide is not stopped by positive measures to reverse the arms race in the very near future.[123] In his words, 'If my arguments are correct, then we cannot put off the matter any longer. We must throw whatever resources still exist in human culture across the path of this degenerative logic. We must protest if we are to survive.'[124] (One at least of Thompson's 'points of no return' in the slide to war, namely the INF deployment of 1983, has now been passed, but it is waning anxiety rather than resignation and despair which has caused the subsequent decline of the disarmament campaign.)

The subtle and qualified nature of the alarmists' arguments has been characteristic of the recent war scare as a whole. It has been a scare of the head rather than the heart, based upon technical worries about military hardware rather than upon grave international confrontation, and inducing pessimism rather than panic. The spectre of World War Three, although it has unquestionably dominated the anxiety of the past decade, proves on inspection to be strangely elusive – war always seems to be thought of as waiting in the wings or lying just around the next bend. This should not, however, be taken to mean that the alarm itself has been in any way insubstantial or unreal. Although there has been nothing like the gut anxiety of the 1930s and 1950s, this seems to have been due as much to differences in the underlying character of the scare as to a lower absolute level of fear. Whether the recent concern about war has actually been justified is, of course, another matter altogether, and one which will be discussed at length in the chapters to come.

4 The Reasons for the Scare

It is very difficult to objectively assess what has prompted the recent upsurge of anxiety about World War Three, for two principal reasons. In the first place, there has been such a wide variety of disturbing strategic developments over the past decade that it is hard to say which of them has played the greatest part in sparking the revival of alarm. In stark contrast to the 'age of peace' in the 1970s, when 'doomwatchers' from both sides of the political spectrum faced an uphill struggle in trying to convince people that all was not as tranquil as it seemed, the 1980s have witnessed so many frightening events that the burden of proof in debates about the risk of war has come to rest almost as heavily upon those who are *not* seriously alarmed.

This leads on to the second major difficulty facing any attempt to assess the causes of the recent war scare, namely the bitter disagreements within British society about the issues involved. Those who themselves see a grave risk of war naturally have a different perspective upon what has caused the fears of others than do those who remain sceptical of the danger of conflict. Policy views appear also to have a role, with hawks tending to attribute the upsurge of anxiety to causes such as the Russian military build-up and the invasion of Afghanistan, while doves lay greater stress upon the part played by other events like the Cruise and Trident missile decisions, the American nuclear accidents, and the publication of the official civil defence handbook *Protect and Survive*.[1] It is not so easy to reconcile these claims by saying that 'different things have worried different people', because many disarmers have claimed that the true cause of hawkish alarm has been a blinkered Cold War mentality, while several hard-liners have asserted that the real cause of the revival of anti-nuclear protest has been successful Soviet nuclear intimidation.[2] As one hawkish commentator wrote:

> Twenty years ago the unilateralist campaign was essentially one of moral protest based on an assumption of nuclear superiority: these were weapons so dreadful that it was immoral to have a defence policy that made us even contemplate using them upon others. Today the unilateralist cause is fuelled by fear based on an assumption of nuclear vulnerability: these are weapons so

dreadful that it is foolish to have a defence policy that might make others more likely to use them upon us.[3]

The present study will attempt to judge the validity of these conflicting interpretations of what has caused the recent war scare, by making a detailed examination of the issues involved. First, the question of which strategic developments have aroused most alarm will be addressed by asking which courses of events Britons have feared might lead to a Third World War. Then, the deep causes of the recent war scare will be analysed by trying to get beyond such one-sided explanations as 'the arms race' or 'the Soviet threat', and by discussing the fundamentally disturbing nature of the current state of heavily armed deterrence.

I WHENCE THE THREAT TO PEACE?

The problem of what causes wars is unquestionably the most contentious issue both in military history and in defence policy debates. Scholarly disputes have raged over the causes even of long forgotten conflicts, and the origins of more recent wars have provoked even greater disagreement because of the passions aroused and the continuing search for 'objective' revision and reappraisal.[4] Given the controversy surrounding the causes of individual wars which have already taken place, it may readily be imagined that the search for an overall theory of why international conflict occurs has produced many conflicting hypotheses, either 'confirmed' or (more often) shattered by each new war that breaks out.[5] It thus comes as no surprise that the question of what might possibly bring about a Third World War at some future date has provoked extensive disagreement within British society in recent years.

One aspect of the perennial dispute about the causes of wars which has become especially prominent over the past few decades is the problem of whether conflict is more likely to arise as a deliberate act of policy or through an unplanned collision between the states involved. Opinions on this issue are often clouded by a failure to distinguish between ultimate and immediate causes of war. Confusion of this kind seems certainly to have underlain the bitter dispute between A. J. P. Taylor and Hugh Trevor-Roper over Nazi culpability for World War Two, with Taylor focusing upon the 'accidental' nature of the actual outbreak of war in September 1939, while Trevor-Roper was more concerned with the underlying thrust of Hitlerian expansionism.[6]

Similar confusion appears to dog contemporary speculation about the likely causes of World War Three, with hawks frequently stressing Soviet malevolence but suggesting that war itself would probably come through miscalculation, while doves sometimes assert that the arms race might inadvertently produce a situation in which one side is driven to a deliberate pre-emptive strike.[7] To try to resolve this ambivalence, the ultimate and immediate causes suggested by Britons for a possible Third World War will here be separated, and examined in turn.

Ultimate causes of war

The experience of the 1930s seems to have greatly reinforced what Donald Watt called 'the sin theory of international relations', whereby 'States, like characters in a detective thriller, could be classified into criminals and victims, aggressors and objects of aggression'.[8] This black-and-white notion remains highly influential to this day, especially in the provisions of the United Nations Charter and in the stereotyped scenarios of 'potential aggression' which characterise official NATO strategy. However, speculation about the actual *causes* of war has very rarely been couched in such simplistic and Manichean terms. Even during the Falklands conflict with Argentina in 1982, British commentators tried to take a detached view of the tangled claims and mutual misperceptions which led to the outbreak of hostilities.[9] The way in which the sin theory does tend to influence thinking about the causes of war is by concentrating attention upon the *relative* responsibility of individual nations, rather than upon political or technical processes affecting the international community as a whole.

British views on which bloc would be more responsible for World War Three range all the way from the official dictum that NATO will never attack anyone and that any hostilities must therefore be initiated entirely by the Warsaw Pact, to the extreme left-wing image of imperialist aggression against a peace-loving socialist camp.[10] Most opinions, however, seem to fall somewhere between these two dogmatic extremes, and to assign at least some of the potential blame to both blocs. Hawkish observers who see the main threat to peace as being an expansionist Soviet drive for world domination often assert that a major contributory cause of conflict could be the West's own weakness and irresolution, tempting Russia to try to hasten her 'historically inevitable' triumph by military means.[11] Doves who have a very different image of the Soviet Union as a defensive, status quo power nevertheless readily admit that her paranoid fear of encirclement or attack could increase the danger posed by the allegedly provocative and bellicose stance of the West itself.[12]

Many observers see some truth in *both* these interpretations of the international situation, and are therefore less able than either hawks or doves to suggest an easy way to reduce the risk of war by means of unilateral amendments to Western policy.[13] Russia is often seen as threatening the peace less because of the imperial march of Soviet communism than because of the internal instability of the Soviet empire, whose alleged decay is compared by some to the disastrous decline of the Austro-Hungarian empire before 1914.[14] The peril of the West's own posture is widely believed to flow less from weakness or assertiveness *per se* than from an unpredictable vacillation between these two extremes, increasing the danger of a collision through miscalculation.[15] As Laurence Martin said in his Reith lectures of 1981:

> Conditioned by its ideals to feel guilty about the use of force, democratic opinion is addicted to crusades: if not against some foreign foe, on whom we project all the blame for our being in conflict, then against the idea of armed force itself. Today, American public opinion, notoriously moody in this way, is on the former tack, while more and more Europeans are taking the other. The danger of such emotionalism leading to intemperate action has been amply demonstrated in the past.[16]

Many Britons have tended to see the danger of a Third World War as stemming from the competition between the superpowers themselves, rather than from the confrontation between the Eastern and Western blocs as a whole. This has allowed observers to take an artificially detached view of which side poses the greater threat to peace, as if Britain herself stood aloof from the whole affair.[17] Doves, in particular, have been equally critical of both superpowers, and have often asserted that it is the United States whose policies now entail the greater risk of war.[18] In E. P. Thompson's words:

> If you press me for my own view then I would hazard that the Russian state is now the most dangerous in relation to its own people and to the people of its client states . . . The United States seems to me to be more dangerous and provocative in its general military and diplomatic strategies, which press around the Soviet Union with menacing bases.[19]

Opinion polls reveal striking support for this 'even-handed' condemnation among the public at large. In a 1982 survey, just as many respondents said that America was likely to attack Eastern Europe as said Russia was likely to attack Western Europe within the next five-year period, with the respondents' political allegiances affecting only the *absolute* level of risk perceived.[20] In 1981, another survey found that the United States was considered almost as likely as the Soviet Union to start a nuclear war.[21] Although 42 per cent of poll respondents in 1983 said that Russia posed the greater threat to world peace (compared to only 12 per cent who said this of America), no less than 39 per cent of respondents stated that there was nothing to choose between the two superpowers in this regard.[22]

What does seem to distinguish fears of the United States and the Soviet Union is the perceived *character* of the threat which each poses to the peace of the world. Although British images of Russia tend to be far less monolithic and Manichean than those prevailing in the United States, poll respondents in 1980 did assert by a ten to one majority that there was a real Soviet military threat to Europe.[23] Both superpowers are thought to have built up their armed forces primarily to defend themselves from attack, but the Soviet Union is seen as having a much greater wish to extend its power over other countries, and a much lower commitment to world peace.[24] America seems to be seen as threatening the peace more because of the alleged irresponsibility and unpredictability of her foreign policy, with two-thirds of British survey respondents throughout the past decade stating that they had little or no confidence in the ability of the United States to deal wisely with the problems of the world.[25]

The notion that American impetuosity might provoke a disastrously reckless reaction to a delicate international crisis is far from new. Such fears were widespread in the original Cold War, with Bertrand Russell going so far as to assert that 'We in Britain are not prepared to place the future of our species in the hands of semi-literate paranoids compulsively acting out their sick hates and their blind malice.'[26] Fear of American recklessness declined after the peaceful resolution of the Cuban missile crisis, but was revived in 1980 by the election of the notorious hawk Ronald Reagan as US President.[27] Some British commentators suggested that Reagan's consistently hard-line approach might actually be safer than the vacillation of President Carter,[28] but the popular image of 'Ronnie Ray-Gun' as a trigger-happy nuclear cowboy made the public at large consider the new administration as more of a threat than a bulwark to world peace, with nine times as many survey respondents in 1981 saying that US foreign policy increased the risk of nuclear war than thought it made the situation safer.[29]

Nuclear disarmers have tended to be the most fervent prophets of American culpability for World War Three, and have frequently argued that not only the policies but also the interests of Europe and the United States have come to diverge.[30] Two specific issues are usually cited in this connection. The first is the increasingly global character of the superpower confrontation, which has led to fears that Britain might be dragged into a Soviet-American conflict sparked outside the NATO area. As one commentator wrote, 'Probably the main risk now is that in a conflict outside Europe, for example the Middle East, the Americans might use, or threaten to use, nuclear weapons against the Soviet Union from British bases and so involve us in a nuclear war.'[31]

The second issue which has worried the disarmers concerns the tangled question of 'theatre nuclear war'. The ambiguities of NATO's 'flexible response' strategy have prompted many in CND to accuse the United States of deliberately planning to distance herself from, and thereby 'win', a nuclear war with Russia. In Thompson's words, 'it is thought by persons in the Pentagon that a "theatre" nuclear war might be confined to Europe, in which, to be sure, America's NATO allies would be obliterated, but in which immense damage would be inflicted upon Russia west of the Urals, while the soil of the United States remained immune . . . This has been seen as the way to a great victory for "the West", and if world-wide nuclear war seems to be ultimately inevitable, then the sooner it can be aborted by having a little theatre war the better.' Disarmers make frequent reference to the appalling statement of a renegade American admiral that 'We fought World War One in Europe, we fought World War Two in Europe, and if you dummies let us, we'll fight World War Three in Europe.'[32] The supposed compliance of European governments with this sinister plan tends to be explained by allegations of blind fear of Russia and unthinking subservience to the USA.[33]

Although the theatre nuclear war scare fits in very well with the 'sin theory' of international relations, doves have usually tried to avoid assigning blame to individual nations or blocs, and have instead described the danger of World War Three in terms of impersonal processes affecting the international community as a whole. World poverty, economic stagnation and the depletion of natural resources have all been cited as possible contributory causes of a global conflict, and some socialists have claimed that the danger flows from the alleged worldwide exploitation of the producing classes,[34] but by far the most prominent peril in dovish eyes has been the arms race. Continued competitive acquisition of weapons is said to pose technical and psychological dangers which are hurling mankind at an accelerating pace towards a catastrophic Third World War.[35] As one disarmer put it:

The nuclear arms race is leading us to the brink of irreversible escalation, to the point of no return. Beyond that is the final abyss. We face the imminent prospect of the extermination of the human race. It must be stopped – and there is very little time left to stop it.[36]

Perhaps the most striking aspect of the arms race concept is that the perils involved have tended to be taken for granted by observers on all sides of the political spectrum. A few commentators have challenged the notion that arms races inevitably lead to war, but most sceptics have tended to pay lip service to the risks of the arms race while concentrating upon other perils such as the Soviet threat.[37] This lack of a direct challenge to the arms race notion has meant that the dangers which are assumed to be involved have often not been clearly defined. The one specific peril on which there seems to be widest agreement is that of nuclear proliferation to the Third World, although this does not now appear to cause as much anxiety as it did in the 1960s.[38] Doves have tended to focus their attention upon the more immediate dangers said to flow from the East/West arms competition itself. The technical dangers thought to be entailed in the manipulation and modernisation of the superpower arsenals will be discussed at length in Chapter 5. Psychological risks are also said to exist, in the shape of institutionalised militarism and the whipping up of a war psychosis. E. P. Thompson has persistently stressed this particular dimension of the arms race, in polemical warnings of the 'degenerative' state of deterrence and the independent downward momentum of the Cold War confrontation. In his words:

> Deterrence theory proposes a stationary state: that of MAD. But history knows no stationary states. As deterrence presides, both parties change; they become addicted; they become uglier and more barbarous in their postures and gestures. They turn into societies whose production, ideology, and research is increasingly directed towards war. 'Deterrence' enters deeply into the structure, the economy, and the culture of both blocs. This is the reason – and not this or that advantage in weaponry, or political contingency – why nuclear war is probable within our own lifetimes. It is not just that we are preparing for war; we are preparing ourselves to be *the kind of societies* which go to war.[39]

An integral part of Thompson's argument is that there is no longer any substantive conflict behind the Cold War confrontation, and that the real danger lies not in the opposing bloc but in the menacing security establishments of both sides, feeding off each other to maintain the frozen hostility of the late 1940s.[40] This assertion has been strongly challenged by several defence commentators, who argue that the arms race is driven not by its own momentum but by traditional mechanisms of power politics, with danger arising when the distribution of power becomes imbalanced.[41] Michael Howard has drawn a parallel with Thucydides' assessment of the causes of the Peloponnesian War, namely that 'What made war inevitable was the growth of Athenian power, and the fear this caused in Sparta.'[42] Many commentators (including Howard) concentrate on the dangers of an imbalance of power in favour of the Soviet Union, but others have asserted that the peril of the current situation lies in the fact that *both* superpowers feel power and influence slipping from their grasp.[43]

Hawks and doves do seem to agree on a wide range of 'neutral' dangers in the present international situation, such as the turmoil in the Third World, the economic travails facing rich and poor nations alike, and the sheer intractable complexity of the interlocking global problems of the 1980s.[44] However, the nature of the threat to peace in the East/West confrontation itself is the subject of fundamental disagreement both among informed commentators and within the public at large. Disputes rage over whether the danger lies in Soviet expansionism or American recklessness, in power politics or the arms race, or in a combination of all these things. The implications of this disagreement for the causes of the recent war scare will be examined later in the present section, but first, attention will be turned to the specific events which Britons consider would be the most likely triggers for World War Three.

Immediate causes of war
British commentators have suggested a very large number of possible causes for the actual outbreak of a Third World War. Even those observers who assert that war is almost inconceivable usually specify certain improbable contingencies in which conflict might actually occur. More alarmist commentators (especially doves) tend to put forward many different suggestions as to what might spark an East/West war.[45] These suggestions are rarely mutually exclusive, and it is often asserted that the likeliest cause of World War Three would be an unmanageable *combination* of pressures and crises.[46]

There are obviously an infinite number of possible scenarios for the outbreak of a Third World War, so that most writers refrain from making detailed predictions, being careful to specify that any scenarios they might construct are purely illustrative in intent. The one issue on which commentators do usually express fairly firm opinions is the fundamental question of whether World War Three would arise as an act of deliberate policy or through an unintended sequence of events. British observers have suggested five broad sets of causes along the spectrum between accident and design, namely human or technical mishap, the escalation of an independent crisis to embroil the superpowers, a deliberate act by one bloc which miscalculates the opposing side's resolve and leads to an inescapable confrontation, a pre-emptive strike provoked by fear of enemy attack, and deliberate, cold-blooded aggression. These five causes (by no means mutually exclusive) will now be examined in turn.

The spectre of accidental war aroused fairly widespread anxiety twenty-five years ago, in the days of the 'hair-trigger nuclear alert'.[47] In recent years, however, it has been mainly the disarmers who have continued to claim that counterforce instability and the multiplication of nuclear delivery systems are inexorably increasing the risk of a war by technical malfunction or by human incompetence or madness.[48] Other commentators have become increasingly sceptical about such warnings, partly because of a low estimate of the risk of such a mishap, and partly because of disbelief in the idea that sheer accident could spark off such a profoundly political process as a war.[49] However, the public at large, bombarded by sensationalist stories of American nuclear mishaps, appears to have a much lower faith in the safety of the deterrent infrastructure, with one in four poll respondents in 1983 saying that nuclear weapons are most likely to go off by accident, and one in five stating that this is the most probable cause of a Third World War.[50]

The idea that war might result from the escalation of an independent regional crisis seems to dominate the thinking of all but firm believers in political rationality or Soviet malice. In Lawrence Freedman's words, 'If World War Three begins, it is unlikely to be a conscious decision of superpower leaders. More likely they will be dragged into it by ambitious or irresponsible clients in circumstances they, the superpowers, do not fully understand.'[51] The mechanics of this growing superpower entanglement are rarely discussed, but most observers seem to believe that it could occur through an incremental escalatory process which distorts or pre-empts successive political decisions, thus evading the obvious irrationality of a sudden leap to all-out war. Doves see nuclear weapons as the most likely vehicle for such automatic escalation, and most Britons appear to believe that, once such weapons were introduced, rationality would collapse and the holocaust would be virtually guaranteed.

Many possible flashpoints have been suggested for such an escalating superpower confrontation, but the general consensus seems to be that the initial crisis is more likely to take place outside Europe than within it. Although several commentators have asserted that World War Three might grow out of an anti-Soviet rising in Eastern Europe, a more frequent suggestion (especially from doves) has been that the prime danger lies in the Third World. In the words of former Prime Minister James Callaghan, 'I used to believe that the world would be fairly safe from all-out nuclear holocaust provided both sides showed restraint in Europe. Now I think that widespread conflagration in other parts of the world could develop into a nuclear conflict.'[52] This opinion finds strong support among the public at large, with only one in ten poll respondents in 1983 stating that a Third World War was most likely to stem from a political crisis in Europe, while no less than one in three said that it was most likely to arise from a conflict between other nations somewhere else in the world.[53]

By far the most feared extra-European flashpoint, and probably the single most influential scenario for the start of World War Three, has been a new flare-up in the Persian Gulf. Ever since the Iranian revolution and the Soviet invasion of Afghanistan the Gulf region has dominated British anxiety about a superpower collision, and this preoccupation has persisted as the Iran/Iraq war has escalated to threaten the vital oil supplies from the area. Scenario after scenario has begun by positing a political breakdown in Iran drawing in either US intervention forces to secure the oilfields or Soviet forces to quell Moslem nationalism, with the other superpower feeling compelled to send troops in reply thus sparking a direct confrontation.[54] Expert analysts have argued that such overt military intervention is far less likely than political and economic pressure and that even if it occurred the crisis would not necessarily escalate into a Third World War, but individuals casting around for the likeliest path to an East/West conflict have nevertheless tended to view the Persian Gulf scenario as the least incredible road to war.[55]

Many commentators have suggested that an East/West confrontation might arise not through a totally independent crisis but through a deliberate superpower initiative which miscalculates the resolve of the opposing bloc. Hawks, especially, have argued that Russia might underestimate the West's determination and unintentionally provoke war by invading a neutral neighbour such as Yugoslavia or Iran.[56] Attempted Western interference with the Soviet Union's East European glacis is considered another possible source of war by miscalculation.[57] Moderate and dovish commentators seem to be rather less worried by the danger of miscalculation than they were during the period of overt superpower brinkmanship in the original Cold War, although an idea which now arouses even greater alarm than then is that one side or the other might actually initiate direct hostilities in the belief that such hostilities could be kept limited in intensity and extent. In the words of one disarmer:

> What frightens me is that some future US leader, cornered by his inability to regenerate his country's economy, to assert American influence abroad, and to maintain his popularity, might believe that it is possible to use nuclear weapons without escalation as a demonstration of power.[58]

The factor which is apparently considered most likely to provoke the escalation of a local collision between the blocs into full-scale war is the advantage accorded by modern military technology to the side which gets its blow in first. Hawks have often argued that the benefits of surprise as revealed in the Arab/Israeli wars of 1967 and 1973, together with the stress placed by Soviet strategists upon seizing the initiative in any conflict with the West, might lead to a pre-emptive Russian conventional strike against Western Europe in a period of grave superpower confrontation. As Neville Brown put it, there is 'a real possibility of instant and massive attack by the Warsaw Pact at some stage – a possibility conceptually in line with Korea in 1950, Czechoslovakia in 1968 and the Middle East in 1973'.[59] Doves tend to have a different anxiety, namely that the growing vulnerability of *nuclear* forces to pre-emptive attack would impel both sides in a crisis to fire their missiles first, in fear of the even more terrible consequences which they would suffer if the other bloc succumbed to the same deadly logic. In Nigel Calder's words:

> The reasoning goes as follows. "I am a good guy who would not dream of starting a nuclear war, but I cannot afford to let that bad guy get his blow in first. I know that he knows that I know that, and I just hope he appreciates what a good guy I am, otherwise he might think that I must be getting ready to hit him. But on second thoughts I see that if he knows that I know that he may suspect me of preparing to hit him, he knows that I must expect him to hit me

first, and so he sees I have every good reason to hit him first, even if he thinks I'm a good guy. To forestall that – hell, he's going to hit me tomorrow. You know what? I have to hit him today!"[60]

Truly deliberate war, in the sense of a cold-blooded assault by one bloc upon the other, has been dismissed as extremely improbable by almost all British observers. Doves have tended to argue that such an assault would be in neither side's interest even without the risk of massive retribution, making nuclear deterrence nothing more than a superfluous and perilous provocation. Other commentators have questioned this complacency, but have generally agreed that deliberate war is highly unlikely as long as the threat of nuclear retaliation exists. In informed circles, only a few hard-liners consider there to be any real likelihood of cold-blooded Soviet aggression.[61] However, the prominence of artificial images of such unprovoked aggression in hawkish literature and official Third World War scenarios has encouraged almost one quarter of the public at large to believe that World War Three would most probably arise from a deliberate attack.[62]

Two points are striking about British ideas on the immediate causes which might spark off a Third World War. The first is how relatively insubstantial are the incidents or the provocations considered sufficient to bring about such an unprecedentedly destructive conflict. This will be discussed in detail later in the chapter. The second striking point is that differences of opinion about the immediate causes of World War Three, although far less clear-cut than those concerning the ultimate causes of such a conflict, nevertheless display a fundamentally similar pattern. Hawks tend to stress the danger of deliberate actions by the opposing bloc, while doves concentrate on accidental or independent perils unaffected by the logic of deterrence. The impact of this disagreement on the recent war scare will now be examined in depth.

The impact of disagreement

The lack of consensus within British society about the possible causes of a Third World War suggests that almost all the foreboding events of the past decade have played at least some part in sparking the recent alarm. Different things do seem to worry different people, and what reassures one individual may terrify another. The hawkish contention, referred to at the beginning of this chapter, that all the anxiety may be traced back in the end to the growing Soviet threat seems of highly questionable validity, not only because of the detailed evidence just examined of substantive British anxiety about other perils such as the arms race or possible American recklessness, but also because it is hard to believe that the Russian military build-up has made the British public feel much *more* at risk than in the later stages of the original Cold War, when (despite the actual strategic balance) the dominant perception seems already to have been one of military inferiority and absolute vulnerability to nuclear attack.[63] In Ian Smart's words, 'because people in Western Europe, unlike their counterparts in North America, have felt constantly vulnerable to Soviet military strength since the 1940s, anything less than a quantum change in that strength has little effect on their perception of that vulnerability'.[64]

If there has been any unifying characteristic behind the recent wave of anxiety about World War Three, it seems to lie not in the dominance of one particular 'cause' such as the Soviet threat, but rather in the dominant role played by those who focused their attention upon only one type of danger, whatever that danger might be. The alarm of the past decade seems to have been most enduring and vociferous not among those who saw a devil's dilemma of many conflicting perils, but among those who concentrated upon only one class of risks, which could (they alleged) be sharply reduced by proper Western policies. In other words, concern appears to have been fuelled less by forebodings of inescapable tragedy than by the frustration of those who thought they *could* see a way out, at their inability to convince a divided society to follow them along the path of salvation. This interpretation is supported by the way in which the war scare was dominated by frustrated hawks during the years of *détente*, and by frustrated doves after the hard-line backlash at the end of the 1970s.

In their efforts to override the scepticism of many informed observers towards their policy suggestions, both hawks and doves tried to elicit the support of the public at large. Given the generally low level of popular knowledge about, and interest in, defence issues, this almost inevitably required a resort to simplistic and sensationalist imagery, apocalyptic scare tactics, and crusading appeals to set things right before it was too late. Although the remedies proposed by hawks and doves were profoundly dissimilar, their actual rhetoric often converged, as illustrated by the following two extracts from writers at opposite poles of the political spectrum:

> Our grandchildren may be a handful of savages living in a radioactive desert, perhaps having passed some intervening years as serfs of a regressive tyranny, or they may be the free citizens of a happy and flourishing culture. It all depends on the decisions we

make now, and those decisions in their turn depend upon a real effort of understanding. The dangers are extreme, the rewards enormous.

The stakes could not possibly be higher. The penalty of failure is oblivion: the prize of success is a glorious upsurge of human achievement, with the elimination of fear, suspicion, hatred and violence in international affairs opening the way to the abolition of poverty and of gross inequality between peoples and between classes. Let us go out and win that prize.[65]

Hawkish and dovish alarmism seems to have been not only strikingly similar but also mutually reinforcing. The doves made great play of the war hysteria which they claimed was being whipped up by the Cold Warriors of the NATO establishment, with one writer asserting that, 'The first important step to stamp out the war disease is to excoriate the "1985" mentality, promoted by nostalgic World War II generals and their opposite numbers in the Kremlin.'[66] Warnings by American hard-liners about ICBM vulnerability, and about the possibility of prolonged and limited nuclear exchanges, all served to fuel dovish concern about the delicacy of the balance of terror. The hawks, for their part, contended that the Western peace movements themselves increased the danger of war by tempting Russia to try to take advantage of NATO's apparent weakness and irresolution, just as Hitler had allegedly been encouraged in his aggression by the activities of the Peace Pledge Union. As Neville Brown put it:

> History is laced only too well with examples of radical upheavals leading to results far more ugly than anything their more decent supporters had even begun to suspect was possible. But no such irony would ever have been more bitter than if 'CND' turned out to be an acronym for a Commitment to Nuclear Death.[67]

The policies put forward by hawkish and dovish commentators aroused anxiety not only among their opponents but also among more moderate observers of the international scene. Suggestions that safety lay in such drastic measures as the adoption of a nuclear warfighting posture or the unilateral abrogation of nuclear weapons were viewed with undifferentiated alarm by proponents of a more restrained approach to the strategic dilemma.[68] One terrifying policy proposed by both hawks and doves was the deliberate destabilisation of Soviet hegemony in eastern Europe. Certain hawks advocated this as part of a positive Western strategy to achieve victory in the continuing ideological struggle with Marxism, while many doves saw the internal disintegration of the Warsaw Pact as a vital step towards the creation of a neutral and disarmed Europe.[69] E. P. Thompson gave an unintentionally chilling vision of the instability which would be involved when he wrote:

> There would not be decades of detente, as the glaciers slowly melt. There would be very rapid and unpredictable changes; nations would become unglued from their alliances; there would be sharp conflicts within nations; there would be successive risks. We could roll up the map of the Cold War, and travel without maps for a while.[70]

Alarmists tended to advocate such drastic remedies not because they appeared from their own standpoint to be entirely safe but because, in a climate of rising international tension, they had come to seem less dangerous than a continuation of the status quo.[71] However, to observers with less doctrinaire ideas about the nature of the threat to peace, both hawks and doves often appeared to be inviting mankind to commit suicide for fear of death. Disagreements about the threat thus seem to have made the recent war scare at least partly self-sustaining, with recriminations and alarmist appeals triggered by the darkening international climate serving in themselves to increase overall anxiety. An attempt will now be made to explain why this chain reaction was so successful, with reference to the fundamental conceptual contradictions inherent in the West's deterrent posture.

II THE DETERRENT PARADOX

The central concept of deterrence, 'If you wish for peace, prepare for war', was enunciated by the Roman writer Vegetius sixteen centuries ago.[72] It is only in the nuclear age, however, that the idea of armed strength preventing war itself (as opposed to merely averting military defeat) has acquired widespread acceptance. Even now, grave doubts remain, and Vegetius' maxim was described by a former Chief of the British Defence Staff in 1979 as 'absolute nuclear nonsense'.[73] Incomplete acceptance of the deterrent paradox appears to lie at the heart of the recent war scare, and to provide the most fundamental explanation for the outburst of popular alarm. The role played by the military infrastructure itself in sparking the recent anxiety will be discussed in Chapter 5. Attention here will be concentrated upon two less tangible causes of the renewed concern – the erosion of belief in deterrence theory, and the misleading nature of deterrence rhetoric.

Peace is our profession

NATO adheres firmly to the concept that peace is best maintained through strength, and has for nearly four decades been assiduously planning and preparing for a war it hopes thereby to deter. As one senior British officer put it, 'It cannot be too loudly stated or too often repeated that Deterrence is the name of the NATO game. The whole NATO enterprise is about deterrence and everything within the Alliance in terms of men, weapons, command and control, communications and the political direction and the economic co-operation are there simply and solely to create and sustain this one overriding element'.[74]

The idea that NATO's military preparations are designed to stop war from ever starting has been stressed time and again in official pronouncements over the past few decades. However, this deterrent logic, despite the widespread publicity it has received, seems never to have been fully accepted by the general public. The defence debate of twenty-five years ago did produce a grudging consensus that if both sides had nuclear weapons, neither would dare go to war, but the decline of popular anxiety from the mid-1960s seems to have owed just as much to the drop in international tension and the low profile adopted by the defence establishment as it did to positive public acceptance of the logic of deterrence. When new weapons decisions and the worsening international climate brought the deterrent infrastructure back into the news in the late 1970s, it appears to have been seen less as a guarantee of peace than as an alarming indication of impending war.

This was in many ways natural. Most observers are notoriously bad at risk perception, and tend, in a televisual society, to base their concern upon the frequency with which certain images are presented in the media. This helps to explain the widespread though statistically groundless fear of flying, since airline disasters attract so much more news coverage than do the far commoner accidents on the roads. A better example for the present purpose is provided by the 'Skylab scare' of 1979, when sensationalist media reports about the descending spacecraft prompted widespread precautionary measures despite expert assurances that the chances of personal injury were no more than one in six hundred billion.[75]

There are strong grounds for believing that much of the popular anxiety which has recently developed about World War Three has similarly artificial roots, and that it has been evoked partly by the greatly increased media coverage of defence issues over the past decade. This hypothesis is supported by the fact that the public at large seems to be particularly concerned about the danger of a war by accident, a possibility which is virtually dismissed by most defence experts but which loomed large in several press reports in 1979 and 1980.[76] Popular inability to distinguish between real and hypothetical dangers may thus be the single biggest explanation for the pessimism which media coverage of new defence programmes and of the dispute between hawks and doves has produced.

What must now be assessed is why such limited public acceptance of the deterrent paradox as had developed by the mid-1960s seems to have broken down over the ensuing decade. There appear to be two main reasons. The first is that the defence establishment did not actively try to maintain popular consensus behind the deterrent posture, but took thankful advantage of public indifference to instead seek stability through professionalism and inconspicuous isolation. This worked well at first, but stored up trouble for the future by fostering ignorance and alienation among the public at large.

The public needed no encouragement to put out of mind such a horrific subject as nuclear war. However, the (often necessarily) secretive and clandestine approach adopted by the government in its deterrent preparations made these preparations appear to many observers to be somewhat sinister and conspiratorial. Journalists made periodic 'exposées' of the nuclear issue, speaking of goings-on 'beneath the city streets', or of 'lifting the stone to see what was crawling about underneath'.[77] The low profile adopted by the defence establishment during the 1960s and 1970s seems merely to have ensured that, when the public did rediscover the deterrent infrastructure, sensationalist revelations of what had actually existed all along would serve to fuel whatever anxiety had triggered the reawakening of popular interest.

This process is most strikingly evident from the reactions of the younger generation, brought up during the years of *détente* and the Vietnam war, and with no personal experience of the climate of totalitarian pressure stretching back to the 1930s in which the West's deterrent posture was forged. The defence debate of the past decade has been this younger generation's first real acquaintance with the paradoxes of nuclear deterrence, and they have been seriously alarmed by a military infrastructure which many of their elders regarded as a guarantee of peace. In a 1981 poll, while respondents aged over 54 asserted by a two-to-one majority that Britain's possession of nuclear weapons reduced rather than increased the risk of a nuclear attack, this proportion fell steadily among younger respondents, with a two-to-one majority of the under-25s thinking nuclear weapons made Britain less rather than more secure.[78]

The second reason for the decline in popular acceptance of the deterrent paradox lies in the shift of NATO strategy from massive retaliation to flexible response. Public consensus in the 1960s seems to have been based on the straightforward belief that, if both sides had nuclear bombs, neither would dare go to war. This belief was perfectly compatible with the official doctrine that any serious Soviet aggression would automatically trigger an all-out nuclear exchange. As time passed, however, and the Soviet nuclear build-up made massive retaliation an increasingly less credible deterrent to limited attack, NATO turned to a new strategy which sought to minimise Russian 'escalation dominance' at intermediate levels of the force spectrum. The arcane and deceptive logic which the new deterrence entailed was far harder for the public to grasp than the crude fear of mutual catastrophe which had prevailed twenty years earlier. In Lawrence Freedman's words:

> . . . the whole preoccupation with complex and fantastic weapons and equally complex and fantastic scenarios scares people and confirms nuclear strategy as the preoccupation of Dr. Strangeloves, full of madcap science and devoid of human sensibilities.[79]

Dovish anxiety has tended to be concentrated upon the *nuclear* dimension of the flexible response strategy, with repeated allegations of a shift from pure, old-fashioned deterrence by Mutual Assured Destruction to sinister and perilous notions of warfighting and theatre nuclear exchanges.[80] The disarmers have often asserted that deterrence is now dead, and that the new weapons and strategies are intended not to prevent nuclear war but to limit the damage which its inevitable outbreak will cause. In Thompson's words, 'They are designed to carry us across a threshold from the *unthinkable* (the theory of deterrence, founded upon the assumption that this must *work*) to the *thinkable* (the theory that nuclear war may happen, and may be imminent, and, with cunning tactics and proper preparations, might end in "victory").'[81] Arguments such as these have undoubtedly increased the anxiety evoked among the general public by the many recent media reports on nuclear issues. However, there are strong grounds for believing that the crudely catastrophic model of nuclear deterrence still has much popular resonance, and that an equally potent cause of the new pessimism about World War Three among the public at large has been a failure to grasp the deterrent function of *conventional* forces.

Deterrence is a concept which British observers have generally associated more with a capacity for punishment and retribution than with military strength in general. This distinction parallels that already discussed in Chapter 2 between British images of nuclear and conventional weapons, associated respectively with a catastrophic holocaust and a traditional military contest. Thus, despite frequent official assurances that *all* NATO forces are intended to prevent war, a strong tradition has grown up of distinguishing between nuclear deterrence and conventional defence. The impact of this distinction on the views of the public at large is illustrated by a 1979 opinion poll, in which 70 per cent of respondents said that a principal function of the armed forces was to defend Britain if war occurred, compared with only 20 per cent who thought that the role of the services was to make other states afraid to attack Britain in the first place.[82]

Since so few members of the public appear to have associated conventional forces with deterrence, it is hardly surprising that the hawkish campaign in the late 1970s to win popular support for rectifying the alleged conventional imbalance in Europe increased fears of a Third World War. Film of advancing Russian tanks, or alarmist scenarios for a Soviet blitzkrieg, seem to have made a far more potent impression than did admissions in the small print that the scenarios were hypothetical and that the real danger lay in Finlandisation. Even Sir John Hackett, who postulated considerable NATO force increases, was unable to reassure his readers that war itself would thereby be prevented, since (to paraphrase Thomas Hardy), 'War makes rattling good future history, but deterrence is poor reading'.[83] The widely publicised Western arms increases and military exercises at the end of the 1970s must further have strengthened the impression of impending war, and when Russia actually did invade Afghanistan, even official Army recruitment adverts posed the alarming question 'Where next?'.[84]

Growing popular expectations in the later 1970s of a real Soviet conventional attack did not evoke practical reactive measures until the horror of war was quite literally 'brought home' to the British public by the growing prominence of nuclear issues in 1980 and beyond. This two-stage process seems to go a long way to explaining how popular faith in nuclear deterrence was undermined. There may thus have been more than a grain of truth in Thompson's allegation that the hard-liners were encouraging a 'progress from the unthinkable to the thinkable *without thinking* – without confronting the arguments, their consequences or probable conclusions, and, indeed, without knowing that any threshold has been crossed'.[85] Hawkish alarmists in the 1970s did not have anything like the sinister motives which Thompson alleged, but the practical effect of their dramatic warnings about NATO's conventional inferiority does seem to have been to create an atmosphere of pessimism about the possibility of an East/West conflict, which did much to fuel the ensuing anxiety about a nuclear holocaust.

The role of the 'New Cold War'

Although the recent war scare seems to have been fuelled in large part by disagreements and misunderstandings about the deterrent infrastructure itself, a critical factor both in triggering and in reinforcing anxiety has undoubtedly been the profound darkening of the international atmosphere since the early 1970s. Conflict has been raging in the Third World throughout the post-war era, but what has made this seem particularly perilous in recent years has been the revival of East/West antagonism and the deterioration of superpower relations to their lowest point for over two decades. The combination of belligerent superpower rhetoric with real shooting wars in the Third World seems to have made many people fear that, despite the stability of the European situation, East/West relations might degenerate from their current state of limited antagonism into a catastrophic World War Three.

This logic is reflected in British predictions (discussed in the earlier half of this chapter) as to what might actually *cause* a Third World War. The most striking fact about such predicted causes of East/West conflict is how relatively insubstantial they are. Many observers seem to believe that, in the prevailing atmosphere of tension and suspicion, an accident or crisis could 'trigger off' the unprecedented devastation of a Third World War without the deliberate agency of either side. This contrasts sharply with the experience of the 1930s, when it took the massive provocation of Hitlerian aggression to produce even a 'conventional' conflict between the major powers. It is often alleged that the present situation bears more resemblance to that before 1914, when tension and miscalculation did play a major role in the slide to war, but this analogy has serious defects which will be discussed at length in Chapter 5.

It is at least arguable that the recent acrimony and turmoil of world affairs is evidence less of the delicacy than of the *stability* of the central strategic balance. So secure is deterrence thought to be that many nations (including the superpowers themselves) have felt free to engage in vituperation and even active hostilities, in the confidence that their actions would not provoke a nuclear holocaust. The collapse of the Soviet-American dialogue of the 1970s obviously makes crisis management a much more difficult task, but it is by no means certain that the increased readiness to use military force despite the nuclear threat has made the current situation more dangerous than the largely static superpower confrontation of the 1950s. International affairs is an area dominated by competition and change, and the regional and proxy struggles of the past decade may in some ways have provided a useful safety-valve, relieving the unnatural immobility and tension of the earlier situation during which (as Britain's 1958 Defence White Paper exaggeratedly put it) the world stood 'poised between the hope of total peace and the fear of total war'.[86]

The idea that increased limited conflict need not imply a heightened risk of World War Three is far from new. Defence commentators have long been arguing that nuclear deterrence is less likely to completely stifle international conflict than it is to divert it into other areas such as limited wars, proxy struggles, arms competition and contests of intimidation.[87] Michael Howard argued that the nuclear threat was a double-edged sword, making total war almost out of the question but at the same time prompting 'a return to an earlier and grimmer period in the history of mankind, in which violence, if not actual, was imminent at virtually every level of social intercourse'.[88] Reasoning of this kind has led many informed observers to assert that the current superpower tension and Third World turmoil give no cause for believing that the balance of terror itself is close to being broken.[89] This view, however, seems to carry little weight with the public at large, who continue to see in every belligerent speech or international crisis the spectre of a Third World War.[90]

One of the main reasons for popular preoccupation with the threat of World War Three appears to lie in the misleading nature of official deterrence rhetoric. British foreign policy has traditionally been reactive and pragmatic, and has had to be presented publicly in an even more passive light because of liberal horror of war, and faith in demonstrations of good will.[91] This, and the strictly defensive posture adopted by the NATO alliance as a whole, have driven British officials to avoid any mention of active bilateral competition with the Warsaw Pact, and instead to stress the need to passively deter a possible Soviet attack. Many individuals have bowed even further to liberal sensitivities by concentrating upon the deterrence not of the potential Russian 'enemy', but of war itself. Britain's Minister of Defence stated in 1969:

> The purpose of NATO is not to produce heaven on earth. It is to prevent hell on earth . . . When I say hell on earth, I am thinking about a third world war; for I believe that a general war between East and West in Europe could scarcely fail to end in the thermonuclear holocaust.[92]

The problem with this kind of rhetoric, however admirable the sentiments involved, is that it focuses attention upon the very thing which is being deterred. Instead of encouraging people to take the avoidance of a nuclear holocaust for granted, and to concentrate instead upon the ways in which nations have learnt to continue their competition in the shadow of the Bomb, deterrent rhetoric often helps to perpetuate the idea of a sharp split between total peace and total war. This caused little alarm as long as the East/West climate appeared to be getting progressively less antagonistic, but when crises and tensions erupted as they did at the end of the 1970s, 'deterrence' was thought to be failing, and many observers, with no other peg on which to hang their anxieties, started to worry about World War Three.

Perhaps the most insidiously dispiriting form of deterrence rhetoric is that which asserts that 'deterrence has kept the peace for over thirty years'. This tends to foster the image of a nuclear Sword of Damocles hanging over the world, and gives the impression that deterrence merely postpones its inevitable fall. The gloom is compounded by the fact that very few defence experts predict an escape from East/West competition or the balance of terror in the foreseeable future. A few hawks have suggested that the Soviet threat might diminish through internal problems once the 'window of opportunity' is past, (with one individual going so far as to assert that, 'If we can get through the next five years we shall probably have a reign of unparalleled peace and prosperity').[93] Doves, however, have laid great stress upon the argument that disaster is bound to come sooner or later if the present situation continues, and this view has found considerable echoes among more established defence commentators.[94] Laurence Martin has suggested that mankind has already fallen off the nuclear skyscraper, and that the only hope is to keep on 'extending the fall', while Lawrence Freedman has summed up the current dilemma as follows:

> We are engaged in a long-term holding operation. The success of this holding operation may be a high probability in the immediate future, but it is most unlikely that it can be guaranteed for perpetuity . . . the problem of combining large nuclear arsenals with the shocks and traumas of political change is difficult, as well

as being crucial for our survival. Even if all goes well for many years, this is still going to be a problem that each succeeding generation will leave to the next, until one day no solution is found.[95]

The revival of superpower tension after fifteen years of *détente* seems to have brought home to the public at large the fundamental and systemic character of the East/West confrontation, and to have been more responsible than any other single factor for the development of enduring pessimism about the long-term prospects for avoiding World War Three. This is well illustrated by a comparison of three opinion polls from 1957, 1969 and 1983, all of which investigated what people thought was likely to happen in the world in the ensuing twenty years. The 1983 poll showed a marked decrease in popular expectations of such radical developments as nuclear disarmament or the establishment of peaceful relations between East and West, and although this was not matched by a spectacular increase in predictions of nuclear war, other surveys indicate that the long-term optimism which had characterised the 1960s had by 1980 become substantially eroded.[96]

This development seems to have formed part of a general loss of confidence in the future, which has been gathering pace in Britain for many years. Breakdown of influence abroad has been accompanied by growing unemployment and economic stagnation at home, creating a pervasive atmosphere of decline and decay. The public have been assailed by gloomy forecasts of global catastrophes ranging from the population explosion to environmental pollution and the depletion of natural resources.[97] The ideal of scientific and technological progress has received severe challenges (one of which, opposition to nuclear power, seems to have been directly involved in the revival of protest against nuclear weapons). In circumstances such as these, it is not surprising that many Britons have become pessimistic about the continued avoidance of World War Three, nor that hundreds of thousands have embraced a millenarian crusade to break away from the apparent hopelessness of nuclear deterrence. In the words of one commentator:

> As long as we continue to rely on the balance of terror produced by nuclear arsenals we shall never be free from the inescapable risk that something will go wrong. A small risk endured for a sufficiently long time brings the certainty that the risk will be fulfilled: an alternative to nuclear deterrence must be found if present and future generations are to be guaranteed a chance of survival.[98]

There have been several attempts over the past decade to challenge this image of the deterrent stockpiles as a Damoclean threat hanging over the future of mankind, and to divert attention to the more down-to-earth conventional violence which is already taking place.[99] However, all such attempts seem so far to have foundered in the face of widespread attachment to the notion of a convulsive Third World War. Hawkish efforts in the 1970s to convince people that the real threat was not nuclear war but Soviet global preponderance backfired because of their excessively Manichean approach and their double-edged attempt to redefine the term 'World War Three'. Equally counterproductive in terms of reducing anxiety about a convulsive conflict between East and West has been the shift in official imagery from the apocalyptic Third World War scenarios of the 1950s to excessively technical notions of limited war and escalation dominance. Whether there is any prospect of the World War Three spectre being more effectively challenged in the future will be discussed towards the end of the present study, but first, an attempt will be made to assess why Britons have remained so preoccupied by the questionable threat of total war.

5 The Preoccupation with Full-Scale War

That the troubled international climate of the past decade should have aroused widespread anxiety is quite understandable; what is more contentious is the particular threat upon which that anxiety has tended to focus. Instead of being concerned about sour East/West relations and the bloody conflicts in the Third World as problems in their own right, many people have concentrated upon the risk that such developments might lead to a catastrophic Third World War. Even the long-running bloodbath between Iran and Iraq aroused little popular interest in the West until attacks on Gulf shipping in 1984 seemed to pose the danger of a superpower confrontation. This preoccupation with the threat of high intensity warfare between the superpowers would be understandable if East/West conflict really were likely to take such an apocalyptic form, but there are strong arguments to the effect that the existence of nuclear weapons makes limited operations even more plausible at the great power level than in the various conflicts which have actually taken place between lesser nations over the past few decades. In the words of Michael Howard:

> Perhaps . . . it is necessary, in reassessing the place of military force in international affairs, to rid ourselves of the idea that if such force is employed it must necessarily be in a distinct 'war', formally declared, ending in a clear decision embodied in a peace treaty, taking place within a precise interval of time during which diplomatic relations between the belligerents are suspended and military operations proceed according to their own peculiar laws. We reveal the influence of this concept whenever we talk about 'the next war' or 'if war breaks out' or 'the need to deter war'. If an inescapable casus belli were to occur between nuclear powers, there *might* follow a spasm of mutual destruction which the survivors, such as they were, would be justified in remembering as the Third World War; but such an outcome is by no means inevitable, and appears to be decreasingly likely. It seems more probable that a casus belli would provoke threats and, if necessary, execution of limited acts of violence, probably though not necessarily localised, probably though not necessarily non-

87

nuclear; all accompanied by an intensification rather than a cessation of diplomatic intercourse.[1]

The real peril of the current situation may be that the greater military assertiveness now being displayed by both superpowers will lead them deeper and deeper into the clinging quagmire of international violence and anarchy, a quagmire already encountered by the Soviet Union in Afghanistan and by the United States in Lebanon and Central America. It is in these messy and brutalising circumstances that the use of nuclear weapons might eventually, and after much 'conventional' slaughter, come to seem like a real policy option (just as the atomic bombing of Hiroshima, which now appears so apocalyptic, seemed almost routine after six years of brutalising warfare). The alternative image of the transition from peace to war as a series of distinct and drastic escalatory steps, or as a brink or precipice over which mankind might suddenly topple into the pit of Armageddon, seems in contrast to be profoundly artificial.[2] This chapter will examine the reasons why people so readily focus upon hypothetical images of high-intensity warfare between East and West, instead of upon the low level struggles which are actually taking place among a much wider variety of antagonists throughout the globe.

I WEAPONS AND SCENARIOS

One reason for the widespread preoccupation with the concept of World War Three appears to lie in the unprecedented reliance of modern states upon standing armed forces. The lengthening production time of weapons systems, the growing pace and complexity of modern warfare, and the increasing emphasis upon deterring rather than defeating aggression have combined to preclude dependence upon the mobilisation of a national war effort, and to force nations to maintain large professional military establishments even in time of peace. The Eastern and Western blocs, in particular, have built up their armed forces to a level far exceeding that required in any of the overt conflicts in which they have actually been engaged since 1945. Anxieties arising out of these large-scale military preparations seem to lie at the heart of the widespread influence exerted by the notion of a catastrophic Third World War.

Deterrent contradictions

It was suggested in Chapter 4 that popular understanding of the deterrent paradox is extremely shaky, and that the idea of weapons existing in order *not* to be used enjoys only limited and qualified acceptance. This being the case, people naturally base their images of war not only upon the low level conflicts which are actually taking place but also upon the military stockpiles of the respective blocs. Public preoccupation with World War Three thus appears to stem partly from the prominence of the deterrent arsenals themselves in recent media coverage of the defence issue.

Several factors seem to have contributed towards this concentration on weapons rather than actual wars. The build-up of both sides' military forces, and the introduction of new systems such as Cruise and Trident missiles, have revived interest in the deterrent stockpiles themselves. Arms control talks have also served to focus attention upon the nuclear dimension of the superpower armouries, instead of upon less apocalyptic and more usable categories of force. The bitter dispute between hawks and doves has exacerbated the situation by making nuclear arms control and new military deployments the subject of intense and highly prominent domestic controversy. International political competition also has tended to exaggerate the salience of nuclear weapons, since the revived struggle of will between East and West has taken as its vehicle not the Berlin dispute of earlier years but the deployment of new missiles such as Cruise and the SS-20. Finally, and perhaps most important of all, there has been no continuing conflict such as Vietnam of sufficient immediacy to Western observers to bring images of warfare down to earth and to challenge the artificiality of basing predictions purely upon military hardware.

Standing armed forces can provide an attractive substitute for political analysis in speculation about the likely character of future conflict. Observers may be tempted to cut through the political imponderables surrounding limited warfare by concentrating on what might happen if the generals were given their head and the doomsday stockpiles unleashed. This process seems to go a long way to explaining the prominence of the notion of an all-out nuclear exchange, as well as of the less apocalyptic but equally artificial concept of full-scale conventional hostilities. Both of these images allow quite detailed technical predictions about the likely course of the conflict, but in political terms they are of highly questionable validity, as illustrated by the widespread preoccupation with the question of what accident or miscalculation might 'spark off' a convulsive Third World War instead of with the arguably more realistic question of what kind of conflict the competing blocs are most likely to consciously pursue. As Michael Howard observed:

> However inchoate or disreputable the motives for war may be, its initiation is almost by definition a deliberate and carefully considered act and its conduct, at least at the more advanced levels of social development, a matter of very precise central control. If history shows any record of 'accidental' wars, I have yet to find them.[3]

It is not merely ease of analysis which has accorded prominence to the notions of full-scale conventional or nuclear war. Perhaps more important has been the ambivalent role of 'scenarios' within the defence establishments of both NATO and the Warsaw Pact. Deterrence is not simply a matter of the prophylactic accumulation of massive destructive power – force planning and operational considerations necessitate also the construction of hypothetical scenarios in which that power might actually be used. Ever since the 1940s, the Western Alliance has maintained detailed plans about what to do in the event of a complete failure of deterrence, expressly in order to prevent that failure from ever occurring.[4] The Soviet Union, also, has constructed a strategy for an all-out conflict between the blocs, in order to deter the 'imperialists' from launching such a devastating war.[5] This has created a vicious circle, with each side's strategies feeding into the scenarios of the other to strengthen the idea that East/West conflict would take the form of a convulsive World War Three.

As weapons have become more destructive, many observers have challenged this closed circle of worst-case planning, on the grounds that all-out war would be so massively incommensurate with any conceivable political dispute between the blocs that, in the event, conflict would assume a much more limited form. As one commentator argued, 'The single scenario and the gravest threat are bets which Britain, surprise or no surprise, can only lose. British resources would be better spread across the spectrum of limited, likely and winnable conflicts.'[6] The defence establishment, however, has been distinctly unreceptive to such suggestions, both because of the continuing importance of deterring all-out attack and because to plan for a limited war (quite possibly outside the NATO area) would play havoc with the Alliance's political cohesion and would be impossible in any case without a knowledge of the specific circumstances involved. NATO's main response to Mutual Assured Destruction has been to concentrate upon the artificial concept of full-scale *conventional* hostilities, a notion which (as discussed in Chapter 2) contains severe contradictions, but which was seized on even before its appearance in Soviet strategic writing because it offered a way of avoiding both the patent irrationality of the nuclear holocaust and the political divisiveness of truly limited warfare.

Nothing better illustrates the artificiality of current official scenarios as predictions of what East/West conflict might actually be like than the conduct attributed to the opposing bloc. Russia is usually portrayed as marching steadily to war, for no clear objectives and in complete disregard of the consequences she is likely to suffer. As Duncan Campbell remarked of Operation 'Square Leg' in 1980, 'The exercise assumed that Soviet leaders may be so loony that nothing stops them'.[7] The official justification for this artificiality is that the scenarios are for the purposes of deterrence, and that if NATO can deter cold-blooded Soviet aggression it should also be able to deter less malignant and more realistic actions by the Soviet leadership. However, many observers tend to get quite the wrong impression from the various scenarios and military exercises, and to conclude that a catastrophic Third World War is the *most* likely rather than arguably one of the least likely manifestations of East/West competition.

The knots into which the British government has tied itself in its efforts to reduce popular misinterpretation of defence scenarios are well illustrated by the planned 'Hard Rock' civil defence exercise of 1982. Chastened by the experience of 1980, when the similar 'Square Leg' exercise was widely interpreted as the official view of what East/West conflict would actually be like, Home Office planners in 1982 adopted a deliberately unrealistic attack scenario, avoiding massive casualty levels or the targeting of American bases, in order to deprive CND of campaigning ammunition.[8] Despite this bowdlerisation, the exercise had to be abandoned because of the refusal of many local authorities to co-operate in 'preparing for a Third World War'.[9]

The Hard Rock fiasco illustrates how difficult it is for Western governments to reassure their people about Soviet intentions while at the same time basing their deterrent policies largely upon Russian capabilities, a feat which Dean Acheson once said was 'like asking a man to breathe in and out at the same time'.[10] Artificial defence scenarios are the ultimate embodiment of the paradox of deterrence, encouraging rather than discouraging the widespread tendency to neglect political considerations and to base images of conflict upon tangible military hardware. What effect this has had upon attitudes towards defence policy as a whole will be discussed in Chapter 6, but first, attention will be turned to the dangers thought to flow from the deterrent arsenals themselves.

Technical instability

Many observers see the deterrent stockpiles of East and West less as passive instruments of dissuasion than as an autonomous source of conflict or as a pile of tinder which a careless spark might ignite to engulf the globe. This fear that an East/West conflict might escalate because of the very preparations made to deter it takes several forms. Doves worry that nuclear weapons might be used accidentally or through a collapse of the infrastructure of control, while hard-liners are concerned that imbalances between the arsenals might tempt Russia to launch an attack. A third fear, shared by many observers, is that the military advantages of striking first could drive one side or the other to seize the initiative in escalating the conflict to a new level of intensity. These three sets of concerns will here be analysed from a sceptical perspective, to challenge their tendency to focus attention upon conflicts far more intense than current political differences between the blocs would warrant.

Technical accident or human insubordination leading to the unintentional release of weapons of mass destruction constitute the purest and most direct forms of the peril which is said to flow from the deterrent stockpiles themselves. Accidental nuclear war is a risk which has most definitely caught the popular imagination, as demonstrated by films like *Fail-Safe*, *Dr Strangelove*, and the more recent *War Games*, in which teenage computer gamers inadvertently become hooked up to the Pentagon, with near-disastrous results.[11] Defence experts are less concerned about accidents in peacetime, but do worry that the disruption of the command and control networks in a limited nuclear or even a full-scale conventional war might cause unplanned escalation to the holocaust.[12]

The problem with the notion of accidental nuclear war, and the reason why most defence experts treat it with such profound scepticism, is that the potential dangers are just as evident to governments themselves as they are to outside observers. The nuclear powers have introduced a whole series of safety checks and bilateral agreements to ensure that their deterrent arsenals do not escape political control, so much so that several commentators have questioned whether the weapons could be released even in response to an enemy attack.[13] Alarmists lay great stress upon the risks entailed in shorter warning times and the proliferation of nuclear systems, but often neglect the fact that technological progress may actually make things safer by improving the reliability of equipment and by allowing greater central control through devices such as electronic locks. As for the disruption of command links in wartime, this remains a major concern despite recent improvements in communication systems, but by the time that political control were jeopardised, the conflict would already have reached an intensity far beyond anything which could rationally flow from current East/West antagonism.

Hard-line observers tend to base their anxieties about the military arsenals less upon loss of control than upon alleged imbalances between East and West. It is argued that unless the two sides' forces are maintained in a rough equilibrium, their very imbalance could prompt the stronger side (Russia, in hawkish eyes) to cash in its advantages by launching an attack. Margaret Thatcher declared unequivocally in 1981, 'If we were weaker than the Soviets, the result would be war – a war no less destructive to the West for being unequal.'[14] A refinement of the imbalance idea which has become especially prominent over the past decade is the concept of a 'window of opportunity', with many hawks alleging that the prospective erosion of Russia's position of strength by internal problems and Western reactive measures might encourage her to strike while she still has the chance. As one senior British officer wrote in 1982:

> If ever the risk of military aggression could be considered worth taking, it must surely be now. Inevitably, therefore, the Soviet military advice to the masters of the Kremlin must be: 'If ever you are going to attack do it now. You will never have it so good'. We must expect that attack at any time.[15]

This notion that World War Three might arise through a theoretical imbalance in the deterrent stockpiles themselves seems to be a classic example of compartmentalised thinking. In focusing so heavily upon the military infrastructure, alarmists tend to neglect the fact that it is in neither bloc's interest to exchange the benefits of peace for the horror of war, even if the other bloc seems likely to come off worse. Just because a window is open does not mean that someone is going to jump through it, especially if the window in question is on the seventeenth floor. Wars may have started in the past because of shifting power relationships (usually less through exploitation of transient 'windows of opportunity' than through fear of growing enemy superiority), but in the nuclear age, the absolute costs and risks of using force tend to far outweigh calculations of relative military advantage.[16] The real deterrent to East/West conflict is not the delicate balance of military power but rather the knowledge that, so long as both sides retain their political resolve, hostilities between them risk being devastating, bloody and exceedingly unproductive.

More worrying to many than the dangers of accident or military imbalance is the risk that an East/West confrontation might escalate because one or both sides feel impelled to seize the initiative rather than simply reacting to enemy moves. As discussed in Chapters 2 and 4, doves tend to concentrate on the pressures facing both blocs to destroy opposing nuclear forces rather than waiting for their own to be destroyed, while hard-liners tend to worry about the strong emphasis placed on surprise attack and pre-emption in Soviet planning for nuclear or conventional operations. There has thus developed a widespread fear that if ever a local conflict or even a grave superpower crisis led either side to believe that 'the war' was on, set procedures would be followed and pre-planned strategies would be implemented to produce World War Three, just as mobilisation and the Schlieffen Plan helped to escalate the Balkan crisis of 1914 into World War One.

This concern that current deterrent planning might become a self-fulfilling rather than a self-denying prophecy may not be as justified as is often assumed. In the nuclear age, 'seizing the initiative' by launching an all-out first strike would be akin to committing suicide for fear of death. One need only examine the size and diversity of the superpower arsenals to see how difficult it would be for an attacking state to limit retaliatory damage to 'only' a few tens of millions of casualties, as some hawkish and dovish commentators have suggested.[17] Technological advance is increasing missile accuracy, but it is also making retaliatory systems less vulnerable and providing an ever growing array of means to inflict genocidal revenge upon an all-out aggressor. (Bacteriological advances, for example, may soon give most countries the latent capacity for terrible retribution.) It is true that a nation would probably suffer even worse if its opponent struck first, but the appalling casualty levels at stake virtually guarantee that decision-makers will cling to the last to the hope that the indications are wrong and that no enemy attack will occur.

As for the notion that a grave crisis might tempt one bloc to make a limited pre-emption in the form of a conventional blitzkrieg or a discriminate counterforce strike, this seems to neglect the fact that limited wars are more trials of will than technical military contests. Partial pre-emptive strikes such as the Japanese attack at Pearl Harbor and the Yom Kippur offensive against Israel have in the past served merely to win a temporary military advantage at the expense of fatally strengthening the opponent's will to resist. It is true that Soviet doctrine appears to be giving increasing weight to the concept of a short, shocking conventional blitzkrieg, but this does not mean that Kremlin leaders would launch such an attack except as a very last resort.[18] NATO is too divided to pose a real military threat to Eastern Europe even should the blocs collide through a political crisis there or in the Middle East, and clear-cut aggression might place the Soviet empire more rather than less at risk, by uniting the West and provoking the same kind of righteous anger which led to the liberation of Europe in World War Two. In John Erickson's words, 'Talk of a Soviet *blitz* is much misplaced: as one Soviet general put it, (cogently I think), waging "blitz war" only leads to a "blitz collapse".'[19]

One of the most striking aspects of recent concern about technical instability in the deterrent infrastructure is that all the alleged dangers were markedly more acute during the original Cold War. The risk of accident and uncontrolled escalation was much greater in the days of the 'hair-trigger nuclear alert' than in the current period of hardened communications and second-strike nuclear forces. Strategic power in the 1950s was imbalanced (albeit in favour of the West) to a degree that makes today's minor deviations from parity at wholly superfluous levels of forces appear meaningless by comparison. Finally, both sides in the Cold War were committed to strategies of massive all-out pre-emption should fighting break out, a situation of much greater escalatory instability than in the current era of flexible response and multiple options for force employment.

What seems to have prompted the recent outcry is not an unprecedented level of technical instability but rather an unprecedented degree of sensitivity to, and understanding of, the requirements for stability itself. People are no longer satisfied with even a lessened risk that the deterrent stockpiles might get out of hand or tempt either side to launch an attack, and are demanding still more careful management to ensure that this does not occur. Why such increased sensitivity has developed will be discussed in Chapter 6. Suffice to say here that the risk of World War Three arising out of the deterrent stockpiles themselves is now more theoretical than real, and that although efforts should continue to reduce what danger remains, technical instability is no reason to concentrate exclusively on the risk of a Third World War at the expense of more down-to-earth problems of international violence and anarchy.

II CONCEPTUAL BIAS

It is ridiculous to expect British thinking about such an emotive topic as potential war to be entirely rational and objective. As was pointed out in Chapter 3, many Britons profess pessimism about the long-term avoidance of war but do not accept the implications of this belief by demanding better security policies or by ceasing to plan for the future. The widespread preoccupation with the concept of full-scale hostilities between East and West seems to contain a similarly subjective and irrational element, which will now be examined by focusing in turn upon the two most prominent British images of World War Three – an all-out nuclear holocaust and a full-scale conventional battle.

A nuclear apocalypse
The most obvious and understandable reason why Britons are preoccupied with the threat of a nuclear holocaust is that this is the kind of conflict which would most directly and direly affect the United Kingdom itself. Britons have long been obsessed with the way in which their own homeland might fall prey to hostile action, as witnessed by the various relics of coastal defences scattered around the island's shores.[20] The risk of invasion caused great popular anxiety in the late nineteenth century, despite the predominance of the Royal Navy, and there appeared a spate of alarmist literature, invoking such questionable devices as a foreign wonder torpedo or a commandeered channel tunnel in order to provide a scenario for fighting on British soil.[21] With the advent of aerial bombardment in the First World War, the invasion spectre was largely defused, and public anxiety became concentrated instead upon the threat of poison gas attack from the air.[22] The current British preoccupation with the terrifying but questionable spectre of a nuclear holocaust seems thus to be wholly in line with earlier scares about dire but often unrealistic threats such as gas bombardment or the crossing of Britain's moat.

Nuclear weapons are by no means the only potential threat to the security of the United Kingdom. Commentators have recently tried to draw popular attention to a whole variety of alleged perils, ranging from internal subversion and the cutting-off of overseas resources to sabotage raids, naval blockade and conventional air attack.[23] However the direct and apocalyptic threat of nuclear bombardment seems to have remained for most people by far the most potent expression of how international conflict could affect Britain herself. This is probably because most of the other threats, although they might be more likely to materialise, nevertheless remain as yet equally hypothetical. Spy trials, IRA terrorism and (above all) the Falklands war illustrate that when a 'low level' threat actually becomes manifest it can arouse even more concern than the theoretical possibility of nuclear annihilation. However, when Britons are faced with an array of equally hypothetical threats ranging from a repeat of the 1973 oil crisis to an all-out nuclear attack, horror appears to predominate over 'objective' risk evaluation, leading to a concentration upon the gravest rather than the most likely peril.

This tendency seems to have been encouraged by the feedback effects of media coverage and alarmist rhetoric. Newspapers and television have naturally angled their coverage of defence issues towards those aspects of most interest to the public at large, thereby providing an imbalanced picture of the strategic situation as a whole.[24] Nothing better illustrates the distorting effect of media sensationalism than the issue of private nuclear fallout shelters, which has given rise to dozens of newspaper articles and television reports, a specialist journal, a novel, and a handbook of government guidelines, despite the fact that the number of concrete shelters which have actually been installed appears to be less than a hundred.[25] Since almost all popular impressions of the defence issue are vicariously obtained, the heavy slanting of media coverage towards the nuclear threat facing Britain herself has almost certainly reinforced the widespread impression that the most likely form of East/West conflict is a thermonuclear Third World War.

Public preoccupation with the threat of a nuclear holocaust appears also to have been directly or indirectly encouraged by individuals seeking support for their own policy ideas. Hawkish observers have seized the opportunity of heightened tension to seek to revive popular interest in civil defence, while doves have tried to play upon the public's nuclear fears in order to convince people of the virtues of nuclear disarmament. Peter Watkins' 1965 film *The War Game* seems to have owed its impact less to any unprecedented horror in its portrayal of a nuclear attack than to the fact that the supposed victims came from Rochester rather than Hiroshima, and the recent CND movement has deliberately exploited this natural preoccupation of Britons with their own national vulnerability by producing a whole series of studies about what nuclear attack would mean for the United Kingdom.[26] Even government ministers have sometimes bowed to (and thereby reinforced) the prevailing fixation with nuclear war by issuing dire warnings of the danger of such a calamity if their own policies are not pursued.[27]

Another factor which may have played some part in focusing attention upon the notion of an all-out nuclear holocaust is the long-standing fascination with apocalyptic imagery.[28] The frequency with which nuclear war is described by such emotive terms as 'Doomsday', 'Armageddon' or 'the holocaust' betrays the influence of this apocalyptic undercurrent upon Western thinking about such a conflict, as also does the continuing obsession with the possibility of universal or near-universal death. Nuclear weapons are, of course, devastating enough to warrant such imagery, but the ease with which it is often assumed that there is an increasing risk of an all-out thermonuclear exchange does seem suspiciously similar to the way in which recent scares about other doomsday threats such as population growth, resource depletion or ecological catastrophe have slipped into worst-case analyses and scientifically dubious assertions in order to give the impression that society as we know it is on the brink of collapse.[29] Perhaps the most striking evidence for an apocalyptic input into British thinking about future warfare is provided by the fact that conflict was being seen in such terms even before the atomic age began, with the Mass Observation studies of the 1930s reporting that, when World War Two broke out, 'It was mixed in people's minds with the end of the world . . . and the ultimate chaos of the Shape of Things to Come'.[30]

The threat of a nuclear holocaust has certainly been seized on by apocalyptic literature as one of the most likely methods for the fulfilment of eschatological prophecies ranging from Nostradamus' assertion that the world will end in 1999 to the fundamentalist Christian belief in a final conflict at Armageddon.[31] How much influence such ideas have upon the public at large is difficult to gauge. Astrology and other such dubious phenomena still command widespread popular credence, and there does seem to have been considerable interest in doomsday predictions over the past decade, but religious funda-mentalism appears to be far less influential in Britain than it is in the United States (where its apocalyptic assertions may have some credibility even within the Reagan administration).[32] It is probably true to say that British thinking about future conflict has been influenced by apocalyptic predictions, but that this has served merely to reinforce the many other factors encouraging a concentration upon all-out hostilities.

Some dovish observers have gone considerably further, alleging that people are mesmerised by the prospect of nuclear annihilation, even to the extent of being subconsciously drawn towards the impending catastrophe.[33] In Humphrey's words, 'The Bomb is patently a superhuman weapon: mind-blowingly destructive – and, if we so see it, mind-blowingly magnificent. Small wonder if people's fear is mixed with awe, if they become hypnotised by the Bomb's dread beauty and its fascinating power.'[34] This apocalyptic notion does draw some support from the unhealthy fascination exerted by books and even games about nuclear war, and by the tendency of a few individuals to see such a conflict in terms of a cleansing holocaust or a well-deserved punishment for the sins and failings of technological society.[35] As one novelist portrayed the thoughts of a last survivor:

> Over the centuries we had devised, invented, improved, and our footsteps would stand in the dust of the moon for eternity. Yet by our self-inflicted wounds we lay dying in cellars, scorched and maimed in Red Square and Times Square and Trafalgar Square. Or drifted in the high upper winds as poisonous radioactive products of combustion. I whispered to myself, 'Dear God . . . we did not deserve all this.' But I knew we did.[36]

The most widespread apocalyptic distortion appears, however, to be found in the views of the doves themselves. The disarmament movement has launched a millenarian crusade which positively *requires* the threat of a thermonuclear Armageddon, to provide what Neville Brown described as 'the dark valley of crisis and near-catastrophe that must and will be traversed to reach the celestial city on the hill, a millenium of Peace on Earth'.[37] It is not Freudian psychology but dovish alarmism which has contributed most to the recent scare about an all-out nuclear holocaust. Images of war and violence do certainly hold considerable fascination for large sections of the general public, but this is a phenomenon which seems to manifest itself most strongly at the *conventional* level, and it is to this area that attention will now be turned.

The conventional alternative

There is a curious schizophrenia in British thinking about World War Three, characterised by the uneasy coexistence of two radically different images of what such a war might actually be like. On the one hand is the apocalyptic notion of an all-out nuclear holocaust; on the other is the concept of full-scale conventional hostilities between East and West. Some individuals hold only one of these two divergent interpretations, but many others seem to adhere to both, placing them side by side as different 'scenarios' or 'phases' of a potential Third World War. The conceptual linkage between the notions of a conventional battle and a nuclear holocaust was discussed at length in Chapter 2, but it remains the case that these two images are often considered very much in isolation, as if they were derived from two entirely separate strategic situations. Part of the reason for this 'doublethink' appears to be that the concept of unrestricted conventional hostilities enables people to temporarily ignore the nuclear revolution and to think about war in the old familiar way.

The notion of full-scale conventional warfare provides an artificial conceptual cocoon within which it is possible to see the East/West struggle as a traditional military contest rather than as a struggle of endurance and resolve in the shadow of unlimited destructive power. It has therefore been seized upon by the many thousands of servicemen and civilians who are more concerned with the technical than the political side of the defence issue. Politicians and strategic analysts may view conventional forces as 'hostages' or 'commitments' whose function is to bolster deterrence or to signal by their actions the strength of Western resolve, but the armed services and the general public tend instead to see the role of non-nuclear forces as being to prepare for, and if necessary to fight, a pitched battle with the forces of the Warsaw Pact. The notion of full-scale conventional hostilities provides a framework within which this traditional concept of defence can still be adhered to, even in a thermonuclear age.

There appear to be several reasons why attention has tended to be focused upon the drastic notion of an *all-out* conventional conflict between the opposing blocs, instead of upon hostilities more limited in intensity or geographical extent. The first reason (following on from the argument above) is that this kind of conflict seems not so much like a truly limited war as like a total war without nuclear weapons. Military men therefore feel able to make quite detailed technical plans and predictions without undue concern about political constraints, while other observers are confirmed in the view that war is an all-or-nothing affair in which, once hostilities have broken out, every means (except, perhaps, for instruments of mutual genocide) will be used to defeat the opponent. Both the all-or-nothing approach and the neglect of political considerations are long-standing characteristics of Western liberal thinking about armed conflict, and go a long way to explain the concentration on unrestrained hostilities, whether at the conventional or at the nuclear level.

An equally important explanation for the prominence of the notion of full-scale conventional hostilities is that this is what is anticipated in official NATO planning. The deterrent requirement for worst-case assumptions, the stress placed by Soviet strategists upon a blitzkrieg offensive and the fact that the Alliance's role is confined to defending its own territory rather than engaging in limited conflict outside the NATO area, have all acted to focus attention upon the prospect of all-out conventional war. Britain's own withdrawal from commitments East of Suez, and her distance from the 'front-line' of the Alliance, appear also to have encouraged a concentration upon high-intensity warfare in Europe, (although commitments in Norway, the Mediterranean and Berlin have prompted some interest in the possibility of a more limited confrontation).

Another reason for the readiness of Britons to contemplate all-out conventional conflict between NATO and the Warsaw Pact lies in the fact that full-scale conventional war is not now regarded with anything like as much horror as in the 1930s. This is no doubt due in part to the eclipsing effect of the even greater awfulness of nuclear weapons, but it seems also to stem from a marked shift in British images of non-nuclear war. As was pointed out in Chapter 2, the twin spectres of poison gas and conventional bombing play much less part in popular imagery today than they did fifty years ago, while fighting is generally expected to last for only days or weeks before the stark choice of a negotiated ceasefire or catastrophic escalation. Conventional war seems therefore to be feared now more because it might lead to military defeat or a nuclear holocaust than because it is seen as a horrific prospect in its own right.

The experience of World War Two may have contributed towards this tendency to underrate the horrors of 'conventional' hostilities, since Britain suffered less grievously than many other belligerents, and a smaller proportion of her soldiers than in 1914–18 faced the terrors of the front-line.[38] However, a more potent explanation for the dulled awareness of what a conventional Third World War would mean may be that most Britons now have only a vicarious experience of actual warfare, and have to base their impressions upon books, films, and the glossy images of military hardware in publicity material and recruiting advertisements. Even the recent Falklands conflict with Argentina was too small, brief and remote to give the British public any real idea of the horrors associated with all-out conventional conflict on a global scale.

A murkier aspect of this issue lies in the revived militarism which first arose in the Fascist states and which (in Michael Howard's words) 'combined the glamour of new technology with the promise of escape from the drab confines of bourgeois morality into a colourful and heroic world in which violence was not only permissible but *legitimized*'.[39] The heavy demand in Britain for military toys, games, models, books and magazines, and the fascination evoked by the pervasive images of war and violence in films and pulp fiction, illustrate that this new militarism is by no means dead, despite the advent of thermonuclear weapons.[40] The notion of full-scale conventional hostilities may, indeed, have provided a channel for its continued expression, and the sales achieved by Sir John Hackett's optimistic depiction of a short and sharp Third World War suggest that the politically artificial concept of a detached military contest between the armed forces of East and West holds almost as much fascination for Britons as does the threat of an all-out nuclear attack.[41]

As with the question of what influence apocalyptic imagery has had upon British thinking about a nuclear holocaust, it would be wrong to read too much into the fascination of a minority of individuals with conventional warfare and military hardware. Current popular militarism has reached nothing like the level of 'the glorification of war as a theatrical event of sombre magnificence' in pre-1914 Europe, let alone of the Fascist vision of 'small teams of young heroes, airmen, tank-crews, storm-troops, "supermen" who by daring and violence would wrest the destiny of mankind from the frock-coated old dodderers round their green baize tables and shape a cleaner, more glorious future'.[42] However, just as apocalyptic predilections seem to have smoothed the path for the notion of an all-out nuclear holocaust, so fascination with the technical aspects of full-scale conventional warfare appears to have dulled awareness of its political gravity and the slaughter and dislocation it would cause. This has not led to belligerence and jingoism, but it does seem to have made all-out conventional conflict between the blocs appear a more conceivable occurrence, thereby fuelling anxiety both about the threat of military defeat and about the risk of nuclear escalation. Attention will now be turned to another factor which appears to have increased the preoccupation of Britons with full-scale war, namely the influence of historical experience.

III THE LESSONS OF THE PAST

The present study is far from unique in its recourse to historical precedent to try to make sense of the contemporary situation. Past experience has always played a major role in attempts to understand and interpret the issues of the moment. However, as has been pointed out many times in the foregoing analysis, history can be a treacherous guide because of the possibility of secular changes which make straightforward linear comparisons invalid. Misinterpretation of past experience has for centuries been causing drastic errors of prediction, especially about future wars, and many historians have (albeit often inconsistently) denounced the whole idea of intelligible 'lessons of the past'.[43] In Michael Howard's words, 'Clio is like the Delphic oracle: it is only in retrospect, and usually too late, that we can understand what she was trying to say'.[44] The profound changes introduced into the modern strategic situation by the advent of thermonuclear weapons, while by no means making prior historical experience irrelevant (especially as regards the perennial characteristics of human political behaviour), have made the application of such experience to the present day an extremely complex and potentially misleading task.

Deceptive historical precedent

Perhaps the most deceptive aspect of historical precedent, in the light of recent strategic developments, is the fact that international relations within Europe in the two centuries prior to 1945 were characterised by prolonged periods of peace, punctuated by short but violent outbursts of major conflict. This was not the case in preceding centuries, when wars often lasted for decades or were virtually endemic in the political situation, nor was it the case outside Europe, where the Great Powers and indigenous peoples continued to engage in conflict on a fairly regular basis. However, the image of warfare which has become enshrined in the liberal tradition views war as a distinct and disjunctive phenomenon, an event rather than a process, which serves to interrupt the more normal condition of international peace.[45]

The natural corollary of this episodic view of conflict has been a channelling of speculation into the question of when and how the *next* outburst of convulsive hostilties might arise. People were preoccupied with the thought of a Great European War for decades prior to its actual outbreak in 1914, and, for all the talk of a 'war to end war', the idea that this was only the *first* world conflict was coined even before the Armistice.[46] Anxiety about the probable destructiveness of a second such struggle developed long before there was any clear indication of the likely antagonists, and when hostilities did break out between Britain, France and Germany in 1939, few Britons doubted that they were witnessing the start of World War Two.[47] The confirmation of this belief by the burgeoning global conflict of the next six years established a powerful conceptual pattern, and it is probable that, even had the defeat of the Axis powers actually produced the 'fun and laughter and peace ever after' of which Vera Lynn sang, mankind would still have been haunted by the historically compelling spectre of a convulsive Third World War.

The international climate of the late 1940s was, in the event, even less propitious than that of 1919, and the abstract notion of World War Three soon acquired a stark immediacy with the development of detailed plans and preparations for an all-out conflict between the capitalist and communist blocs.[48] The burgeoning destructiveness of the nuclear arsenals did lead both sides to declare that total war was not inevitable despite their political antagonism, but the plans and preparations continued in the name of deterrence, and the increasingly horrific spectre of a convulsive Third World War continued to over-shadow thinking about international affairs until the improvement of East/West relations themselves in the early 1960s. War scares can, of course, influence later perceptions just as can actual wars, and it is prob-able that the historical basis of the recently revived anxiety about World War Three lies as much in the apocalyptic imagery evoked by events such as the Cuban missile crisis as it does in the original precedent of 1914–45.

What has not so far occurred is the superseding of World Wars One and Two by actual post-war hostilities as the basis for popular thinking about international conflict. Britons have long drawn a clear conceptual distinction between 'Great Wars' centred on Europe and 'limited wars' in the rest of the world, so that conflicts such as Korea and Vietnam, while considerably influencing British perceptions of limited warfare itself, seem to have done little to undermine the widespread fascination with the notion of all-out hostilities. Only at the conventional level has the precedent of World War Two been supplanted by that of more modern conflicts such as those in the Middle East, and even here, considerable recourse to the earlier experience persists.[49] As for the concept of a Cold War confrontation in which the deciding elements are arms competition, brinkmanship and proxy struggles rather than direct armed conflict, this appears to have been too radical a departure from the traditional convulsive image of warfare to have wholly superseded it. The confrontation idea has, as discussed in Chapter 2, acquired considerable prominence within the defence community itself, but even those hawks who proclaim that the Third World War is already in progress do not altogether dismiss the possibility of a thermonuclear 'World War Four'.[50]

It is true that weapons technology has changed so greatly since 1945 that the notions of a spasm exchange of nuclear missiles, or even of a brief and violent non-nuclear conflict, bear almost as little overt resemblance to the grinding struggles of World Wars One and Two as does the alternative image of a continuing Cold War.[51] However, the fundamental similarity is much greater, and, moreover, fits in with the traditional pattern of military predictions based upon historical precedent. Such predictions usually go awry not because they fail to take notice of new strategic developments but because, in taking such developments into account, they fail to see the wood for the trees. New weapons technology is grafted on to the pre-existing strategic framework, without realising how that framework itself will be altered by the change in technique. Thus, French thinkers in the 1920s devised the ultimate instrument of positional warfare at the same time as such static fighting was becoming increasingly obsolete. The Maginot Line embodied the classic blend of innovative hardware and traditional strategic thought.

A similar incomplete integration of new developments seems to dominate the prevailing notion of World War Three. Most Third World War imagery tends to unite the weapons of the 1980s with the strategy of the 1940s – a politically unreal synthesis which multiplies the concept of unrestricted total warfare by the power of the hydrogen bomb to obtain the apocalypse. What this linear extrapolation from past experience neglects is the fact that thermonuclear weapons, by making it inconceivable any longer to engage in all-out hostilities as a rational instrument of policy, have replaced the polarisation between war and peace which characterised international relations in Europe prior to 1945 by a continuous spectrum of armed violence with no rational upper limit. In this new situation, the idea of a distinct and convulsive Third World War has become increasingly anachronistic. There are strong grounds for believing that the pattern of Great Wars has been broken, and that, however long people continue to be mesmerised by the historical mirage of World War Three, it is in the messy and unspectacular regional struggles, arms build-ups and political confrontations of the past four decades that the true future of international conflict lies.[52]

The search for analogy
The deceptive effect of historical precedent upon popular thinking about modern warfare has been exacerbated by a deliberate recourse to analogies with the past in an attempt to make sense of the present international situation. This phenomenon has been most marked with regard to the extremely contentious question of what might *cause* a war. It is in this profoundly political area that historical experience has most to contribute even in the changed strategic environment of the

thermonuclear age, so that analysis and discussion of how World War Three might actually arise has tended to be dominated by the promulgation of various supposed 'lessons of the past'. Unfortunately, this deliberate search for historical analogies has naturally laid stress upon the similarities rather than the differences between the current strategic situation and that of earlier eras, thereby obscuring the changes which have taken place since the age of total war.

A few commentators have sought historical parallels in events as long ago as the Peloponnesian War or the various conflicts of the Roman Empire, but the vast majority have restricted their attention to the much more widely known experiences of World Wars One and Two.[53] For some observers, the 'lessons' taught by the outbreak of these two struggles are essentially similar, with the two deductions most commonly drawn being that it is dangerous to assume that hostilities will be over by Christmas, and that the greatest danger of World War Three is from miscalculation, since (to quote one commentator) 'Neither the Kaiser nor Hitler had any conception that they were starting a world war; still less that they would lost it.'[54] Where common features are seen between 1914 and 1939, they tend to be particularly readily extrapolated into the future. In the words of one observer:

> I have a lurking fear that, just as the First World War began not on the frontier between the Western allies and the German empire but in remote Sarajevo, and just as the flashpoint for the Second World War was the Polish Corridor and not the Western front, so it could be that the Third World War could begin, shall we say, in Central America, or in Southern Africa, in the oilfields of Iraq or as a result of some miscalculation among the warring factions in South East Asia.[55]

Usually, however, the First and Second World Wars have been regarded as exemplifying two very different causes of international conflict, with World War One being associated with miscalculation and an arms race while World War Two is seen in terms of unprincipled aggression and an imbalance of power.[56] Disagreement about which policies would best reduce the risk of war in the contemporary era has tended to focus around these divergent 'lessons of the past', prompting serious debate over whether the current situation is more like 1914 or 1939.[57] As E. P. Thompson lamented, 'Today the "lesson" of World War II has stuck in the public mind while the "lesson" of World War I has been forgotten. Because it is widely believed that military weakness and appeasement "caused" World War II, many people now condone new forms of militarisation which will, if unchecked, give us World War III.'[58] The competing claims of the various protagonists in this debate about whether the present state of affairs bears more resemblance to 1914 or 1939 all too often tend to obscure the central fact that the current situation is profoundly dissimilar from *both*.

The 1914 analogy, based as it is upon events which have almost faded from living memory, has tended to find more resonance among informed observers than among the public at large. Doves have seized upon the supposed precedent of World War One, making much of Foreign Secretary Edward Grey's remark that 'great armaments lead inevitably to war', and drawing a parallel between the disastrous mobilisation race of 1914 and the alleged first-strike instability of the current superpower arsenals.[59] More moderate commentators have been sceptical of the idea that the First World War was sparked off by an unrestrained arms race, but have often seen a distinct analogy between the miscalculations and blunders of 1914 and the confusion and complexity of contemporary international affairs.[60] During the East/West confrontations of the early 1960s, both Kennedy and Macmillan were haunted by the spectre of August 1914, and a similar anxiety resurfaced at the end of the 1970s when the world seemed to be drifting into a minefield of strategic instability and interlocking crises, making many fear the advent of a second Sarajevo.[61]

The central defect of the 1914 analogy is that commentators have been so busy drawing ingenious parallels such as that between the Soviet nuclear build-up and Tirpitz's expansion of the Imperial German Navy that they have failed to pay sufficient attention to the fundamental difference between attitudes to war in the 1900s and 1980s. Most people in 1914 expected a brief and glorious clash of arms, and viewed this prospect with jingoism and militaristic fervour.[62] It was only the unforeseen horror and slaughter of the trenches which made the outbreak of war seem such a catastrophic event, and which prompted so detailed a post-mortem on the distinctly unremarkable causes which set it in train. In the 1980s, by contrast, fear of escalation to an annihilating nuclear holocaust has made the advocacy of *any* directly hostile action against the opposing bloc appear like criminal lunacy. There is a chance that blunder and miscalculation could embroil one or both superpowers in a messy regional conflict, but to argue on the basis of 1914 that such insubstantial causes might 'spark off' a full-scale Third World War is to ignore the profound shift which has been taking place in attitudes to warfare ever since the carnage in Flanders seventy years ago.

The 1914 analogy has dominated the intellectual side of the recent anxiety in Europe, but far more influential at the popular level has been the memory of appeasement and Hitlerian aggression prior to World War Two. Despite Anthony Eden's disastrous attempt to apply the 'lessons of the 1930's' in the Suez crisis of 1956, the Nazi analogy has retained its force, and one of the things which doomed the Argentine attempt at a bloodless annexation of the Falkland Islands in 1982 seems to have been the clear parallel in British minds with Fascist actions fifty years earlier.[63] Hawks have repeatedly exploited this deep neurosis about another Munich by taking every opportunity to compare the Soviet threat with that posed by Nazi Germany, and the conceptual linkage has been further strengthened by the tendency of many observers to draw rhetorical parallels with potent experiences such as the Battle of Britain or the outflanking of the Maginot Line.[64]

The problem with such simplistic analogies with the 1930s is that they tend to suggest that mankind is heading inexorably for another convulsive war, or at least that such a war constitutes the most immediate and pressing threat. In some cases, the proponents of such analogies have intended to create exactly this impression, but often (as was discussed in Chapter 2) the present danger is seen to lie in proxy defeat and Finlandisation rather than in a catastrophic World War Three. This has usually been far from obvious from the analogies themselves, especially when direct parallels have been drawn between the current situation and a specific point in the slide to war five decades ago.[65] In the later 1970s, however, there were many statements similar to Harold Macmillan's assertion that, 'Speaking honestly, I would say that we are now at 1935 or 1936', and surprisingly few observers tried to challenge the image of 'the gathering storm' by pointing out that, even if the Soviet regime really were as evil as the Nazis, it would be rational neither for it nor for the West to initiate the unprecedented devastation of an all-out Third World War.[66]

Britain is not the only country where perceptions of future conflict have been strongly influenced by the experience of the early twentieth century. Americans, although now preoccupied by the additional 'lessons' of Korea and Vietnam, tend to give the appeasement analogy as much if not more credence as it evokes in Britain itself.[67] In the Soviet Union, also, the experience of the 'Great Patriotic War' continues to dominate thinking about major conflict.[68] The preoccupation of both superpowers with the danger of surprise attack may in part be a reflection of their searing memories of Pearl Harbor and Operation Barbarossa.[69] In West Germany in 1980, Chancellor Helmut Schmidt repeatedly stressed the supposed analogy with 1914, while the dilemma of the Moscow Olympics boycott was particularly keenly felt because of the experience of the Berlin Olympics in 1936.[70] The recent war scare thus seems to have been as heavily influenced by historical precedent outside Britain as within it.

It has been suggested that policy makers would approach current events more objectively if they did not know much history at all.[71] However, it appears to be precisely such relative ignorance of the past which prompts the most grievous misuse of historical precedent, since individuals draw powerful 'lessons' from their own simplistic understanding of whatever searing events they or their parents have experienced. As Ernest May has argued, the only way to reduce misinterpretation of historical precedent is to *expand* awareness of what has gone before, thereby bringing home the variety and complexity of past events, and highlighting secular changes which make straight-forward linear comparisons invalid.[72] How historical examples might be used to encourage the development of a more realistic perspective upon the current strategic situation will be discussed towards the end of the present study. First, however, attention will be turned to the question of what impact the recent war scare has had upon policy views in the British defence debate.

6 The Impact of the Scare

The recent wave of anxiety about World War Three has been intimately associated with the renewed debate about defence as a whole. Various different images of a Third World War have been put forward in an attempt to attract support for particular kinds of security policy. Some commentators have tried to frighten people into following their recommendations by alarmist warnings of the danger of war, while other observers (or even the same ones at different times) have tried to defuse opposition by reassurances about the stability of the current situation. In this chapter, an analysis will be made of how the World War Three spectre has influenced the British defence debate, to determine who (if anyone) has actually benefited from the widespread preoccupation with the threat of a Third World War.

I EFFECT ON OPINIONS

Many dimensions must be taken into account when assessing how the recent war scare has affected British opinions about security policy. Not only does the scare appear to have influenced attitudes towards specific weapons programmes such as Cruise and Trident, but it also seems to have affected opinions on foreign policy issues such as East/West relations and the American alliance, not to mention its effect on attitudes towards the actual *use* of military force in a future crisis. It is also important to distinguish the impact of the recent upsurge of anxiety from the impact of the Third World War concept itself, which dominated thinking about East/West conflict even during the era of *détente*. These two influences will here be examined separately, to determine whether opinions on security policy are affected more by the very notion of World War Three or by the fear that such a conflict might actually occur.

The Third World War concept

As discussed in Chapter 2, Britons have a variety of different images of World War Three. However, by far the most prominent concepts are those of an all-out nuclear holocaust and of a full-scale conventional battle. The impact of these two images upon policy views will here be assessed, by focusing in turn upon British opinions about military preparations, alliance relationships, and the use of force against the Eastern bloc.

Concentration on the spectre of an all-out nuclear holocaust instead of on less apocalyptic nuclear tasks such as alliance symbolism, political intimidation and even limited nuclear options has prompted a widespread belief in the pointlessness of nuclear overkill, on the grounds that if both superpowers already have enough nuclear weapons 'to blow up the world several times over', new systems of whatever type can serve little purpose except to make the rubble bounce.[1] The holocaust concept has particularly prejudiced people against 'usable' nuclear weapons like the neutron bomb, since these are felt to pose grave dangers of starting the slide into an all-out spasm exchange.[2] British scepticism about the value of civil defence precautions appears also to have been fuelled by this apocalyptic and all-or-nothing attitude to nuclear war.

What the holocaust image has not done is to convince people of the disarmers' logic that, since nuclear war would destroy the world, the weapons themselves are no defence and Britain should get rid of them as soon as possible. Opinion polls reveal that, although *new* nuclear systems are widely seen as superfluous and dangerous, there is strong support for maintaining existing weapons as a deterrent to attack. A survey in 1983 found that, while respondents opposed by a majority of three to two the installation of American Cruise missiles, a similar majority rejected the idea that existing US nuclear bases in Britain should be expelled.[3] More strikingly, over half of respondents in a 1981 poll said that the United Kingdom should 'maintain her current nuclear capability', compared to less than one in four who said that nuclear weapons should be abandoned, and less than one in five who said the force should be improved.[4]

The effect of Third World War imagery upon British attitudes towards non-nuclear forces seems to have been similarly ambivalent. On the one hand, the notion that full-scale conventional war is a real threat and that first nuclear use would not save NATO without triggering catastrophic escalation has prompted many commentators to press for a more robust non-nuclear posture.[5] An opinion poll in 1983 found that supporters of nuclear weapons believed by a six to one majority that Britain should also maintain strong conventional forces, with three to one backing for this policy even among advocates of nuclear disarmament.[6] However, there has never been sufficient political will either in government or among the public at large to provide the human and material resources necessary for a truly firm conventional defence, and this parsimony seems to stem largely from the all-or-nothing belief that nuclear weapons will ensure continued peace in Europe or will make traditional fighting irrelevant should deterrence fail and World War Three break out.

Turning to opinions about alliance relationships, the Third World War spectre seems to have had as double-edged an influence as it has had upon attitudes towards military preparations. On the one hand, fear of thermonuclear devastation has made Britons less concerned about amassing a stronger alliance than their opponents, and more concerned about not being dragged into war through somebody else's dispute. Forty-six per cent of poll respondents in 1981 said that Britain should become neutral rather than siding with the United States, and almost as many respondents that same year said that Britain should take no military action against a Warsaw Pact assault, whether conventional or nuclear, upon continental Western Europe alone.[7]

Counterbalancing this unwillingness to get involved in a potentially apocalyptic conflict has been the widespread belief that Britain could not stand aside from World War Three even if that was what she wanted. Scenarios of an all-out nuclear holocaust or of a full-scale Soviet blitzkrieg leave Britain little chance of escaping involvement, and so provoke less discussion of opting out than if strategic discussion revolved around limited conflicts in Iran, Yugoslavia or even West Germany. British supporters of NATO have relied heavily on the concept of a full-scale Third World War, meeting calls for a more independent security policy involving the withdrawal of the Rhine Army or the ejection of American bases by asserting that Britain's strategic position means she is bound to be attacked in any European conflict, regardless of her defence posture. In the words of the 1981 Defence White Paper, 'Whether we like the fact or not, and whether nuclear weapons are based here or not, our country's size and location make it militarily crucial to NATO and so an inevitable target in war.'[8]

The disarmers, as the principal exponents of the view that any use of nuclear weapons would inevitably escalate into a holocaust destroying belligerents and neutrals alike, have faced particular contradictions in arguing that Britain could achieve safety by distancing herself from nuclear preparations. Some peace activists have contended that removing nuclear bases would leave no targets to be attacked, but most have fallen back upon the argument that nuclear disengagement in Europe would reduce the overall danger of conflict by creating a buffer zone between the blocs and by removing the temptation for America to try to fight a 'theatre' war in the region.[9] Cast in these terms of which security policy stands the best chance of preventing war altogether, collective security and the NATO alliance have fared considerably better in British opinion than if the issue were framed in terms of whether to risk being drawn into a potentially apocalyptic conflict, with poll respondents in 1983 asserting by over nine to one that Britain should remain a NATO member.[10]

Where unwillingness to risk an apocalyptic Third World War *has* made itself felt is in British attitudes towards active competition with the Soviet bloc. Even such low level measures as condemnatory rhetoric, economic sanctions and the 1980 Olympics boycott have aroused considerable opposition among those concerned not to jeopardise the climate of *détente*. Overt advocacy of active Western participation in a proxy struggle with the Soviet Union has been confined to a minority of hawks,[11] and as for the suggestion that Western troops should be committed to direct hostilities with Soviet forces, on however limited a scale, this proposal has been virtually taboo (except in hypothetical scenarios) ever since the Berlin blockade.[12] Only 4 per cent of poll respondents in 1980 advocated a direct American military response to the Russian invasion of Afghanistan, and only 2 per cent said that Britain herself should send troops to fight the Soviet invaders.[13] The Falklands crisis demonstrated British willingness to use force against lesser powers threatening British interests, but the spectre of World War Three seems to act as a potent deterrent to intervention against Russia herself.

How Britons might feel about using force if faced with a grave Soviet challenge is very difficult to gauge, since people are notoriously bad at predicting in advance what their reactions might actually be. The collapse of British resolve during the Munich crisis of 1938, and the resolution displayed a year later despite earlier contrary indications such as the Peace Pledge Union and the King and Country debate, are salutary warnings of the danger of taking peacetime attitudes towards the use of armed strength as a reliable guide to how people might feel if it ever came to the point.[14] However, peacetime thinking is important in its own right, not only because an apparent lack of resolve can lead aggressors to miscalculate as the Argentinians did in 1982, but also because if people came to believe that the consequences of resistance were worse than those of surrender, they might accommodate themselves to outside threats without any attack having to take place. It is therefore worthwhile to assess how the Third World War concept has affected the hypothetical willingness of Britons to resist Soviet aggression.

The notion that war might be confined to the conventional level has enabled servicemen and civilians alike to see national defence in terms other than thermonuclear annihilation, and has helped to maintain a high degree of public resolve behind the idea of standing up to the Russians even if deterrence should fail. The Oxford University Union in 1981 threw out the Queen and Country resolution which it had passed before the nuclear age began, and poll respondents in 1983 asserted by an eight to one majority that it would be better to fight in defence of Britain than to accept Russian domination.[15] As discussed in Chapter 5, however, this traditional image of armed defence has had the drawback of suggesting that full-scale conventional war might be sparked off by relatively minor political causes, thus undermining public confidence in NATO's deterrent strategy and sharpening fears that the Alliance's supposed non-nuclear inferiority might lead either to swift military defeat or to catastrophic nuclear escalation.

The concept of a mutually suicidal nuclear holocaust has had the opposite effect of reassuring many people that neither side would ever dare to cross the nuclear threshold in the first place, but this has been counterbalanced by the widespread belief that if it did ever come to the point, any humiliation would be preferable to risking the inconceivable catastrophe of an all-out nuclear exchange. Even hard-liners have shied away from the dilemma of 'suicide or surrender' by arguing that what matters is avoiding the choice altogether, and only a few commentators have stuck openly to the position that nuclear war would be preferable to subjugation.[16] Britons have been reluctant to state the opposite conclusion for fear of appearing unpatriotic or undermining deterrence, but one Tory MP in 1976 did frankly state, 'If I were offered the choice, I should prefer to be red than dead, and so would any rational human being.'[17]

Opinions within the general public on this extremely painful issue appear to be fairly evenly divided, with 36 per cent of poll respondents in 1980 saying that Britain should resist Soviet expansionism even at the price of a nuclear war, while 33 per cent of respondents in 1983 said that it would be better to surrender to the Russians than to face the consequences of a nuclear attack.[18] Because of the widespread belief that any use of nuclear weapons would inevitably escalate to the holocaust, debate on this issue has revolved less around the question of what level of nuclear war Britain should fight before giving in than around the problem of NATO's dependence on first nuclear use to repel conventional attack. The current pressure for the West to end its reliance on using nuclear weapons first thus seems to have been directly fuelled by the perception that full-scale conventional conflict and an all-out nuclear exchange are the two most likely alternatives for World War Three.

Perhaps the most far-reaching effect of Third World War imagery has been to encourage Britons to view the security issue in apolitical terms. Scenarios for a Soviet conventional blitzkrieg take little account of the Kremlin's practical motivations, while the nuclear holocaust is (in Michael Howard's words) 'widely seen as a *Ding an Sich*, unrelated to the existing political situation or to any security requirements likely to arise out of it'.[19] The effect of these apolitical images has been to reinforce the split between hawks and doves, by giving each group its independent technical nightmare without a common political basis on which the dispute can be reconciled. Disagreement on defence policy thus appears to be rooted as much in the World War Three concept itself as in the recent wave of alarm about such a conflict, and this issue will now be examined further by assessing what effect the increased anxiety of the past decade has itself had on British opinions about security policy.

The recent alarm

Increased anxiety about war has been only one among many influences on recent British thinking about defence, so that changes in the balance of opinions cannot necessarily be ascribed to the war scare *per se*. In fact, there seem to have been surprisingly few shifts in British views on security policy since the era of *détente*, and most of these shifts appear to have stemmed from causes other than heightened fear of war. Lord Chalfont did adopt a more hard-line position because of increased concern about the Soviet threat, while defence correspondent Andrew Wilson espoused unilateral nuclear disarmament on moral grounds when he realised that nuclear war might actually occur, but the vast majority of individuals in the recent strategic debate already held (or at least inclined towards) their present views long before the war scare began.[20] This continuity will now be examined by discussing the evolution of British opinions on defence policy and foreign policy since the era of *détente*.

Overall public support for nuclear disarmament does not appear to have markedly increased over the past decade, despite the striking resurgence of CND. Surveys reveal that up to a third of Britons agreed with the CND case in the early 1980s, but this is no higher a proportion than supported nuclear disarmament during the years of *détente*.[21] A 1980 poll found that the number of people 'objecting to' nuclear weapons was not very much greater among those who thought there was likely to be a nuclear war within the next decade than among more complacent respondents.[22] It is true that there developed majority opposition to specific nuclear systems such as Cruise and Trident, but this seems to have been due less to heightened fear of war than to the British public's ingrained distrust of any innovation which disturbed the status quo; by the time INF deployment commenced at the end of 1983, more people had come to accept than to challenge the missile programme.[23]

At the political level, the Labour Party has once more embraced the cause of unilateral nuclear disarmament, but this also seems to have been due less to the war scare itself than to outside influences. In the early 1980s the Labour Party drifted out of the hands of the parliamentary old guard into the control of left-wing activists and long-time disarmers such as Michael Foot, prompting the defection of right-wingers to form the SDP, and causing sufficient popular disenchantment to bring about a Tory landslide in the 1983 general election.[24] A more real shift of British opinions as a whole occurred in the later 1970s, when increasing anxiety about the Soviet threat produced a greater willingness among politicians and the public at large to spend more on conventional forces. However, this mood did not persist despite the heightened war fears of the 1980s, and not even the Falklands War arrested for long the development of renewed dissatisfaction (both popular and governmental) with the burden of defence expenditure.[25]

Turning to the foreign policy arena, anti-Americanism is another feature of British thinking which has become particularly evident over the past decade but which may not be directly attributable to war fears themselves. For one thing, opinion polls conducted during the era of *détente* already indicated majority agreement with the idea that British foreign policy depended too much upon that of the USA.[26] More importantly, recent increases in anti-American sentiment may be traced directly to the more independent and hard-line stance adopted by the United States on security issues, particularly under the Reagan administration.[27] Indeed, this heightened dissatisfaction with US policy seems itself to have fuelled the recent war scare in Britain, rather than the other way around.

As to the influence of increased anxiety upon the willingness of Britons to help in the defence of other nations, a comparison of poll results from 1975 and 1980 shows a noticeable rise in popular support for sending British troops or military supplies to allied or neutral states subjected to communist attack.[28] Soviet assertiveness in the later 1970s, culminating in the invasion of Afghanistan, thus appears to have bolstered rather than sapped British willingness to oppose further communist expansion. As was pointed out in the previous section, however, Britons have remained very reluctant to take action against

Russia when it actually came to the point, and the principal nightmare behind the recent war scare has been that ill-conceived US intervention against the Soviets in the Persian Gulf might spark off a global confrontation. The overall conclusion must therefore be that British opinions about security policy have not changed radically since the era of *détente*, and that fear of war is only one of several influences which have caused such shifts as have occurred.

This conclusion flies somewhat in the face of the notion that the past decade has witnessed a dramatic breakdown of the previous British security consensus, but the image of a shattered consensus itself requires considerable qualification. It is true that anxiety about war has undermined confidence in the efficacy of NATO's deterrent strategy and has prompted many observers to propose major or minor policy amendments which might make the situation more secure. However, most of these policy disagreements seem already to have been latent in British society during the period of *détente*, concealed only by the fact that dissenters either did not feel impelled to enter the security debate or were unable to make themselves heard in the prevailing climate of apathy and acquiescence. What has really changed over the past decade is not so much the *character* of British opinions about defence, but rather the fervour with which such opinions are debated, not only within the narrow and relatively like-minded 'defence community' but also among outsiders and the public at large. How important the recent war scare has been in prompting this more far-reaching debate will now be discussed at length.

II EFFECT ON ACTIVISM

How many people theoretically support or oppose a particular security policy is in many ways less important than how much people care whether the policy is implemented or not. This fact is illustrated by comparing the recent defence debates in France and Holland; opinion polls in the two countries reveal very similar proportions of latent popular opposition to established security policy, and the stark contrast between the respective defence debates seems to stem largely from the difference between the assertiveness of the Dutch peace movement and the acquiescence of the French public on the security issue.[29] An analysis will now therefore be made of how large a part fear of war has played in encouraging both hawks and doves in Britain to press their views more actively over the past decade. The chapter will then conclude with an overall assessment of who has benefited and who has suffered from the impact of the recent war scare upon the British defence debate.

Cause or effect?

There has undoubtedly been a close interrelationship between heightened alarm about war and increased discussion of security policy over the past decade. Both hawkish and dovish commentators have justified their proposals for change by warning of the dangers inherent in present policies, and the media has likewise spiced its coverage of the defence issue with sensationalist references to the possibility of World War Three. The problem is one of distinguishing cause from effect. Did growing fear of war spark off the renewed security debate, or has the recent war scare itself been a by-product of increased discussion, acrimony and alarmism about the defence issue? This question is very difficult to answer because the correlation noted in Chapter 4 between alarmism and dissatisfaction with existing security policies could be due either to the fact that anxiety about war impelled people to press for a new approach to defence, or to the fact that opposition to the status quo on quite different grounds prompted the issuing of dire warnings about the danger of World War Three in an attempt to frighten others into supporting the amendments proposed.

One way of tackling this problem is to use a historical yardstick, and to ask whether fear of war has impelled more or fewer people to take an interest in defence today than it did twenty-five years ago. Indicators such as media coverage and the size of CND demonstrations suggest that the security debate of the past decade has been at least comparable in intensity to that which occurred in the late 1950s and early 1960s. What must now be assessed is whether other influences than fear of war have played a greater or lesser part in triggering recent defence discussions, as well as whether any secular changes have occurred since the Cold War period to make the British security debate more or less responsive to outside stimuli.

British thinking about defence and foreign policy has always been strongly influenced by other criteria than the strategic situation itself. Moral revulsion from a policy which threatens the mass annihilation of opposing civilians has recently prompted tens of thousands of religious or liberal-minded individuals to protest unconditionally against nuclear weapons, and has brought most British Churches into the defence debate.[30] However, the Bomb caused at least as many ethical qualms in the 1950s when it was new to everyone and not just to the younger generation, and it is noticeable that today's CND has come to rely upon sophisticated strategic arguments rather than depending as it once did largely upon moral outrage.[31] A similar argument applies to the role of social factors in sparking the recent wave of anti-nuclear protest – modern British society may be plagued with tensions and problems, but the drab conditions of the 1950s provided an equally fertile soil for dissent in the shape of the 'Angry Young Men'.[32] Neither moral nor social stimuli for anti-militarism thus appear to have been markedly more potent over the past decade than they were twenty-five years ago.

Relative economic hardship has certainly increased since the days when Macmillan assured Britons that they had 'never had it so good', but this may not in fact have been such a powerful catalyst of security debate as is often assumed. Hard-liners bemoaned the priority given to welfare spending in the later 1970s, but at least defence budgets were steadily increasing, in stark contrast to the cuts imposed by Duncan Sandys twenty years earlier. In the 1980s, debate has focused not upon conventional forces but upon the much less costly nuclear programmes, and although the multi-billion pound price tag of the new Trident system has given rise to the slogan 'Jobs not Bombs', a 1982 opinion poll found that only half as many respondents disagreed with the Trident purchase on grounds of cost as opposed it because they 'objected to nuclear weapons'.[33] Judging by how few people today compared to the 1950s cite defence or foreign policy as one of Britain's most important problems, economic worries appear to have served more to divert attention from remote considerations such as international affairs to more immediate issues like unemployment and the cost of living than to spark off a defence debate on economic grounds.[34]

One factor which does seem to have had more influence upon the recent security debate than it did during the Cold War is party politics. In the 1959 election, the bipartisan defence consensus had not yet been broken, and in 1964, public concern was dwindling and Alec Douglas-Home was unable to capitalise on Labour's ambivalent stand on the nuclear issue.[35] In the later 1970s, by contrast, Margaret Thatcher (like Ronald Reagan in the United States) deliberately cultivated the growing dissatisfaction with *détente* by campaigning for a harder line against the Soviet Union, and Labour's subsequent shift to unilateralism gave voters a real choice of strategic options and made defence a major issue in the 1983 election campaign. However, both political parties were as much following as leading the sentiments of their supporters on the security question, so that it cannot be claimed that the recent defence debate was whipped up purely for party advantage. Domestic politics has served to amplify and channel British discussion of the security issue, but the global extent of the recent defence debate indicates that the controversy does not have its roots in such narrowly national factors.

The recent round of weapons modernisation by both blocs provides a more universal cause for debate, and, moreover, one which has directly affected Britons through the Cruise and Trident missile decisions. However, even more new military programmes were in train in the late 1950s and early 1960s, including highly contentious schemes for US missile bases in Britain and for the modernisation of Britain's own deterrent force. The same applies to disagreements over strategy. NATO's current posture of first use and limited nuclear options has caused a great deal of controversy over the past decade, but virtually all the associated problems of credibility and escalation control were being discussed in the 1950s debate over massive retaliation, despite NATO's theoretical nuclear superiority over the Warsaw Pact.[36] Both hawks and doves have tended to give the impression that recent strategic developments are new departures requiring radical remedial measures, but the reality is that the problems of conventional weakness, counterforce instability and even strategic defence have existed for decades, and were being discussed in theory long before they arose in practice.[37]

This does not necessarily mean that the heightened security debate of the past decade must have been due to increased anxiety about World War Three. Less apocalyptic perils such as Finlandisation and the loss of overseas resources have caused just as much concern among hard-liners as has the spectre of a convulsive conflict. However, this is also far from new; one of the main criticisms of the 1950s doctrine of massive retaliation was that it might lead to Western withdrawal and humiliation in real-world crises, while Britons were even more sensitive to 'out of area' threats in the Cold War period when their own world role remained large. Furthermore, doves had their own down-to-earth concern in the 1950s in the shape of fallout from atmospheric nuclear testing, a threat which has drastically diminished since the Test Ban treaty of 1963. It is thus hard to resist the conclusion that, although the recent defence debate has had many other causes than anxiety about a Third World War, these additional stimuli have been no more prominent over the past decade than they were twenty-five years ago.

The most appropriate model to explain the relationship between the recent war scare and the associated security debate seems to be one of deep mutual interaction. Britons have been motivated to take an increased interest in defence for a wide variety of reasons and have freely invoked the spectre of World War Three to try to win support for their own policy proposals, but heightened fear of war has also played its own independent role in impelling both the alarmists and their audience to take an active part in the renewed security debate. Anxiety about a Third World War thus does appear to have played a major (if far from exclusive) role in expanding British discussion of the defence issue. The question which remains is why the recent war scare should have been as effective in sparking debate as was its predecessor twenty-five years ago, if (as previous chapters have argued) recent fears have been characterised more by sensationalist alarmism than by gut anxiety about the international situation.

This paradox does not seem to be accounted for by changes in the World War Three spectre itself. The feeling that there is less and less that individuals, or even Britain herself, can do to influence the current strategic situation has spurred some people to try to reassert control over their own destinies by pressing for radically new defence policies which would not leave their fate in the hands of remote politicians, foreign generals, or rogue computers, but it has driven many more into attitudes of resigned powerlessness and apathetic fatalism.[38] The notion that a Third World War might be limited to conventional fighting has caused hawks to worry about military defeat and doves to fear catastrophic escalation, but has motivated far less popular protest than the direr threat of nuclear annihilation. Shifts in World War Three imagery thus do not explain why a less imminent perception of threat than in the Cold War period should have triggered a comparably sized defence debate.

As was hinted in Chapter 5, the solution seems in fact to lie in the development of increased sensitivity about any threat to peace, however theoretical and remote. People in today's relatively secure international environment have become even less tolerant than they were twenty-five years ago of the remotest possibility that a Third World War might actually come. Just as the tremendous advances in medical science over the past two centuries have not reduced fears of disease but have instead served to focus anxiety upon those diseases like cancer which still remain incurable, so the shift in attitudes to the avoidance of World War Three from a profound hope in the 1950s to a confident expectation in the 1970s seems now to have made even the theoretical possibility that such a conflict might occur sufficient to cause widespread outcry against the defence policies involved. The Third World War scare of the past decade thus appears, despite its air of artificiality, to have markedly influenced the wider defence debate, and who has benefited from that influence will now be discussed in detail.

The balance of advantage

Ten years after the Third World War scare in Britain resumed, indications of who has reaped the most advantage remain ambivalent. On the one hand, defence spending has been substantially increased, nuclear modernisation programmes carried through, and a hard-line conservative government elected with large majorities on two successive occasions. On the other hand, an unprecedented number of Britons have been roused to active opposition to established security policies, and the major opposition party has committed itself to a radically anti-nuclear defence programme. This ambivalent impact fits in with the analysis presented earlier in this chapter, since it was argued that the war scare has had either a minimal or a double-edged effect on actual *opinions* about security policy, and has boosted the activism of hawks and doves alike. What will now be assessed is whether alarmists have simply been wasting their time, or whether scare tactics can in some circumstances succeed (or prove positively counterproductive) in building support for particular defence policies.

One reason for thinking that alarmism can bring results is that the Third World War spectre has very different policy implications depending on one's image of World War Three. The hawkish notion of a full-scale conventional war caused by Soviet blitzkrieg aggression tends to build support for higher defence spending, while the dovish image of a nuclear holocaust sparked by an uncontrolled arms race tends to increase hostility towards the existing security infrastructure. It is true that dramatising one of these spectres can also help to raise apprehensions about the other, but for either hawks or doves to admit that there is very little risk of East/West conflict even along their most feared path could help their opponents to secure a monopoly of Third World War imagery, and hence to slant the policy debate in their favour.

A second reason why alarmism need not always be fruitless is that, in the absence of a lively defence debate such as has recently been fuelled by fear of World War Three, apathy prevails and a free hand is given to whoever currently controls the levers of power. It is for this reason that many security experts in the later 1970s cultivated popular anxiety in order to challenge what they saw as the Labour government's parsimony towards defence, while in the 1980s the roles were reversed and the reigning hard-liners defended the stability of the status quo in an attempt to defuse the alarmist onslaught of the disarmament movement. An enduring pattern has thus emerged, in which whoever is in power tries to reassure dissenting outsiders into acquiescence, while those out of power employ scare tactics to impel more of their latent supporters to stand up and campaign for their proposed policy amendments.

Things are not, of course, quite so simple in practice, and it is necessary to introduce some more specific data into this theoretical model of the benefits and drawbacks of alarmism. In the first place, the British defence establishment tends, regardless of which party is in power, to take a somewhat more hard-headed and security-minded approach than do large sections of the public at large. The result is that any extension of the defence debate to wider sections of British society tends to call into question the previously accepted verities of NATO strategy and nuclear deterrence, and to provoke an outburst of anti-militarism from idealists who had distanced themselves from the security issue until driven to protest by anxiety about World War Three. This is exactly what has happened over the past decade, and the hawkish attempt in the later 1970s to gain support by breaking through the apathy of the public at large has proven to be distinctly double-edged.

Counterbalancing this latent dovish sentiment is the tendency for outside opinion to swing towards established security policy the more intensely the issue is debated. The longer and more far-reaching defence discussions become, the more support official policies receive in the polls, and the more diluted and qualified become the criticisms of those who based their opposition on strategic rather than moral or ideological grounds. Such a shift of opinions took place in the early 1960s, and is also clearly evident from the heightened defence debate of 1983, when it helped to doom the Labour Party's radical challenge in the general election.[39] Thus, whereas alarmism can be a double-edged weapon for hard-liners, for doves it can be a wasting asset, and (as in the fable of the Sun and the Wind) proponents of disarmament may in the long run achieve greater success through the indirect effects of apathy, financial stringency and complacency about international affairs than through their present policy of scaremongering and direct confrontation with the defence establishment.

Although it is difficult to see who gains through unjustified alarmism about World War Three, it is easier to see who loses. Britain as a whole is less likely to follow the safest and most effective defence policy if that policy is evolved by unrealistic concentration on the threat of a Third World War at the expense of more down-to-earth security threats. The problem is exacerbated if anxiety about war gives rise to a polarised, ill-informed and sensationalist defence debate as has happened over the past decade. It is understandable that both hawks and doves have invoked the potent spectre of World War Three in an attempt to win support for their preferred policies, but those more restrained commentators who have consistently questioned the imminence of

East/West conflict and have tried to shift the security debate into more realistic channels have performed a considerably more valuable service for Britain as a whole.[40]

7 Conclusion

British speculation about possible conflict between the major powers has long been dominated by two fundamental questions – what form might such conflict take, and how likely is it to occur in the foreseeable future. In the era of total war, a tendency developed to consider these questions independently of one another, as if the primarily military problem of what might happen once hostilities began had only limited relation to the primarily political issue of how likely war was to be declared in the first place. However, since the advent of thermonuclear weapons, it is arguable that the likelihood and nature of conflict have become inextricably interlinked, with limited antagonism over a specific political issue being far more likely than a sudden slide into all-out hostilities, and with only the uncertainty and passion associated with any use of military force serving to shore up the once clear-cut distinction between war and peace. In this new situation, it would in many ways appear sensible to abjure separate discussion of the likelihood and nature of East/West hostilities, and instead to ask the single question of what type of conflict the competing blocs are most likely to pursue.

What seems to have happened in recent years is that British speculation about future warfare has fallen between these two stools, failing to adopt either a wholly compartmentalised or a wholly integrated approach to the likelihood and nature of East/West conflict. Conceptual bias, historical precedent and the paradoxical logic of deterrence have encouraged Britons to concentrate upon the prospect of high intensity warfare between the blocs, regardless of the prevailing level of political antagonism. This preoccupation with the military aspects of full-scale war has not, however, been isolated from speculation about the *likelihood* of conflict, with notions of 'arms races' or 'windows of opportunity' leading many people to believe that there is a serious risk of a high intensity conflict actually breaking out. The recent war scare thus appears to have its roots in fundamental confusion within British society about the relationship between the likelihood and nature of East/West hostilities, between the military and political dimensions of East/West competition, and between the two radically different concepts of total and limited war. This conceptual confusion will now be explored further by an attempt to set the war scare of the past decade in a wider temporal context, both in terms of the preceding era of *détente* and in terms of how British thinking about East/West conflict might develop in the future.

The instability of acquiescence

Edward Gibbon wrote, 'instead of inquiring *why* the Roman Empire was destroyed, we should rather be surprised that it had subsisted so long'.[1] A similar consideration applies to the demise of the unconcern which had prevailed in Britain about defence and East/West relations during the 1960s and 1970s. Although there is every reason to believe that this complacency was justified and that the strategic situation was indeed extremely stable, the foundations upon which the complacency was actually based appear to have been paradoxically delicate and artificial. Far from being grounded in a reassuring belief that the East/West contest was politically unlikely to escalate into a markedly more intense form of competition, popular unconcern seems to have rested upon the much less solid criteria of ignorance, acquiescence and faith in a burgeoning *rapprochement* between the opposed blocs. These negative grounds for complacency were highly vulnerable to adverse strategic developments, and instead of inquiring why anxiety about war revived in the later 1970s, we should rather be surprised that the artificial (if justified) unconcern of the preceding era had subsisted so long.

At the root of the instability of British attitudes towards the East/West relationship appears to be the tension between maintaining deterrence and pursuing *détente*. Britain's solution to this dilemma has been to delegate military preparations and contingency planning to a corps of professional specialists, thus enabling society as a whole to adopt a much more relaxed attitude towards the Soviet bloc. In Laurence Martin's words, the military have become like 'latter-day remittance men, given a small slice of the family income on condition that they go off and pursue their unsavoury activities quietly where they will not embarass decent folk'.[2] It might at first be thought that this division of responsibility between deterrence and *détente* would have acted to calm worries about World War Three, by freeing the public at large of the need for constant schizophrenia about Soviet capabilities and intentions, and thus allowing them to take a more objective view of relations between East and West. Unfortunately, the long-term effect which the professionalisation of the defence effort has had upon popular thinking appears to have been exactly the opposite, for reasons which will now be discussed.

In the first place, the delegation of defence to a self-contained corps of specialists seems to have encouraged the security establishment in the years of *détente* to content itself with unconcerned acquiescence rather than positive support from the population at large. Widespread public indifference must have come as a welcome relief to the defence community after the CND protests of the Cold War era, and the daunting task of trying to break through this indifference to create and maintain a popular defence consensus was abjured in favour of technocratic internal debates about how to make NATO strategy credible in an age of superpower parity.[3] Labour governments were especially concerned to let sleeping dogs lie, due to the anti-nuclear bias of their own activist supporters. The defence establishment thus tended to become introverted and élitist, forfeiting any partial consensus which had been built up among the general public by the defence debate of the late 1950s and early 1960s, and relying almost entirely upon apathy and unconcern to damp down the latent popular unease about security policy. This latent unease seems to have played a major part in the revival of controversy and alarm in the later 1970s, particularly when exploited by hawks and doves seeking popular support for their own radical policy alternatives.[4]

The ignorance fostered during the years of *détente* both by popular indifference and by official reticence appears also to have contributed strongly to the recent war scare, by encouraging the public to rely upon simplistic and misleading criteria for an understanding of the strategic situation. Tangible military hardware has overshadowed political considerations in influencing images of East/West conflict; questionable historical analogies have been used as a substitute for original thought about contemporary strategic problems, and the paradoxical concept of deterrence has encouraged a focusing of attention and alarm upon the very thing being deterred. All these processes have reinforced people's natural preoccupation with the kind of high intensity conflict which would most directly affect Britain herself, and have made such a conflict appear markedly more conceivable than might have been suggested by a less superficial analysis of the strategic situation. In default of any real public debate about the political dimension of East/West relations, the professionalisation of defence thus seems to have acted less to remove worst-case planning from the foreign policy arena than to actively channel popular thinking about relations with the Soviet bloc into the defence forces' own field of military preparations and World War Three.

The public remained reassured about East/West relations only so long as the international climate appeared to be growing progressively more secure. As soon as this gradual improvement was checked by the increased incidence of Third World crises together with the stagnation of the SALT process and the acceleration of superpower arms competition, fears of World War Three began to revive. The renewed anxiety seems to have been due in part to a lack of historical perspective, and sceptics of the war danger have repeatedly emphasised that the present situation, although relatively more tense than that of the early 1970s, contains nothing like the technical and political instabilities of the original Cold War (not to mention the massive instability which it took to set off World War Two). However, one of the effects of *détente* appears to have been to increase the public's expectations of the avoidance of East/West conflict and to make people less tolerant of even the slightest risk that such a conflict might actually come. Although gut anxiety about war is less now than it was in the 1950s or 1930s, recent peace protests have been on just as large a scale as those in the earlier eras. This increased sensitivity suggests that the assertion that 'we have seen worse before' provides only limited reassurance, and that Britons are likely to remain concerned as long as they see East/West relations in terms of a continued confrontation with a finite risk of sparking off a catastrophic conflict.

This questionable image of an armed peace in which the main danger is that of a convulsive war seems to have been strengthened, at least in the minds of the general public, by the experience of *détente*. East/West relations in the 1960s and 1970s appeared to correspond more to the peaceful interludes of the era of total war than to the state of active, low intensity competition which the Soviet Union understood by the term 'peaceful coexistence'. Many British spokesmen positively stressed the idea of a sharp polarisation between peaceful relations and a catastrophic World War Three, in order to attract popular support for the policy of *détente* with the odious Soviet regime and to defuse criticism of the technical vulnerability of NATO to limited attack.[5] The notion that the alternative to *détente* was a catastrophic Third World War was reassuring as long as people believed that the superpowers would therefore choose *détente*, but it became a source of considerable anxiety as soon as indications began to appear of a more competitive and conflictual relationship between East and West. How the unstable popular acquiescence of the 1960s and 1970s actually broke down, and the implications of this breakdown for British thinking about defence and foreign affairs, will now be examined in detail.

Controversy and concern
The principal cause of the recent wave of anxiety about World War Three has been a lack of consensus upon two fundamental issues – how

best to visualise East/West competition, and how best to achieve the Western goal of maintaining peace with freedom. Controversy about these two issues has existed ever since the original Cold War, but was damped down during the years of *détente* by the seemingly progressive improvement of the East/West climate. When tension returned, even at a comparatively modest level, the controversy was revived, and with it anxiety about the risk of a Third World War. It is because of this apparently systemic link between controversy and concern that the actual development of the recent war scare is in many ways less remarkable than the fact that it was postponed for so long by the inconclusive acquiescence of the era of negotiations.

Perhaps the greatest single cause of the recent alarm about a Third World War has been confusion about whether East/West competition should be seen in terms of total or limited conflict. For reasons which were discussed at length in Chapter 5, Britons have been reluctant to fully accept the idea that the advent of thermonuclear weapons has fundamentally changed the characteristics of conflict between the major powers, by making high intensity warfare so destructive that competition is diverted into other channels such as arms build-ups, political confrontations, proxy struggles, and (as a last resort) the application of limited military force in an attempt to face down the opponent in a trial of will. Although this limited war model has won considerable support in Britain (especially among defence experts), notions derived from the era of total war have remained extremely persistent, producing widespread fears that the heightened tension and competition between the United States and the Soviet Union might 'spark off' a convulsive World War Three, just as the antagonism between Britain and Germany twice precipitated all-out conflict in the first half of the twentieth century.

The anxiety of the past decade appears to have been prompted less by the Third World War concept itself than by the incomplete breakdown of this concept in favour of the new image of a limited contest of endurance and resolve in the shadow of effectively unrestricted destructive power. It is noteworthy that the war scare started not with a *resurgence* of the traditional image of a convulsive World War Three but with a challenge to this concept by hard-liners such as Alexander Solzhenitsyn concerned about 'Finlandisation' and defeat without war. Although intended to diminish the widespread preoccupation with the threat of high intensity conflict, this challenge seems actually to have had the opposite effect, especially when bolstered by easily misinterpreted arguments about the political implications of Russia's alleged war-winning capability.

Anxiety appears to have been greatest among those who did see a risk of limited conflict, but who continued to view it in the total war terms of a technical military contest rather than in terms of a political struggle of wills. Conceptual confusion of this sort seems to have underlain dovish concern about the shift from 'pure' mutual assured destruction to flexible response and limited nuclear options, as well as hawkish alarm about Western vulnerability in artificially self-contained military contests at various levels of the force spectrum. Nothing better epitomises the damaging confusion between the two radically different concepts of total and limited conflict than the hybrid notion of full-scale conventional hostilities, which has undermined confidence in the suicidal irrationality of major war, without diverting attention away from the technical characteristics of the deterrent stockpiles and towards the extreme political gravity of modern high intensity warfare.

Almost as important in prompting the recent war scare as the lack of consensus about how to visualise East/West competition has been the bitter controversy over whether the best way to avert conflict is to prepare for peace or to prepare for war. When the stagnation of *détente* eroded the apathy and acquiescence of the early 1970s, it was those individuals who thought they could see a clear way forward if only the rest of society would follow their advice who tended to become most anxious about the possibility of a Third World War. The conflicting nature of their suggested remedies meant that it was impossible to ease the frustration of all the individuals concerned, and the increase in the West's defence preparedness from the late 1970s onwards served only to shift the burden of anxiety from the hawks to the doves. Disagreements about defence policy increased concern also among less committed individuals, both by encouraging scaremongering and alarmist warnings to try to frighten people into supporting a particular policy and by focusing attention upon the deterrent stockpiles rather than upon the much less apocalyptic character of East/West relations themselves.

Although controversy about defence policy does seem to have played a large part in sparking the recent war scare, the influence has not been all one way. There are strong grounds for believing that the increase in anxiety about World War Three has itself been a major factor in the revival of the wider defence debate. Alarm does not seem to have substantially changed actual opinions, and there is little evidence that scaremongering has been of decisive benefit either to the hawks or to the doves in their efforts to shift overall attitudes towards defence policy in their own favour. However, the intensity and radicalism of the defence debate itself has been considerably increased by heightened anxiety about a Third World War, with the appearance of a wide variety of campaigning organisations each attempting to 'save the world' by promoting its own individual policy ideas. Anxiety thus seems to encourage disagreement rather than consensus, and there is every reason to believe that, if East/West relations were to worsen yet further, the effect would be to deepen policy divisions within British society rather than to unite people behind one particular line. Whether this vicious circle of concern and controversy can be broken will now be discussed in depth.

Towards a new consensus?

British alarm and disagreement about security have declined considerably since the early 1980s. Partly because of habituation to continued East/West tension and partly because of the gradual toning down of superpower rhetoric, peace demonstrations have become smaller and most Britons have come to believe that World War Three is a long-term danger or will not occur at all.[6] Controversy about defence has also become less bitter as both hawks and doves have strained to capture the middle ground by appearing moderate and reasonable and as debate has shifted away from new nuclear deployments towards the issues of conventional defence and President Reagan's 'Star Wars' scheme, neither of which have as much immediacy nor provoke such clear-cut divisions among British observers as does the nuclear issue.[7] However, the war scare itself is far from over; considerable anxiety and discord remain, and although concern is likely to slowly diminish if present trends continue, a new weapons controversy or a grave superpower confrontation could revive the alarm and protest of five years ago.

The British security establishment has been striving for the past few years to find a way of placing the nation's defence effort on a more stable domestic footing. Attention has generally revolved around the rebuilding of the security consensus which is thought to have broken down at the end of the 1970s.[8] Michael Howard, however, has broadened the discussion to include the deflation of unjustified fear of war by arguing that NATO must design its defence posture not only to deter the Soviet Union but also to 'reassure' the Western Europeans themselves of their continued security. In his words, 'Above all we must stop being frightened, and trying to frighten each other, with spectres either of Soviet "windows of opportunity" or of the prospect of inevitable self-generating nuclear war.'[9] An analysis will now be made of the remedies which Howard and others have proposed, in order to determine how reassurance and consensus might most effectively be pursued.

The British government has to some extent fallen back upon its traditional policy of maintaining a low profile on defence in order to avoid arousing unnecessary anxiety and dissent, and has repeatedly stressed the unlikelihood of war while avoiding mention of those controversial subjects like civil defence and limited nuclear options which caused so much concern in the early 1980s. This negative stance, however, is insufficient without an accompanying positive attempt to shape public perceptions of the strategic situation; otherwise, as happened in the era of *détente*, the defence establishment runs the risk of fostering ill-informed ideas, sensationalist imagery and conspiratorial suspicions of the kind which fuelled the recent outburst of alarm. The security debate of the past decade has removed many of the obstacles to a more positive domestic strategy on the defence issue by breaking through popular apathy and by exposing the public to many unfamiliar concepts which were common currency within the defence community; it would be tragic if the security establishment were to lose the ground which has been so painfully gained over the past few years by relapsing into introversion now that the storm seems to be passing and the debate appears to have been won.

Many defence experts have suggested that the road to consensus lies through subtle policy shifts such as more energetic pursuit of arms control, greater European defence co-operation or a stronger conventional posture. It is argued that such policies would defuse controversy by simultaneously addressing both hawkish and dovish concerns on issues like East/West arms competition, Europe's dependence upon the United States and NATO's reliance on first nuclear use.[10] However, the disputes which have arisen about these specific issues over the past decade are merely symptoms of a more fundamental and long-standing controversy over the nature of the Soviet threat and the role of military force in the nuclear age. Subtle technical fixes such as 'conventionalisation' finesse rather than confront this basic controversy and so have only limited value in enhancing domestic consensus; like the 'twin track' compromise on INF they may attract sufficient political support to be carried into effect, but they do not resolve the fundamental dispute over whether peace is best preserved by preparing for peace or by preparing for war.[11]

If the defence community is truly to reduce domestic disagreement and alarm, it must transcend the managerial approach of trying to avoid public notice or evolving subtle compromise solutions, and must make a greater effort to set popular thinking about security within its proper political context. In Lord Carrington's words, 'We must be seen to be taking the broad view. The dehumanization of the East/West relationship would be the quickest road to catastrophe I can imagine.'[12] This need for a more outgoing discussion of the political background of military preparations has been recognised by many defence experts,[13] and the efforts which have already been made in this field have helped to diminish fears that war might start merely through the accumulation or imbalance of military hardware. What specific measures might be taken to further heal the rift between defence and foreign policy in the British security debate will now be discussed in detail.

The first requirement is to expand discussion of East/West relations beyond the narrow sphere of arms control talks to include the broader political imperatives towards conflict and co-operation between the blocs.[14] It is true that British observers disagree profoundly about the enigma of Soviet intentions, but the past decade has shown that trying to evade this controversy by basing defence preparations solely on Soviet capabilities may actually produce worse disagreements by inflaming the inevitable dispute about the Soviet threat with a series of artificial technical scares about 'windows of vulnerability' or destabilising 'first strike' missiles. Better to grasp the nettle of disputes about Russian hostility by using what data is available to discredit extreme views and to narrow the range of sensible debate beyond the current face-off of those who believe in unremitting Soviet malice and those who see both blocs as helpless prisoners of uncontrolled military bureaucracies and frozen Cold War antagonism.[15]

A second task is to encourage Britons to view limited conflict between the blocs less as a detached military contest and more as a struggle of will for concrete political objectives. This might be done by inviting greater discussion of what values and interests the West should defend, how much effort the Soviets might make to threaten those interests, and what costs and risks the West should accept to counter such threats. There will undoubtedly be profound disagreements (for example over how to secure oil supplies from the Persian Gulf), but a more political approach to potential conflict could help to reassure Britons about the stability of the current international situation. Even a desperate Soviet empire would have much less to gain from attacking the West than the West would lose if it gave up the fight, and this knowledge will deter Kremlin leaders as long as they know they cannot destroy NATO's *capability* to resist. A comparison of real political incentives could thus be far more reassuring than NATO's current agony over the hypothetical dilemma of whether to use nuclear weapons against a Soviet Union driven by some inconceivable motive to launch a full-scale conventional attack and prepared to make a pre-emptive nuclear strike if its advance is thwarted.

The current lack of political incentive for either bloc to use military force except for limited objectives such as subduing ideological threats among weak neighbour countries does not, of course, guarantee that East/West conflict will remain on such a restrained level. Should the superpowers collide over some local issue, concern about reputation and prestige could drive the blocs into an escalating struggle of resolve more and more disproportionate to the original war aims. However, past superpower crises suggest that the countervailing influence of nuclear dread will remain extremely strong, and that if a conflict does get out of hand it will not be through swift escalation to a convulsive Third World War but rather through a local conflict intended to be quickly settled dragging out into a prolonged battle of attrition. Both blocs are now well aware of how difficult it is to disengage from military commitments, but the risk of becoming entangled in a more and more bloody and unproductive struggle of endurance and resolve remains real, and should be made to play a larger role in British thinking than does the politically artificial spectre of World War Three.

Preoccupation with the all-out use of the military stockpiles of East and West might be reduced by portraying these stockpiles less as a deterrent to hostile action and more as a neutral insurance against the escalation of a crisis or conflict for military rather than political reasons. It should be argued that the principal purpose of defence preparations is to further enhance the technical stability of the East/West relationship by persuading both sides that no form of attack can deprive the opponent of the capability to resist as he desires without causing such losses that he might resort to more drastic means in retaliation. Emphasising *bilateral* stability could help to diminish current anxieties, by assuring doves that NATO is concerned not to acquire a first-strike capability against the Warsaw Pact, and by making current planning for full-scale Soviet aggression seem more theoretical and less Manichean. The overall impression should be that armed forces *per se* serve merely to underpin the strategic environment of limited antagonism by depriving both blocs of any prospect of a purely military victory, and that if force is used it will be to achieve a specific political objective rather than to exploit (or forestall enemy exploitation of) technical instability in the deterrent stockpiles themselves.

Many defence experts (especially hard-liners) have taken the opposite approach to diverting attention from the Third World War spectre, and have argued that military forces, far from merely deterring their own large-scale use, have all sorts of political functions as symbols of resolve or instruments of intimidation which are more important than their potential use in war. However, whether theoretical superiority at one level of the force spectrum is politically useful in an age of mutual assured destruction is unclear, and the scenarios which have been devised to show how such superiority might hypothetically be of benefit in an actual conflict have served to increase rather than decrease preoccupation with the threat of World War Three.[16] If military sufficiency were instead pursued in the name of technical stability, this might erode the conceptual linkage between inadequate deterrent forces and low level political challenges, thereby encouraging people to see outbursts of tension and local conflict as evidence less of the *failure* of central deterrence than of confidence in its robustness and stability.

Probably the best way of encouraging Britons to take a more political view of defence is to set the current strategic situation in its historical perspective. As was pointed out in Chapter 5, simplistic analogies with the past may be highly misleading, but they nevertheless remain one of the most potent influences upon British thinking about defence and so should be pursued in order to encourage more realistic historical comparisons. Current events are already widely compared with the years preceding World Wars One and Two, but these analogies are unnecessarily disheartening – there was nothing like the present fear of mutual devastation to arrest the slide to war in 1914, while the Soviet Union today is nowhere near as bent on aggression as was Hitler's Germany. It would be better if more reference were made to post-war experiences, when both nuclear weapons and the East/West confrontation were already in existence.

Several telling comparisons suggest themselves from the post-1945 period. Korea, Vietnam and the Cuban missile crisis are just as powerful illustrations of the conflicting errors which can lead to war as are Munich, Pearl Harbor and Sarajevo, and they do not have the disadvantage of suggesting that one single mis-step would trigger Armageddon. The fact that the relatively serious political and military instabilities of the Cold War era did not spark off World War Three reassures one of the stability of the current age of agreed boundaries and secure second-strike capabilities. Russia's invasions of Hungary, Czechoslovakia and Afghanistan, and her clumsily coercive diplomacy towards the European neutrals, are more suitable illustrations of the Soviet threat to weaker states with incompatible ideologies than is a mere tallying of raw military power. Popular unfamiliarity with such examples may be overcome by invoking fresher historical memories: the fate of Solidarity in Poland indicates the limits of the peace movement's pan-European crusade, the continued violence in Lebanon and in the Iran/Iraq war illustrates the real-life quagmire to which appeals to force may lead, and Britain's own battle for the Falklands shows that local forces and the perceived willingness to fight over a specific political issue are far more important deterrents to limited aggression than is the overall balance of military power.

It will not be possible (nor is it desirable) to fully defuse British alarm and controversy on the defence issue. The closed nature of communist society will continue to foster widely varying interpretations of the Soviet threat, and the lack of any historical experience of direct fighting between nuclear powers will similarly encourage widely differing views on what might happen should such fighting occur. However large an emphasis is placed on the political roots of international conflict, doves will remain convinced that the deterrent stockpiles pose grievous dangers in their own right, while hard-liners will continue to dread (and sometimes to pursue) politically meaningful military superiority. There is thus no hope of building a true security consensus in Britain, nor of fully discrediting the deeply-rooted spectre of a convulsive Third World War. All that can and should be done is to encourage a somewhat more sensible and realistic defence debate – a decidedly preferable alternative to the often polarised and hysterical discussions of the past decade. It is the task of political leaders and of the security community to shape such a better informed debate within British society as a whole, rather than returning to the introverted and managerial approach which contributed so much to causing the recent war scare.

Appendix: The Opinion Poll Evidence

Public opinion polls have provided one of the most important categories of source material for the foregoing analysis of British thinking about World War Three. Attitudes towards the value of such opinion surveys tend to fluctuate markedly, ranging from uncritical acceptance when the results happen to support an individual's own point of view, to outright scepticism when the results are distasteful or appear to be at odds with other more 'practical' indications of popular feeling. The strengths and limitations of the opinion poll technique have already been discussed in considerable detail in social science literature, but since the conclusions of such analyses tend to filter down only in de-based and partisan form into the acrimonious public debate surrounding the findings of political surveys, a brief attempt will now be made to assess how reliable and informative the opinion poll evidence actually is in reflecting popular attitudes towards the specific issue of a possible Third World War.

Technical characteristics
British polling organisations have between them asked several hundred questions related to defence and foreign affairs over the past decade alone. Almost all the resultant data (except for that not publicly available) has been examined for the purposes of the present study. Hundreds of survey results from the period before 1975 have also been analysed, in order to set the recent war scare in its historical context. Given the large amount of data involved, it might be thought that the opinion poll evidence would provide ample information about popular attitudes to the defence issue. Unfortunately, however, the survey material has several shortcomings which make it a much less adequate guide to public reactions during the recent war scare than the number of questions alone might suggest.

In the first place, the spread of data tends to be somewhat unbalanced, with very few surveys conducted during the 1970s when anxiety about war first began to revive, and later polls concentrating upon the nuclear issue rather than upon wider aspects of defence and foreign affairs. Secondly, many recent surveys on defence have been conducted on a 'one-off' basis, making chronological comparisons difficult because of the well-known dependence of poll responses upon the exact way in which questions are phrased.[1] Finally, although most survey results have been broken down according to social factors such as sex, age and class, virtually no information has been available about cross-correlations between attitudes on different aspects of the defence issue. These deficiencies have limited the value of the mass of survey data, and have left some tantalising gaps in the coverage of the field concerned. Much valuable evidence does, however, exist, and in view of the fact that the polls were carried out quite independently of the present study, it is fortunate that the survey evidence sheds as much light as it actually does upon British thinking about World War Three.

Although conducted by several different organisations, almost all the polls under discussion were carried out using a standard technique developed over many decades (primarily in the United States) for the scientific investigation of public opinion. Each survey involved between 500 and 2000 street or doorstep interviews conducted in Britain over a period of 2 to 8 days. The selection procedure used was that of multi-stage quota sampling, wherein between 40 and 100 local authority areas are selected at random, and interviewers in each area must approach a set number of respondents of previously specified sex, age and social class. If necessary, the final totals are then weighted to conform to the correct proportional distribution of these interlocking social groups within the adult population as a whole. The object of the exercise is, of course, to provide an accurate and objective estimate of how feelings are running among the entire mass of the British public.

It is not possible to assess the reliability of the quota sampling technique by applying traditional statistical theory, because respondents are not selected by a purely random and impersonal process. However, empirical methods involving the comparison of two or more exactly parallel surveys on the same issue do allow the likely magnitude of chance variation in poll results to be fairly accurately determined. Gallup estimate that, if 1000 respondents were interviewed and 40 per cent of them were found to be in agreement with a particular proposition, the chance that an exactly similar poll involving a different body of respondents would find the percentage of agreement to be either less than 32 per cent or more than 48 per cent is under one in a hundred, while there is at least a 50–50 chance of the difference being 2 per cent or less. Although such levels of uncertainty and imprecision cast some doubt on the reliability of the standard opinion poll technique for making detailed electoral predictions, errors of a few per cent are perfectly tolerable when considering the broad characteristics of British thinking about defence and foreign affairs.

More worrying, because more insidious, than chance variation is the possibility of systematic errors affecting all polls alike. There are several ways in which the sample of interviewees may become unrepresentative of the population as a whole, ranging from the refusal of some people to cooperate with the survey, to imbalances either within each quota band or across non-quota variables. How, for instance, did interviewers react to passers-by wearing military uniform or CND badges? Systematic bias is disturbing because it is so hard to pin down, but there are nevertheless good reasons to believe that any errors involved are of no greater significance for present purposes than those caused by chance variation. Polling has come a long way since the Literary Digest debacle of 1936, when systematic discrimination in favour of middle-class voters by techniques such as telephone interviews and mailed questionnaires produced an error of 19 per cent in predictions of the American presidential election.[2] It is reasonable to assume that the modern survey organisations are well aware of such glaring pitfalls, and that their sampling methods give a tolerably accurate estimate of the responses which would be obtained if the poll questions were asked of every single adult in Britain. A much greater cause for concern is the question of whether bare opinion poll statistics can ever give a true impression of the actual feelings of the general public.

Empirical limitations

The central problem with the opinion poll technique is that it relies on active investigation rather than passive observation of popular reactions to the issues of the day. This is useful in that it allows enquiries to be sharply focused onto the specific area of interest, but it is damaging in that it forces the investigators themselves to impose a detailed conceptual framework within which standardised 'yes or no' opinions may be expressed. Flexibility and ease of analysis are thus paid for by an increase in the risk (familiar throughout scientific experimentation) that the act of measurement may distort the very thing being measured. It is this interventionist character of the survey technique which arouses most scepticism about the value of opinion poll evidence, and an attempt will now be made to assess just how prejudicial the pollsters' own role has been to the accuracy with which survey data reflects popular thinking about defence and foreign affairs.

The most obvious distorting influence upon poll results is the way in which questions are phrased. Replies on a given issue may be considerably affected not only by leading questions or emotive terminology but also by less obvious factors such as the impact of previous questions in the survey, the range of response options offered, or the identification of one particular option with government policy or the status quo. Popular ignorance about defence makes surveys on this issue particularly susceptible to response distortion, both because questions may not be fully understood and because the efforts of the pollsters to make the issues clear make tendentious presentation even harder to avoid. However, the survey organisations are aware of the pitfalls involved, and take great pains to make their enquiries as unbiased as possible. Multiple response options and open-ended questions have done much to mitigate the structured artificiality of the opinion poll technique. The real problem underlying the variability and inconsistency of survey replies is not bias or incompetence among the pollsters themselves, but rather the public's own indifference to, and lack of firm opinions about, the issues concerned. In Frankel's words:

> Public opinion polls are notoriously unreliable because the volatility of political attitudes is directly proportional to the lack of salience of and information about the issue involved. Hence even the best conducted public opinion poll cannot tell much about the degree of commitment of the respondents to the attitudes they profess to hold about defence, an issue-area about which they have only limited, if any, interest. As we hold considered opinions about and have stable attitudes to only such matters to which we have given some thought in the past, the odds are that responses to the pollsters' questions on issues of defence would not be well considered and, however carefully they are graded, do not express consistent and committed attitudes.[3]

Volatility of opinions may not actually have been such a problem over the past decade as Frankel's comments might suggest. As was discussed in Chapter 2, the recent war scare has been characterised by the development of an enduring pessimism about the long-term prospects for avoiding World War Three, a state of affairs very different from that during the original Cold War when John Strachey noted drastic swings between 'a complacent view that nuclear war was too remote a contingency to take seriously, and a panic view that it was likely within a few weeks or months'.[4] Although poll results in the 1980s have undoubtedly been influenced by news reports of nuclear issues and international crises, the effect of such news stories seems to have been to cumulatively increase the underlying level of anxiety rather than to produce major fluctuations in popular attitudes on a day-to-day basis. Much more worrying than the idea that survey results are worthless because public opinion may change overnight is Frankel's more subtle contention that actively eliciting the views of a thousand or so poll respondents may artificially manufacture opinions about issues which are in reality completely ignored by the vast majority of the public at large.

The critical variable appears to be the level of detail involved. Surveys which introduce concepts and dilemmas unfamiliar to the general public do run a grave risk of yielding unrealistic results, as illustrated by the polls about limited nuclear war which were discussed in Chapter 2. However, it is far from clear that the entire field of defence and foreign affairs may any longer be held to be an inappropriate subject for survey analysis. Frankel was writing in the era of *détente*, when popular indifference about security policy was at its height. In recent years, the climate has profoundly changed, and it seems inconceivable that more than a small minority of the population have given no thought at all to such prominent questions as whether or not Cruise missiles should be based in Britain, or how likely it is that there will be a Third World War. Although only a small proportion of those whom the polls suggest to be anxious about war or opposed to current policies have actually been motivated to action, the proportion so motivated has nevertheless been greater than on almost any other political issue in recent history. Public opinion on defence and foreign affairs may be inchoate, ill-informed and irrational, but it has become increasingly hard to maintain that it does not exist at all.

The fundamental limitation of the opinion poll evidence used for the present enquiry seems to be less that the picture it gives of popular thinking about defence is artificial than that it is incomplete. How the public reacts to issues as complex and emotion-laden as those of war and peace depends heavily upon psychological processes which cannot readily be analysed in the rational terms of the survey technique.[5] Cognitive dissonance allows incompatible opinions to be held about different aspects of the defence issue, a fact which goes a long way to explain why poll responses vary according to which particular priority the question stresses most. It is difficult, for instance, to assess public attitudes towards NATO's strategy of first nuclear use, because many survey respondents who oppose this policy in principle nevertheless assert that Britain should be 'defended at all costs'.[6] Psychological defence mechanisms such as wishful thinking may distort the 'rational' dimension of an individual's beliefs, even leading to an apparent decrease in anxiety when the danger of war seems most acute. It is hardly surprising that psychological factors play such a large part in popular speculation about the likelihood of war, since, given the apocalyptic image which most people have of World War Three, asking 'When do you think war will come?' is almost equivalent to asking the taboo question, 'When do you think you will die?'. The Mass Observation studies of the 1930s illustrate the complexity of popular reactions to the threat of a devastating war, and one extract in particular speaks volumes for the inadequacy of mere opinion poll statistics:

> We don't bother much about it . . . Not because we are not thinking about it. Life's too short to keep on with war, war, war. I don't think they will and I hope they don't. That's what I think . . . It's too much to cope with, and we can't do anything.[7]

The unquantifiable nature of such individual attitudes makes it tempting to discount modern survey data altogether, on the grounds that there are so many possible pitfalls and sources of error associated with the opinion poll technique that none of its conclusions may truly be trusted unless suggested anyway by more 'practical' forms of evidence. This, however, would be just as much of an over-reaction as it is to say that historical precedent is useless because of the pitfalls of simplistic 'lessons of the past'. Survey material may be extremely useful provided its limitations are clearly recognised. The 'scientific' character of opinion poll data, while perhaps appearing faintly ridiculous in view of the pervasive irrationality of popular beliefs, nevertheless represents an invaluable supplement to the subjective estimation of public opinion through personal experience, especially when attempting to make comparisons between attitudes in different nations or at different periods of time. As long as survey results are treated with care, and as long as they are used in conjunction with other indicators of popular feeling, they have considerably more to contribute towards an understanding of what the British public actually thinks about defence than sceptics often admit.

As was pointed out in Chapter 1, the survey evidence used in the present study was collected from the unpublished files of the polling organisations themselves, whose addresses may be found at the end of the Bibliography. Those wishing to pursue further the topic of recent popular thinking about defence should not, however, approach the pollsters directly without first examining two recent books which concentrate exclusively on analysing poll data on the security issue in different NATO states – *Defence and Public Opinion* by David Capitanchik and Richard Eichenberg, and the more up-to-date and comprehensive work *The Public and Atlantic Defense*, edited by Gregory Flynn and Hans Rattinger.[8] Neither book adopts the present author's policy of quoting poll results in full and of using other indications of popular thinking besides survey data, but this enables both works to cover a wider range of survey material than does the present study, and they should therefore be the first resort for readers wishing to know more about public opinion on broader aspects of the defence issue.

Notes and References

1   INTRODUCTION

1. War fears in the period from 1945 to 1975 are well described by Smart (1975).
2. At the dates shown, Gallup asked Britons, 'How much risk of a world war do you think there is in the situation in Vietnam?'

	A great risk	Some risk	No risk at all	Don't know
October 1966	14%	46%	31%	9%
April 1972	6%	37%	40%	17%

At the dates shown, Gallup asked Britons, 'Do you think that the present situation in the Middle East presents a serious risk of a world war involving the major powers, some risk, or no risk at all?'

	Serious risk	Some risk	No risk at all	Don't know
June 1967	33%	50%	17%	—
October 1973	30%	48%	20%	2%

3. See 'Hedge against the holocaust', *The Sunday Times*, 13 April 1980, and 'The peace protesters of cold comfort camp', *The Times*, 10 December 1982.
4. For a variety of perspectives on why the upsurge of alarm occurred, see Adelphi Papers 182–4 (1983) and B. Kent, 'Why is there a new wave of peace activism in the UK?', in Newman (1982).
5. See Palme (1982), English (1984) and 'The World against the Bomb', *Sanity*, November 1983.
6. See Sanders (1983) and Wasserman (1983).
7. See 'Why the general is refighting World War III', *The Times*, 19 June 1982 and 'Acting Armageddon', *Radio Times*, 22–28 September 1984.
8. See Noel-Baker (1978) and E. P. Thompson, 'Resurgence in Europe and the Role of END', in Minnion (1983).
9. In January 1983, respondents were asked, 'What is the likelihood that US–Soviet hostilities will escalate into a Third World War?'

	Very likely	Somewhat likely	Not likely	Don't know
Great Britain	20%	31%	44%	5%
United States	13%	38%	44%	5%
West Germany	10%	24%	66%	—
Netherlands	10%	21%	60%	9%
France	7%	33%	54%	6%

(Poll reported in *Newsweek*, 31 January 1983.)
10. See '400,000 join in Netherlands' biggest protest', *The Times*, 23 November 1981 and 'Street battles rage as Reagan speaks', *The Times*, 12 June 1982.

11. See Driver (1964).
12. See, for example, Close (1979) and 'Pope warns world of nuclear war disaster', *The Times*, 2 January 1980.
13. See Nixon (1980), Schell (1982) and 'Soap opera Armageddon', *The Sunday Times*, 11 December 1983.
14. See, for example, 'Thatcher dismisses minister over defence cuts speech', *The Times*, 19 May 1981.
15. See J. C. Garnett, 'British Strategic Thought', in Baylis (1977).
16. See the various works by these authors in the Bibliography.
17. See Crozier (1978) and P. Rogers (1981).
18. For a discussion of the problems facing defence commentators in reaching out to the public at large, see L. Ruehl, 'The Media and the Image of Defence Policy: Europe', in Adelphi Paper 182 (1983).
19. See, for example, Owen (1972), Burrows (1972) and Carver (1982).
20. See, for example , Brazier (1980) and Allaun (1981).
21. See, for example, Campbell (1982), Tucker (1982) and Prins (1983).
22. See 'The Bomb back on the Agenda', *The Times*, 15 September 1980.
23. See Minnion (1983).
24. See, for example, Koenig (1981), Bradley (1982), Robinson (1983) and Berman (1983).
25. See J. Frankel, 'Defence, Public Opinion and Parliament', in Gregory (1975) and D. Capitanchik, 'Public Opinion and Popular Attitudes towards Defence', in Baylis (1977).
26. In January 1980, Gallup asked, 'As far as you know, do we have any nuclear weapons located in Britain or not?'

    Yes 63%   *No* 9%   *Don't know* 29%

    In September 1980, Gallup asked, 'Can you tell me what the following initials stand for – NATO?'

Correct	29%
Incorrect/borderline	11%
Had heard of, but did not know initials	52%
Had not heard of	8%

27. See Capitanchik (1982).
28. For a more detailed overview of the internal structure of the British security debate, see L. Martin, 'The Domestic Context of British Defence Policy', in Flynn (1981).
29. See, for example, Frankel (1975) and I. Beckett (1981).
30. The British defence debate of the 1950s and 1960s is discussed in great detail by such authors as Snyder (1964), Driver (1964), Rosecrance (1968), Pierre (1972), Bartlett (1972) and Groom (1974). For some sketchier studies of the more recent British security debate, see Capitanchik (1982), Foot (1983) and Coker (1984).
31. N. Brown (1977), Pentz (1980).
32. See, for example, Macmillan (1972), pp. 388–405 and 'UK feared invasion by Stalin', *The Times*, 4 January 1982.
33. The author's own views on the war danger are summarised in his article 'World War Three: A Historical Mirage?', *Futures*, August 1983.

2 IMAGES OF WORLD WAR THREE

1. Liddell Hart (1937) p. 269.
2. On British military planning before World War One, see Gooch (1974).
3. See Morgan (1980), ch. 3.
4. See I. F. Clarke (1966), pp. 200–2.
5. See Kahn (1962) and 'The War Game', *Sanity*, Dec./Jan. 1980/81.
6. On US planning in the 1920s for a possible war with Britain, see A. J. P. Taylor (1979), pp. 158–61.
7. C. Foxley-Norris, 'The UK and a Third World War', in RUSI (1982), p. 56.
8. See 'Left seeks dismissal of defence chief after Peking speech', *The Times*, 2 May 1978 and F. Pym, *HCJ* 978/1256, 12 February 1980.
9. See, for example, 'Will Japan lead us to World War III?', *New Statesman*, 8 September 1978.
10. See, for example, Hackett (1982), ch. 19.
11. See, for example, J. Nott, *HCJ* 7/128, 23 June 1981.
12. See, for example, Kidron (1983), map 8.
13. See Neild (1981) p. 15.
14. Hackett (1982), Bidwell (1978).
15. In March 1981, Gallup asked, 'In case of war, to what extent do you think we could trust "..." as an ally?'

	A great deal	*Up to a point*	*Not at all*	*Don't know*
USA	62%	25%	7%	5%
Norway	37%	30%	10%	23%
Denmark	32%	34%	9%	24%
W. Germany	22%	47%	20%	10%
Greece	7%	34%	34%	25%
France	6%	45%	42%	7%
Italy	4%	33%	47%	16%
Turkey	3%	23%	46%	27%

16. In November 1983, Gallup asked, 'If Britain's security was threatened by a Russian attack, how much confidence do you have in the United States to do whatever is necessary to defend Britain, even if this risked a direct attack against the United States itself?'

    A great deal 17%; *A fair amount* 27%; *Not very much* 31%; *None at all* 21%; *Don't know* 4%.

17. See, for example, Lord Paget, *HLJ* 406/1314–16, 1 April 1980, G. Pattie in the *Sixth Report from the Expenditure Committee*, Session 1978–79, HC 348, p. 130 and 'Memory of 1940 may be behind devotion to the deterrent', *The Times*, 27 January 1981.
18. Clausewitz (trans. 1976) p. 7 & p. 88.
19. For an excellent analysis of this outlook, see Howard (1978).
20. Laurie (1979) pp. 68–9 & 111–2.
21. See, for example, Zuckerman (1982).
22. See, for example, Russett (1981).

23. See the *Statement on the Defence Estimates, 1976*, Cmnd 6432 (HMSO) paras. 29–32.
24. See, for example, Crozier (1978) and Nixon (1980).
25. See, for example, M. Harbottle, 'The Need for New Perspectives in Military Thinking', in Tromp (1982).
26. US pressure for such a course is hypothesised in Hackett (1978) pp. 282–5.
27. For an example of such views, see 'For the Unification of the Struggle against Imperialist War Preparations with the Programme of Social Transformations', *Red Flag*, 10 February 1984.
28. E. P. Thompson (1982) p. 17.
29. Howard (1983) p. 82.
30. See, for example, Conquest (1979).
31. Soviet thinking is well analysed by Vigor (1975) and Holloway (1984).
32. See D. Campbell, 'The Way to World War III', *New Statesman*, 10 October 1980.
33. See, for example, Crozier (1978) and Prins (1983).
34. For a justification of this approach, see Hill-Norton (1982).
35. See, for example, Hackett (1978) and R. Nixon, 'The West is losing World War III', *Now*, 21 March 1980.
36. For a typical example of such compartmentalisation, see Kingston McCloughry (1960).
37. See, for example, A. J. P. Taylor (1979).
38. Moulton (1970) p. 130.
39. See, for example, R. Thompson (1974) p. 175.
40. See Solzhenitsyn (1976).
41. Crozier (1978) p. 9.
42. Ibid, p. 184.
43. This concentration on the military rather than the ideological threat is evident from Thatcher (1980).
44. This fear was expressed by Walker (1975).
45. See, for example, Wall (1977).
46. See, for example, Lord Carrington, *HLJ* 370/236–7, 29 April 1976.
47. These two scenarios are outlined in Solzhenitsyn (1978) p. 60 and R. Butt, 'Will the Russians win without a shot?', *The Times*, 29 January 1976.
48. See Thatcher (1977) pp. 42–3 and Nixon (1980).
49. Bidwell (1978) p. 7. See also R. Thompson (1981).
50. *Statement on the Defence Estimates, 1981* vol. I Cmnd 8212–I (HMSO) paras. 108–9.
51. See, for example, Adelphi Paper 102 (1973) and Northedge (1974).
52. *Statement on the Defence Estimates, 1975* Cmnd 5976 (HMSO) para. 21; *Statement on the Defence Estimates, 1976* Cmnd 6432 (HMSO) para. 26.
53. *Nuclear Weapons and Preventing War* (MOD Public Relations leaflet, 1981).
54. These two viewpoints are exemplified by R. W. Howe (1981), and L. Martin, 'The Role of Military Force in the Nuclear Age', in Martin (1979).
55. For a detailed analysis of the concept of Finlandisation, and of its extensibility to other European countries, see Ginsburgs (1978).
56. See, for example, Le Bailly (1976) and Lord Chalfont, 'Facing up to the Dangerous Decade', *The Times*, 2 June 1980.

57. This point is well brought out in L. Freedman, 'NATO Myths' (1981) pp. 57–8.
58. See, for example, P. Rogers (1981).
59. M. Harbottle, 'The Need for New Perspectives in Military Thinking' in Tromp (1982) pp. 17–18.
60. See, for example, Hackett (1978) ch. 9.
61. See, for example, W. S. Thompson (1982).
62. These scenarios are suggested by Owen (1980) p. 21 and Bidwell (1978) ch. 11.
63. Monckton (1968) p. 31.
64. Such a ploy over the island of Spitzbergen is hypothesised in detail by Leopold Labedz, in his article 'The Fall of Europe', *Now*, 18 January 1980.
65. See, for example, A. Kershaw, *HCJ* 930/121–4, 19 April 1977.
66. Such an assault on the UK was suggested by N. Lyell, *HCJ* 8/651–2, 9 July 1981 and by Lord Cranborne, *HCJ* 12/172, 5 November 1981.
67. See, for instance, Pocock (1973), and 'The soft underbelly of NATO', *Daily Telegraph*, 8 February 1979.
68. See, for example, Le Bailly (1976) and J. R. Hill, 'Maritime Forces in Confrontation', *Brassey's Annual , 1972.*
69. A purely maritime conflict was suggested by Lord Orr-Ewing, *HLJ* 383/384, 12 May 1977 and by J. Cronin, *HCJ* 932/778, 19 May 1977.
70. See, for example, Baker (1982).
71. See, for example, Hackett (1978) ch. 18 and S. Menaul, 'War in Space: Fact or Fiction?', *Protect and Survive Monthly*, August 1981.
72. Possible weapons developments over the next century are discussed in Langford (1979).
73. See N. Brown (1977) p. 192 & pp. 297–9.
74. Hackett (1978).
75. Bidwell (1978).
76. Ibid, p. 7.
77. *Statement on the Defence Estimates, 1981*, vol. I Cmnd 8212–I (HMSO) para. 317.
78. See, for example, J. F. Dunnigan, *The Next War* (New York: Simulations Publications Incorporated, 1978).
79. See J. Wellbeloved, *HCJ* 931/486–7, 19 May 1977.
80. See, for example, Lord Chalfont, 'The West must act to defend itself while it still has the chance', *The Times*, 15 March 1976.
81. See, for example, Hackett (1978) pp. 312–3.
82. For a detailed discussion of the surprise attack issue, see H. Stanhope, 'New Threat – or Old Fears?', in Leebaert (1979).
83. See 'Britain studying use of chemicals as wartime retaliation against gas attack', *The Times*, 3 April 1980 and 'Britain has no defence against attack by poisons', *The Times*, 16 August 1980.
84. Only a handful of books have appeared on this neglected issue, most notably R. Clarke (1968) and Harris (1982).
85. See S. Summerskill, *HCJ* 929/1477–9, 7 April 1977.
86. See Hackett (1978) pp. 207–20 and 'Volunteers queue to join Home Guard', *The Times*, 2 March 1982.

87. Harold Macmillan thought in 1962 that the great conventional battle in Germany 'would last three hours, or at the most three days'. See Macmillan (1973) p. 354.
88. Compare the analysis in Vigor (1983) with that in Vigor (1975) pp. 158–9.
89. In May 1980, NOP asked, 'If there is a World War, do you think it will be a nuclear war, or do you think only conventional (non-nuclear) weapons will be used?'

    Nuclear 46%; *Conventional* 31%; *Both* 16%; *Don't know* 7%.

90. Some of the complexities involved are discussed in *The Military Balance, 1982–1983* (IISS, 1982) pp. 129–33.
91. See the *Statement on the Defence Estimates, 1980*, vol. I Cmnd 7826–I (HMSO).
92. See, for example, the Labour Party Defence Study Group (1977) pp 59–63 and the European Security Study (1983).
93. In January 1980, Gallup asked, 'Which side – NATO or Russia and the Warsaw Pact – has the strongest military forces?'.

    NATO 13%, *Warsaw Pact* 59%; *Both equal* 6%; *Don't know* 22%

94. This point is well brought out in John Garnett's article on 'Limited "Conventional" War in the Nuclear Age', in Howard (1979).
95. 'General manoeuvres', *The Sunday Times*, 25 June 1978.
96. See Hackett (1978) and the Alternative Defence Commission (1983).
97. See *Statement on the Defence Estimates, 1980*, vol. I Cmnd 7826–I (HMSO) para. 221.
98. See, for example, Howard (1983) pp. 112–4.
99. Chichester (1982) p. xii.
100. In January 1983, Gallup asked, 'If there is a Third World War, do you think it will be a nuclear war, or do you think only conventional, non-nuclear weapons will be used?'

	All	Con	Lib	SDP	Lab
Nuclear:	58%	54%	55%	60%	67%
Conventional:	28%	34%	31%	30%	18%
Don't know:	14%	12%	14%	11%	15%

101. See, for example, Barnett (1970) and Dinter (1983).
102. R. Bonner Pink, *HCJ* 9/360, 22 July 1981.
103. See, for example, Bellamy (1981) and Mearsheimer (1982). An interesting pulp fiction treatment of a protracted conventional Third World War is provided in Rouch (1980).
104. See, for example, J. E. Powell, *HCJ* 8/299–302, 7 July 1981.
105. See Lord Paget, *HLJ* 415/475, 3 December 1980.
106. J. Nott, *HCJ* 8/277–9, 7 July 1981.
107. See, for example, Martin (1982) p. 87 and J. Critchley, *HCJ* 987/845–7, 26 June 1980.
108. See *Statement on the Defence Estimates, 1976* Cmnd 6432 (HMSO) para. 29.
109. See, for example, Lord Hill-Norton, *HLJ* 423/21–2, 20 July 1981.
110. Retaliatory offensives are advocated in Huntington (1983) and Dinter (1983).

111. The British nuclear deterrent has been justified by some observers as a bargaining device in case of military defeat. See J. Amery, *HCJ* 986/1848–51, 19 June 1980 and J. Critchley, *HCJ* 8/610–11, 9 July 1981.
112. It could, of course, be argued that the late 1970s interest in Nazi occupation regimes was a surrogate for concern about the taboo subject of subjugation by the Soviet Union. See Longmate (1975) and Deighton (1978).
113. In January 1983, Gallup asked, 'Who do you think would win if it came to a war between the West and Russia?'

    West   25%; *Russia*   25%; *Nobody would win*   33%; *Don't know*   17%.
114. J. C. Garnett, 'Limited "Conventional" War in the Nuclear Age', in Howard (1979) pp. 84–5.
115. See Martin (1982) pp. 24–7.
116. In October 1981, NOP asked, 'If there was a nuclear war, how likely do you think it is that you personally will survive?'

    Certain   0%; *Very likely*   2%; *Fairly likely*   3%; *Fairly unlikely*   11%; *Very unlikely*   34%; *Certain not*   42%; *Don't know*   8%.
117. The preferred formulation is that NATO will never use *any* weapons unless it is attacked. See P. Blaker, *HCJ* 40/166–7, 29 March 1983.
118. See, for example, Neild (1981) p. 18 and M. Clarke (1982) p. 130.
119. In January 1983, Gallup asked, 'Who is more likely to initiate a nuclear attack in Europe: the United States or the Soviet Union?'

    United States   28%; *Soviet Union*   48%; *Don't know*   24%.
120. See, for example, P. Rogers (1981) pp. 98–100 and C. Foxley-Norris, 'The UK and a Third World War', in RUSI (1982) pp. 63–4.
121. See Hackett (1978) chapters 24–6, Lord Renton, *HLJ* 406/329–30, 5 March 1980, and J. Loveridge, *HCJ* 987/1318, 1 July 1980.
122. 'Haig reveals NATO might fire nuclear shot to warn Russia', *The Times*, 5 November 1981.
123. J. H. Robertson, *HCJ* 12/403, 10 November 1981.
124. See Kissinger (1979) p. 219 and Owen (1980) pp. 21–2.
125. *Statement on the Defence Estimates, 1981*, vol. I Cmnd 7826–I (HMSO) para. 221.
126. For sceptical views, see N. Calder (1981) p. 42 and Lord Gladwyn, *HLJ* 400/1345, 26 June 1979.
127. Lord Trenchard, *HLJ* 425/1425, 9 December 1981.
128. See Hackett (1978), Lord Zuckerman, *HLJ* 415/429, 3 December 1980, and N. Brown, 'The Church and the Bomb' (1982) p. 5.
129. See, for example, Laurie (1979) p. 93.
130. See, for example, Lord Chalfont, 'New Dimensions of Nuclear Madness', *The Times*, 25 July 1977.
131. Lord Hill-Norton, 'Watchdog of the Sea-Lanes', *The Times*, 18 August 1980.
132. See, for example, S. Menaul, *The Times*, 10 January 1981 and P. Gallois, 'The war in Europe which is most likely to occur will have no resemblance whatsoever to the war of 1939–1945', in Tromp (1982).
133. See J. Kilfedder, *HCJ* 977/722, 24 January 1980 and C. Soley, *HCJ* 983/1075, 28 April 1980.

134. Smith (1980) p. 47.
135. See Lord Gladwyn, *HLJ* 408/823–5 and L. Freedman (1980) pp. 133–5.
136. In December 1983, MORI asked, 'I am going to read out a list of statements some people have made for or against having nuclear weapons in Britain. Please would you tell me whether you agree or disagree with each one: 'A war in Europe involving nuclear weapons would not necessarily lead to a nuclear attack on America.'

Agree strongly 14% *Tend to agree* 31%; *Neither agree nor disagree* 6%; *Tend to disagree* 27%; *Disagree strongly* 14%; *No opinion* 7%.

137. Macdonald (1981) p. 21.
138. See, for example, 'How vague Reagan words raised a storm in NATO', *The Times*, 22 October 1981.
139. See Lord Chalfont, 'Nuclear threat: someone has to sound the alarm', *The Times*, 16 August 1976.
140. See L. Freedman, 'Strategic Weapons in the 1980s' (1981) p. 47.
141. N. Calder (1981) pp. 149–50.
142. See Lord Mountbatten (1980), Lord Carver (1982) and J. Nott, *HCJ* 3/140, 14 April 1981.
143. See, for example, Howard (1983) p. 144, and J. Cox, 'A "Limited Nuclear War"', in *New Left Review* (1982).
144. See A. C. Brown (1979) and D. Healey, *HCJ*, 707/1332, 3 March 1965.
145. 'Avoidance of War: Mr Chamberlain on his "Prime Duty"', *The Times*, 4 July 1938.
146. For such a scenario, see Montgomery (1956).
147. See, for example, Howard (1983) pp. 133–50.
148. See Campbell (1982) ch. 12 and Lord Chalfont, 'Why Russia may think she can win a nuclear war', *The Times*, 2 August 1976.
149. See, for example, Briggs (1982) and 'Acting Armageddon', *Radio Times*, 22–28 September 1984.
150. In September 1980, Gallup asked, 'If nuclear weapons were used against Britain, do you think that Britain as a nation would or would not survive it?'

Would 26%   *Would not* 60%   *Don't know* 14%

151. Mountbatten (1980).
152. See Campbell's *New Statesman* articles such as 'World War III: An Exclusive Preview', 3 October 1980, and his book *War Plan UK* (1982).
153. See P. Evans, 'The UK Front', in RUSI (1982).
154. See Shute (1957), Roshwald (1959) and *Dr Strangelove, or how I learned to stop worrying and love the Bomb* (Columbia Productions Ltd, 1963).
155. See, for example, M. Clarke (1982), Goodwin (1982) and Greene (1982).
156. See 'The War Game', *Sanity*, December/January 1980/81, 'Soap opera Armageddon', *The Sunday Times*, 11 December 1983 and 'Acting Armageddon', *Radio Times*, 22–28 September 1984.
157. See the Home Office publication *Protect and Survive* (1980) and E. P. Thompson (1980).
158. Briggs (1982).
159. See 'Nuclear safety book "could save 15 million"', *The Times*, 17 March 1980 and Openshaw (1983).

160. Such a sinister aim is divined by Bolsover (1980).
161. In December 1983, MORI asked, 'If there were a nuclear attack, what do you think would be *your* chance of survival? Please give me a score out of ten. A score of ten would mean you thought you were certain to survive. A score of nought would mean you thought you were certain that you would *not* survive.'

0	1	2	3	4	5	6	7	8	9	10	No opinion
60%	7%	8%	6%	3%	11%	1%	1%	1%	0%	1%	1%

162. See L. Freedman, 'Does civil defence claim too much?', *The Times*, 26 March 1980. In September 1983, Gallup asked, 'What difference do you think civil defence would make to people's chance of survival?'

      A great deal 11%; *Some* 19%; *A little* 33%; *None at all* 28%; *Don't know* 9%.

163. See Macdonald (1981) p. 16–17, F. Allaun, *HCJ* 977/731–2, 24 January 1980 and J. Cowley, *The Times*, 14 August 1980.
164. N. Hepburn, 'Horsemen', *The Listener*, 27 March 1980.
165. Long-term effects are stressed in Campbell (1982) and Openshaw (1983).
166. For a useful overview of the nuclear winter debate, see *Strategic Survey, 1984–1985* (IISS, 1985) pp. 23–7.
167. See the frighteningly vivid descriptions of the effects of nuclear war by civil defence advocates such as Sibley (1977) and Popkess (1980).

3   THE NATURE OF THE SCARE

1. In July 1975, Gallup asked, 'Would you say there is much danger of World War, or not much danger?'

   Much danger 15%; *Not much danger* 71%; *Don't know* 14%.
2. 'Never another war – Nixon', *The Times*, 10 March 1971.
3. See H. Wilson (1979) p. 177 and Buchan, *The End of the Post-War Era* (1974) pp. 4–10.
4. Howard (1974) p. 4.
5. See, for example, Northedge (1974), Howard (1976) p. 143 and L. Martin, 'The Utility of Military Force', in Adelphi Paper 102 (1973).
6. Carrington (1970) p. 5.
7. Baynes (1972) p. 91.
8. See, for instance, 'Missing Persons: Where have all the marchers gone?', *Sanity*, August 1973.
9. Owen (1972) p. 15.
10. See, for example, Wall (1977) and Lord Chalfont, 'The West must act to defend itself while it still has the chance', *The Times*, 15 March 1976.
11. See, for example, Pentz (1976) and I. Smart, 'Deadly accuracy of new missiles raises war risk', *The Times*, 17 January 1974.
12. Howard (1983), pp. 14–15.
13. See Bartlett (1972) pp. 228–37 and Pocock (1973).
14. J. Hackett, 'Defining the True Purpose of NATO: What should be understood', *The Times*, 6 February 1968.

15. Solzhenitsyn (1976) p. 18.
16. See 'Mrs Thatcher attacks Russia on eve of detente pact', *The Times*, 28 July 1975 and 'Thatcher warning on Soviet strength', *The Times*, 20 January 1976.
17. Thatcher (1977) p. 41.
18. See Chalfont (1966).
19. Lord Chalfont, 'Obsolete Strategy that keeps five million men under arms', *The Times*, 19 August 1974.
20. Chalfont explained this change of emphasis in his article, 'We dare not give anything away while the Soviet military build-up goes on', *The Times*, 4 April 1977.
21. See, for example, Bonds (1976) and Churchill (1977).
22. See, for example, E. F. Gueritz, 'Don't put off until tomorrow', *RUSI Journal*, December 1978.
23. See, for example, 'Tory Pledge on Defence – New 'Iron Lady' Warning by Mrs Thatcher', *Daily Telegraph*, 20 April 1979 and 'Lord Chalfont urges vote for Tories', *Daily Telegraph*, 1 May 1979.
24. See, for example, 'World faces greatest danger, says Pym', *Daily Telegraph*, 9 March 1979 and 'Grave dangers lie ahead, says next Defence chief', *Daily Telegraph*, 23 March 1979.
25. See Hackett (1978), Bidwell (1978), 'NATO: A Special 5-page report', *The Times*, 26 May 1978 and 'Would we lose the next war?', *Now*, 9 November 1979.
26. See P. Wright, 'Why does nobody recognize the growing nuclear peril?', *The Times*, 6 August 1975.
27. See B. T. Feld, 'The hands move closer to midnight', *BOAS*, January 1980.
28. See 'Europe is second safest continent, says Schmidt', *Daily Telegraph*, 10 March 1979 and F. Mulley, *HCJ* 965/42, 26 March 1979.
29. R. Maudling, *HCJ* 927/229, 1 March 1977.
30. See 'African conflicts could be fanned into world war – Mr Callaghan', *The Times*, 7 June 1978 and E. Stevens, 'The arms race, not a Russian blitz on Europe, is the real threat', *The Times*, 26 January 1977.
31. See, for example, Lord Chalfont's articles, 'As the arms balance tilts against the West, "doomwatching" is less of a joke', *The Times*, 6 September 1977 and 'This frightening conspiracy of silence', *The Times*, 4 September 1978.
32. In October 1977, Gallup asked, 'Here is a sort of scale. Would you, with the help of this card, tell me how you assess the chances of a world war breaking out in the next ten years?'

(0=*No danger*; 100=*War certain*)

0	10	20	30	40	50	60	70	80	90	100	Don't know
45%	8%	7%	7%	4%	10%	2%	3%	2%	1%	4%	6%

In July 1979, Marplan asked, 'How likely is it that Britain will be involved in a major war':

Percentage saying very or quite likely:

	All	Conservative	Labour	Liberal
Within five years	11%	9%	15%	8%
Within ten years	24%	20%	28%	24%
By the year 2000	40%	37%	41%	35%

33. See 'Soviet action "the worst threat since world war"', *The Times*, 10 January 1980 and 'War fears emerge in Commons statement', *The Times*, 24 April 1980.

34. Sir John Hackett had hypothesised crises in precisely these countries as the sparks for his own conflict scenario. See Hackett (1978) chs 5 & 9.

35. See, for example, 'RAF "needs more fighters and quickly"', *The Times*, 29 November 1979, and 'Mock war will involve drafting 30,000 troops to Germany and a nuclear "threat" to Britain', *The Times*, 21 March 1980.

36. See 'Computer is shut down after second missile alert', *The Times*, 9 June 1980 and 'Mr Whitelaw calls for civil defence effort and scorns defeatists', *The Times*, 6 September 1980.

37. 'Soviet threat to Romania foreseen by ex-defence chief', *The Times*, 1 May 1980.

38. Lee (1981) p. xi.

39. See 'Soviet moves bring decade of danger, Pym says', *The Times*, 11 October 1980, Lord Chalfont, 'Facing up to the dangerous decade', *The Times*, 2 June 1980 and J. D. Lunt, 'The decade of danger', *Army Quarterly*, October 1980.

40. See, for example, '"Armageddon" call for civil defence corps', *The Times*, 21 January 1980.

41. E. P. Thompson (1980) p. 53.

42. See, for example, Barnaby (1980), Pentz (1980) and Joyce (1981).

43. See, for example, Kahler (1979) and Lee (1981).

44. N. Calder (1981) p. 153.

45. See, for example, Popkess (1980), R. Banks, *HCJ* 979/619–30, 20 February 1980 and 'A lethal failure of duty', *The Times*, 19 January 1980.

46. See, for example, 'Cruise missiles in Britain', *The Times*, 27 February 1980 and 'Our survival may be at stake – Restore the Civil Defence', *The Sunday Times*, 13 April 1980.

47. See 'How to take shelter', *The Sunday Times*, 27 April 1980 and B. Kent, 'Notes from the Concrete Grass Roots', in E. P. Thompson (1980).

48. In May 1980, NOP asked, 'Do you think that some time in the future there will be a Third World War?'

	All	Men	Women	18–34	35–54	55+	Con	Lab	Lib
Yes	65%	64%	66%	69%	64%	63%	60%	67%	62%
No	25%	29%	22%	23%	27%	25%	28%	24%	33%
Don't know	10%	8%	12%	8%	9%	12%	11%	9%	6%

49. See Szabo (1983).

50. This focus is evident from the *Fifth Report from the Foreign Affairs Committee*, session 1979–80 (HC 745).

51. See 'Hard Line stops, Reagan says', *New York Times*, 16 October 1984 and 'Cordial Gorbachov joins calls for peace and goodwill', *The Times*, 17 December 1984.

52. See Marshall (1982) and D. L. Tucker, 'Will your Pet survive?, *Protect and Survive Monthly*, May 1982.

53. See, for example, P. Rogers (1981) and Prins (1983).
54. See 'Three minutes to midnight', *BOAS*, January 1984.
55. See Coker (1984) and 'How CND has changed', *Sanity*, November 1983.
56. See Coker (1985) and 'Nuclear debate cut off', *Boston Globe*, 16 February 1985.
57. See, for instance, 'Deterrent has preserved peace, Minister says', *The Times*, 27 March 1981.
58. See, for example, Segal (1983) and N. Brown, *An Unbreakable Nuclear Stalemate* (1982).
59. D. Carlton, 'Potential threats to European stability', in Gutteridge (1982) pp. 179–80.
60. In December 1984, Gallup asked, 'Do you think that another world war is likely during the next 25 years?'

    Yes, likely   36%; *No, not likely*   54%; *Don't know*   10%.

61. In January 1983, Gallup asked, 'Do you think that some time in the future there will or will not be a Third World War?'

	All	Men	Women	18–34	35–44	45–64	65+	Con	Lab	Lib	SDP
Yes	46%	43%	49%	53%	42%	43%	40%	38%	53%	44%	61%
No	35%	43%	29%	33%	40%	36%	35%	44%	30%	29%	27%
Don't know	18%	14%	22%	14%	18%	20%	25%	18%	18%	27%	12%

62. In March 1980, the BBC asked, 'Within the next ten years, how likely do you think it is that there will be a nuclear war involving Britain?'

    Very likely   11%; *Quite likely*   21%; *Not very likely*   36%; *Not at all likely*   25%; *Don't know*   8%.

63. The results of the above poll are shown correlated with those of the accompanying question, 'Do you ever find yourself worrying about the possibility of a nuclear war?'

	Very likely	Quite likely	Not very likely	Not at all likely	Don't know
Worried	6%	11%	13%	5%	3%
Not worried	5%	9%	23%	20%	5%

64. See Schell (1982) pp. 138–52 and N. Humphrey, 'Four minutes to Midnight', *The Listener*, 29 October 1981.
65. For attempts to apply statistical methods to the prediction of future conflict, see L. F. Richardson (1960) and Sagan (1981) pp. 323–8.
66. B. T. Feld, *The Times*, 24 October 1974.
67. See Schlesinger (1965) p. 357 and Sorensen (1965) p. 705.
68. See, for example, 'China says that the world is accelerating towards another war on a global scale', *The Times*, 27 December 1975.
69. See, for example, 'Tory leader visits garden of futility', *The Times*, 11 April 1977.
70. See, for example, 'A long and wistful look at the arms race', *The Times*, 29 May 1978 and E. P. Thompson, 'Notes on Exterminism, the Last Stage of Civilisation', in *New Left Review* (1982) pp. 24–5.
71. Lord Brockway, *HLJ* 404/1399–1400, 6 February 1980.
72. In October 1981, NOP asked, 'How likely do you think it is that there will be a nuclear war in your lifetime?'

Certain 3%; *Very likely* 10%; *Fairly likely* 25%; *Fairly unlikely* 21%; *Very unlikely* 21%; *Certain not* 9%; *Don't know* 11%.

73. Brodie (1962) p. 244.
74. See *Civil Defence: why we need it* (Home Office public relations leaflet, 1981).
75. On attitudes to war in Victorian and Edwardian England, see Gooch (1981) ch. 1.
76. This fear is discussed in Bialer (1980).
77. See Laurie (1979) ch. 1 and I. F. Clarke (1966) ch. 5.
78. These two perspectives are found in Liddell Hart (1937) ch. XXV and Madge (1939) p. 49.
79. Wingfield-Stratford (1932) p. 393.
80. See, for example, L. Freedman, 'Europe between the Superpowers', in Segal (1983) pp. 111–12.
81. See, for example, H. Fraser, *HCJ* 946/85, 13 March 1978 and D. Healey, *HCJ* 4/285–6, 7 May 1981.
82. Rotblat (1981) p. 31.
83. At the dates shown (among others), Gallup asked, 'Would you say there is much danger of World War, or not much danger?'

	Much danger	Not much danger	Don't know
January 1951	58%	29%	13%
October 1957	31%	44%	25%
July 1960	42%	40%	18%
September 1961	40%	43%	17%
November 1962	31%	54%	15%
September 1965	28%	57%	15%
February 1968	37%	50%	13%
March 1969	18%	63%	19%
January 1980	57%	34%	9%
May 1980	56%	36%	8%

At the dates shown, Gallup asked, 'How worried are you about the chances of a world-wide war breaking out in which nuclear bombs will be used?'

	Very worried	Fairly worried	Not at all worried	Don't know
March 1958	15%	39%	35%	11%
April 1983	25%	.31%	42%	2%

84. The respective CND campaigns are compared in Minnion (1983).
85. Quoted in Owen (1972) p. 15.
86. In May 1960, Gallup asked, 'Which of these is the most important problem facing the country today':

Defence, armaments and nuclear weapons	23%
International affairs	23%
Economic affairs	11%
Pensions	10%
Roads	7%
Colonial affairs	7%
Housing	5%
Education	4%
Health	3%

Labour relations	2%
Other	1%
No problem particularly important	4%

In May 1980, Gallup asked, 'What would you say is the most urgent problem facing the country at the present time?'

Cost of living	41%
Unemployment	23%
Strikes	7%
Other economic problems	5%
International affairs	4%
Law and order	3%
Increase productivity	2%
Health	2%
Other	11%
Don't know	2%

87. See, for example, 'World faces greatest danger, says Pym', *Daily Telegraph*, 9 March 1979 and Lord Noel-Baker, *HLJ* 415/143, 26 November 1980.
88. Rippon (1981) p. xxv.
89. See, for example, 'World war not inevitable, says Graham Greene', *The Times*, 17 August 1981.
90. J. E. Powell, *HCJ* 977/976–7, 28 January 1980.
91. See A. Calder (1969) pp. 25–6.
92. See A. J. P. Taylor (1965) pp. 454–5.
93. See 'The nuclear family goes underground', *The Sunday Times*, 30 January 1983.
94. In September 1980, Gallup asked, 'If you thought a nuclear attack on your area was likely in the next 24 hours, what would you do?'

Wait and hope for the best	26%
Seek shelter in home or immediate neighbourhood	28%
Try to escape from the area	18%
I don't really know what I would do	22%
Something else	7%

In March 1980, the BBC asked, 'Do you think you know enough about what to do in the event of a nuclear attack on Britain? If not, have you made any attempts to find out for yourself what to do in the event of a nuclear attack, would you rather not know unless one was about to happen, or do you think it is pointless anyway?'

Know enough about what to do	11%
Have made attempts to find out	19%
Rather not know unless war imminent	23%
Pointless anyway	32%
Other	10%
Missing	5%

95. Madge (1939) and Madge (1940).
96. See A. J. P. Taylor (1965) pp. 427–8, Brodie (1962) and Bolsover (1980).
97. Madge (1939) pp. 54–5.
98. See Madge (1939) pp. 52–3 and (1940) p. 30.

99. Madge (1940) p. 134.
100. See Madge (1939) pp. 86–95 and (1940) pp. 34–5.
101. *Sanity*, December 1962, p. 11.
102. See I. F. Clarke (1966).
103. See, for example, Wingfield-Stratford (1932) and B. Russell, 'The Road to Peace', in McAllister (1955).
104. See, for example, G. Smith, 'Defence: Mr Foot's double-think', *The Times*, 24 April 1981.
105. See Groom (1974) pp. 384–6.
106. See Russell (1963) and E. P. Thompson, 'Notes on Exterminism, the Last Stage of Civilisation', in *New Left Review* (1982).
107. See 'West Germans fear Armageddon', *The Times*, 23 April 1980 and 'Belief in the inevitability of war grows in Europe', *The Times*, 3 July 1980.
108. See Capitanchik (1983) chs 4 and 6.
109. N. Humphrey, 'Four minutes to Midnight', *The Listener*, 29 October 1981.
110. Driver (1964) p. 102.
111. N. Humphrey, op. cit. in note 109.
112. Macmillan (1973) p. 217.
113. See Driver (1964) p. 146, C. M. Woodhouse, *HCJ* 668/1465–6, 31 October 1962 and I. Doress, 'Flight from the Bomb', *New Society*, 12 March 1964.
114. Likely public reactions to a grave nuclear crisis are discussed by de Kadt (1964) p. 104, and M. Clarke (1979) pp. 204–5.
115. Sir John Hackett paints a picture of a British population sunning itself and watching television soap operas (albeit under heavy air attack) during a short conventional war. See Hackett (1978) pp. 252–9.
116. See Madge (1939) p. 86.
117. See, for example, R. Conquest, 'Now for the crisis of 1982', *Daily Telegraph*, 5 May 1979.
118. For an exception, see C. Foxley-Norris, 'The UK and a Third World War', in RUSI (1982) pp. 60–1.
119. Neild (1981) p. 129.
120. In March, 1938, Mass Observation asked, 'If you think war is coming, about when do you expect it?'

In the immediate future	18%
Next year or the year after	19%
In the next 5 or 10 years	27%
Later or never	20%
Don't know	16%

(See Madge (1939) p. 56.)

In August 1950, Gallup asked, 'Do you think that there is danger of another world war? If so, when will it begin?'

In 1 year	9%	Soon	5%
In 2 years	18%	Not soon	2%
In 3 years	10%	Don't know when	16%
In 4 to 5 years	4%	No danger	19%
In over 5 years	3%	Don't know	14%

In May 1980, NOP asked, 'Do you think that some time in the future there will be a Third World War? If so, when?'

In 1 year	4%	In 20 years	6%
In 2 years	7%	In over 20 years	3%
In 5 years	17%	Don't know when	12%
In 10 years	12%	Will not occur	25%
In 15 years	4%	Don't know	10%

121. In January 1983, Gallup asked, 'Do you think that some time in the future there will or will not be a Third World War? If you think there will, how long do you think it will be before there is a Third World War?'

1–4 years	5%	20 years	5%
5 years	4%	21–30 years	2%
6–9 years	3%	Over 30 years	4%
10 years	8%	Don't know when	11%
11–14 years	1%	Will not occur	35%
15 years	2%	Don't know	18%
16–19 years	1%		

122. R. Butt, 'Will the Russians win without a shot?', *The Times*, 29 January 1976.
123. See Thompson, op. cit. in note 106.
124. E. P. Thompson (1980) p. 57.

4   THE REASONS FOR THE SCARE

1. Compare, for example, 'Afghanistan: the West's opportunity', *The Times*, 5 January 1980 and B. Kent, 'Why is there a new wave of peace activism in the UK?', in Newman (1982).
2. See, for example, Joyce (1980) and V. Bukovsky, 'Better red than dead is not good enough', *The Times*, 4 December 1981.
3. G. Smith, 'Defence: Mr Foot's double-think', *The Times*, 24 April 1981.
4. See, for example, Robertson (1971) and Halle (1967).
5. The tragic story of attempts to end war by tackling such individual 'causes' as secret diplomacy or arms races is told by Hinsley (1963).
6. See A. J. P. Taylor (1961) and Trevor-Roper (1961).
7. See, for example, Hackett (1978) and P. Rogers, 'The Slide to War', *Sanity*, December/January 1981/82.
8. D. Watt, 'The Historiography of Appeasement', in Sked (1976) pp. 110–11.
9. See the *Sunday Times* Insight Team (1982) chs 3–7.
10. See, for example, *Red Flag*, 10 February 1984, p. 1 and P. Blaker, *HCJ* 40/167, 29 March 1983.
11. See, for example, Churchill (1977).
12. See, for example, Neild (1981).
13. Some observers are confounded by the conflicting imperatives, while others try to make distinctively 'owlish' recommendations. Compare, for example, N. Calder (1981) and Howard (1983).

14. See, for example, 'The decline of an empire', *The Times*, 1 September 1980.
15. See, for example, Heath, 'Alastair Buchan Memorial Lecture' (1980).
16. Martin (1982) pp. 89–90.
17. Such impartiality was criticised in 'Lest we forget, America is on our side', *Sunday Times*, 8 November 1981.
18. See, for instance, J. Dimbleby, 'Europe's destiny – too precious to entrust any longer to Washington?', *The Listener*, 1 October 1981.
19. E. P. Thompson (1980) pp. 49–50.
20. In February 1982, Gallup asked, 'How likely do you think it is that Russia will attack Western Europe within the next five years?', and also, 'How likely do you think it is that the United States will attack Eastern Europe within the next five years?'

	All		*Con*		*Lab*		*Lib/SDP*	
	USSR	*USA*	*USSR*	*USA*	*USSR*	*USA*	*USSR*	*USA*
Very likely	6%	6%	3%	2%	7%	7%	6%	7%
Fairly likely	15%	15%	12%	9%	17%	17%	15%	18%
Not so likely	24%	23%	28%	22%	20%	23%	26%	26%
Not at all likely	48%	49%	47%	62%	50%	45%	49%	46%
Don't know	7%	7%	10%	5%	7%	8%	4%	4%

21. In October 1981, NOP asked, 'If there was a nuclear war, who do you think is most likely to start it?'

Russia 35%; *America* 29%; *China* 3%; *Britain* 0%; *Other* 12%; *Don't know* 21%.

22. In October 1983, Marplan asked, 'Which of the two, America or Russia, do you think is the greater threat to world peace, or are they both equally a threat to peace?'

America 12%; *Russia* 42%; *Both equally* 39%; *Don't know* 7%

23. In January 1980, Gallup asked, 'Do you think that (Russia/the United States) does or does not pose a threat to Britain and other European countries in the military field?'

	Does	*Does not*	*Don't know*
Russia	85%	8%	6%
United States	35%	54%	11%

24. In October 1981, MORI asked, 'On this card are a list of statements that have been used to describe the Soviet Union and the United States. Please read through the list, keeping the United States/Soviet Union in mind. Every time you come to a statement that fits your ideas or impressions of the United States/Soviet Union, just tell me the number of it.'

	USA	*USSR*
Has built up its military power to defend itself from attack	60%	51%
Wishes to extend its power over other countries	31%	70%
Genuinely wants world peace	40%	6%

25. At the dates shown (among others), Gallup asked, 'How much confidence do you have in the ability of the United States to deal wisely with present world problems?'

	Very great	Consid- erable	Little	Very little	None at all	Don't know
January 1975	4%	22%	25%	25%	10%	15%
September 1977	6%	36%	23%	17%	8%	11%
August 1979	5%	19%	26%	28%	10%	12%
January 1980	9%	31%	25%	22%	5%	8%
May 1980	6%	28%	27%	24%	9%	6%
November 1980	4%	15%	26%	27%	12%	17%
August 1981	6%	25%	24%	26%	11%	8%
June 1982	6%	26%	27%	25%	13%	4%
November 1983	4%	15%	22%	31%	20%	7%

26. Russell (1962) p. 9. See also Macmillan (1972) p. 397, and 'Churchill papers cited dangers of US policy', *Boston Globe*, 2 January 1985.

27. See, for example, 'Dirty Ronnie – the men and women of President Reagan's Magnum Force', *New Statesman*, 13 March 1981.

28. See, for instance, Chatham House (1981) p. 6 and Lord Chalfont, 'How Mr Reagan would handle the decade of danger', *The Times*, 7 October 1980.

29. In November 1980, Gallup asked, 'As you may know, Ronald Reagan has been elected President of the United States. Do you think that this will be a good thing or a bad thing for peace in the world?'

    Good thing 26%; *Bad thing* 37%; *Don't know* 37%.

    In October 1981, NOP asked, 'Do you think that the present foreign policy of the United States is making nuclear war more or less likely, or is it making no difference?'

    More likely 57%; *Less likely* 8%; *No difference* 26%; *Don't know* 10%.

30. For an extreme expression of this view, see Kaldor (1978).
31. Neild (1981) p. 18.
32. See *Sanity*, June/July 1981, p. 8, and G. R. La Rocque, 'How a Nuclear War in Europe might be fought', in Tromp (1982).
33. See, for example, Thompson (1980) p. 26.
34. See, for instance, the Socialist Party of Great Britain (1982).
35. See, for example, Noel-Baker (1958) and Joyce (1981).
36. Pentz (1980) p. 15.
37. For a rare direct critique of arms race alarmism, see Howard (1983) pp. 151–70.
38. There have even been suggestions that gradual nuclear proliferation might be a good thing, spreading deterrent stability to a wider range of international confrontations. This argument is made most strongly by Waltz (1981).
39. E. P. Thompson, 'Deterrence and Addiction', in Barnaby (1982) p. 72.
40. See E. P. Thompson (1982).
41. See, for example, A. Barnett, 'Surviving between the Superpowers', *New Statesman*, 12 February 1982.
42. See Howard (1983) pp. 15–22.
43. See, for example, Bull (1978).
44. See, for example, N. Brown (1977) and Barnaby (1980).
45. A typical catalogue of risks is given in P. Rogers (1981) pp. 100–4.

46. See, for example, Hacket (1978) chs 2–9 and N. Calder (1981) pp. 145–6.
47. See, for instance, Burdick (1962), and Liddell Hart (1960) p. 70.
48. See, for example, F. Allaun, *HCJ* 986/28, June 9th, 1980.
49. Such scepticism is evident from Howard (1983) p. 12, and F. Pym, *HCJ* 986/28, June 9th, 1980.
50. In December 1983, MORI asked, 'If nuclear weapons were used anywhere in the world in the next ten years, which of the following do you think would be the most likely cause:

Terrorists deciding to use them	15%
An accident which causes a bomb to go off	26%
The Americans deciding to use them	22%
The Russians deciding to use them	19%
Some other country deciding to use them	12%
No opinion	8%

In January 1983, Gallup asked, 'Which of these causes comes nearest to your own ideas as to how a Third World War would happen?

A deliberate aggression by one side or the other	23%
An uncontrolled arms race	11%
An accidental firing of a nuclear weapon	18%
A political crisis in Europe	10%
A conflict between other nations somewhere else in the world	33%
Some other reason	3%
Don't know	7%

51. L. Freedman, 'Shadow of the Superpowers', in Bidwell (1978) p. 24.
52. J. Callaghan, *HCJ* 977/955, 28 January 1980.
53. See note 50 above.
54. See, for example, 'Mr Benn fears Britain being sucked into war', *The Times*, 25 April, 1980.
55. For a less apocalyptic analysis of possible crises in the Gulf, see Eilts (1980).
56. See, for example, Hackett (1978), ch. 9.
57. See, for example, Carver (1982) p. 94.
58. Kaldor (1981) p. 45.
59. N. Brown (1977) p. 187.
60. N. Calder (1981) pp. 142–3.
61. Utter Soviet malice is assumed in C. Foxley-Norris, 'The UK and a Third World War', in RUSI (1982).
62. See note 50 above.
63. See Daniel (1978) pp. 109–10. In May 1960, respondents were asked, 'All things considered, which country do you think is ahead in total military strength at the present time – the US or the USSR?

US 12%; *USSR* 55%; *Neither ahead* 5%; *Don't know* 28%.
64. I. Smart, 'European Nuclear Options', in Myers (1980) pp. 115–16.
65. Conquest (1979) p. 6 and Pentz (1980) p. 16.
66. Joyce (1981) pp. 177–8.
67. N. Brown (1981) pp. 32–3.
68. See, for example, Owen (1980) and Howard (1983) pp. 116–50.

69. See, for example, Crozier (1978) ch. 11 and F. Halliday, 'The Sources of the New Cold War', in *New Left Review* (1982) p. 322.
70. E. P. Thompson (1982) p. 34.
71. Thompson himself argued this in a letter to *The Times*, 12 November 1981.
72. Vegetius (trans, 1767) p. 89.
73. Mountbatten (1980).
74. Hill-Norton (1978) pp. 21–2.
75. See 'Insurers cash in on Skylab', *Daily Telegraph*, 6 July 1979 and 'Skylab proves a real sell-out in Cornwall', *Daily Telegraph*, 11 July 1979.
76. See 'Atom Terror smash "hushed up" at RAF base', *The Sun*, 6 November 1979; '6 Minute War!', *Sunday Mirror*, 11 November 1979; 'US war brain boobs again', *The Sun*, 9 June 1980; and 'Radiation leak averted in Titan missile explosion', *The Times*, 20 September 1980.
77. See Laurie (1979) and N. Calder (1981) p. 10.
78. In October 1981, MORI asked, 'Do you think the fact that Britain itself has nuclear weapons increases or decreases the risk of a nuclear attack on this country?'

	All	*15–24*	*25–34*	*35–44*	*45–54*	*55–64*	*65+*
Increases risk	33%	46%	39%	32%	32%	26%	19%
Decreases risk	35%	24%	27%	34%	40%	47%	43%
No effect	25%	25%	29%	27%	23%	21%	26%
Don't know	6%	6%	5%	7%	6%	6%	12%

79. L. Freedman, 'NATO Myths' (1981) pp. 57–8.
80. See, for example, P. Rogers (1981) and Prins (1983).
81. E. P. Thompson (1980) pp. 45–6.
82. In July 1979, Marplan asked, 'What do you think is the most important job of the British Armed Forces nowadays? And the second most important?' (Results shown combined.)

To defend Britain if war occurs	70%
To maintain law and order	36%
To help protect the free world	32%
To control civil problems like Northern Ireland	26%
To make others afraid to attack us	20%
To keep up essential services during strikes	15%

83 See Hardy (1919) p. 54.
84. See 'Next?', *The Times*, 29 January 1981.
85. E. P. Thompson (1980) p. 46.
86. *Report on Defence – Britain's Contribution to Peace and Security*, Cmnd 363 (HMSO, 1958) para. 1. The 'safety-valve' argument is made by Towle (1981).
87. See, for example, Blackett (1956).
88. Howard (1972) pp. 8–9.
89. See, for example, Lord Gladwyn, *The Times*, 2 December 1978 and *Strategic Survey, 1981–1982* (IISS, 1982) pp. 1–12.
90. In August 1983, Gallup asked, 'Do you think that the present situation in the Middle East presents a serious risk of a world war involving the major powers, some risk, or no risk at all? And what about the present situation in Central America, do you think that presents a serious risk of a world war involving the major powers, some risk, or no risk at all?'

	Serious risk	Some risk	No risk at all	Don't know
Middle East	24%	57%	14%	5%
Central America	23%	50%	19%	7%

91. See Frankel (1975).
92. D. Healey, *HCJ* 779/236, 4 March 1969.
93. P. Wall, *HCJ* 5/203, 19 May 1981.
94. See, for example, A. Roberts, 'The Critique of Nuclear Deterrence', in Adelphi Paper 183 (1983) pp. 5–6.
95. L. Freedman (1978) pp. 25–6 and L. Martin, ' Merely to talk calmly about it gets you a Strangelove image', *The Listener*, 5 November 1981.
96. In December 1957, Gallup asked, 'Looking ahead to 1978, that is in 20 years time, which of these things do you think will have happened by then?'

Russia and the West will have worked out a way of
living peacefully together 46%
An atomic war between Russia and America 19%
Russian Communism will have collapsed 17%
Western Capitalism will have collapsed 7%
Civilisation as we know it will be in ruins 7%

In December 1969, Gallup asked, 'Looking ahead to 1990, that is in 20 years' time, which of these things do you think will have happened by then?'

Russia and the West will be living together peacefully 37%
All countries will have ceased to manufacture H-bombs
or anything like them 24%
Atomic war between Russia and America 10%
Russian Communism will have collapsed 12%
Capitalism and the Western way of life will have
collapsed 13%
Civilisation as we know it will be in ruins 15%

In March 1983, Gallup asked, 'Looking ahead to the year 2000, that is not quite 20 years' time, which of these things do you think will have happened by then?'

Russia and the West will be living together peacefully 26%
All countries will have ceased to manufacture nuclear
weapons or anything like them 16%
Nuclear war between Russia and the West 15%
Russian Communism will have vanished 10%
Capitalism and the Western way of life will have collapsed 13%
Civilisation as we know it will be in ruins 14%

97. See Maddox (1972).
98. Goodwin (1982) p. 13.
99. See, for example, R. Thompson (1981) and 'Old wars still leave you dead', *The Sunday Times*, 21 March 1982.

5 THE PREOCCUPATION WITH FULL-SCALE WAR

1. Howard (1970) p. 206.
2. The image of a 'final abyss' occurs frequently in Mountbatten (1980).
3. Howard (1983) p. 12.
4. On early Western planning for World War Three, see A. C. Brown (1979).
5. See Mackintosh (1960) and Baylis, *Soviet Strategy* (1981).
6. Cable (1983) p. 38.
7. D. Campbell, 'The Way to World War III', *New Statesman*, 10 October 1980.
8. See Campbell (1982) pp. 48–53.
9. See 'Councils blamed as civil defence exercise shelved', *The Times*, 15 July 1982.
10. Quoted in L. Martin, 'Shadow over Europe', *The Listener*, 26 November 1981.
11. See Bischoff (1983).
12. See, for example, Bracken (1983) and Posen (1982).
13. See, for example, Ford (1985).
14. M. Thatcher, *HCJ* 12/28, 4 November 1981.
15. C. Foxley-Norris, 'The UK and a Third World War', in RUSI (1982) pp. 60–1.
16. See Lebow (1984) and Howard (1983) pp. 7–22.
17. See, for example, Lord Chalfont, 'Why Russia may think she can win a nuclear war', *The Times*, 2 August 1976 and P. Rogers, 'The Slide to War', *Sanity*, December/January 1981/82.
18. Moscow's attachment to blitzkrieg theory, but only as the least bad military option, is discussed in Vigor (1983).
19. J. Erickson, in the *Fifth Report from the Foreign Affairs Committee*, Session 1979–80 HC 745 (HMSO) p. 37.
20. See Warner (1980).
21. See Gooch (1981) ch. 1 and Morgan (1980) ch. 3.
22. See I. F. Clarke (1966) ch. 5.
23. See, for example, Crozier (1970), Le Bailly (1976), Wall (1977) and 'Warfare by Chemicals most likely, Tories say', *The Times*, 2 July 1980.
24. See, for example, J. Paxman, 'If the Bomb drops', *The Listener*, 20 March 1980 and 'Britain and the Bomb', *Daily Mirror*, 6 November 1980.
25. See 'Fall-out shelter family miss home comforts', *The Times*, 28 October 1980; 'Is a Nuclear Shelter the last thing you need?', *Sunday Times Magazine*, 3 May 1981; *Protect and Survive Monthly*, Blumenfeld (1981); and *Domestic Nuclear Shelters: Technical Guidance* (Home Office, 1981).
26. See, for example, Greene (1982) and Openshaw (1983).
27. See, for example, 'African conflicts could be fanned into world war – Mr Callaghan', *The Times*, 7 June 1978 and 'Carrington gives stern warning to unilateralists', *The Times*, 28 October 1981.
28. The history of such imagery is discussed in Kermode (1967).
29. This common pattern of alarmism is discussed in Maddox (1972).
30. Madge (1940) p. 40.
31. See, for example, Berlitz (1981), Goetz (1982) and Hill (1982).

32. See 'Reagan's Apocalypse Now', *Guardian*, 21 April 1984.
33. See, for example, E. P. Thompson (1980) pp. 56–7.
34. N. Humphrey, 'Four Minutes to Midnight', *The Listener*, 29 October 1981.
35. See, for example, Laurie (1979) pp. 278–81 and 'Armageddon in your living room', *The Times*, 5 April 1983.
36. Graham (1979) p. 209.
37. N. Brown (1981) p. 28.
38. The nightmare faced by those who did find themselves at 'the sharp end' is detailed by Ellis (1980).
39. Howard (1983) p. 68.
40. See, for example, Rouch (1980) and Wargames Research Group (1979).
41. See 'Why the general is refighting World War III', *The Times*, 19 June 1982.
42. See Gooch (1981) pp. 38–9 and Howard (1976) pp. 119–20.
43. See, for example, A. J. P. Taylor (1979) p. 175 and J. Gooch, 'Clio and Mars: The Use and Abuse of History', in Perlmutter (1981).
44. Howard (1983) p. 195.
45. See Hinsley (1963).
46. See Repington (1920) p. 391.
47. See Lukacs (1976) p. 53.
48. See A. C. Brown (1979).
49. See, for example, 'Allies reenact Second World War battle', *The Times*, 23 September 1980.
50. See, for example, Crozier (1978) p. 10.
51. See N. Brown, 'The Changing Face of Non-Nuclear War' (1982).
52. This argument is developed in my article 'World War Three: A Historical Mirage?', *Futures*, August 1983.
53. Analogies with ancient wars are drawn by Mandelbaum (1981) and Luttwak (1976).
54. H. Hanning, *The Times*, 25 August 1981.
55. Lord Oram, *HLJ* 425/192, 10 November 1981.
56. These conflicting historical perils were pointed out by defence minister John Nott, in *HCJ* 1000/219, 3 March 1981.
57. See, for example, Allaun (1981) p. 9.
58. E. P. Thompson (1982) p. 9.
59. See Grey (1925) pp. 89–90, and A. J. P. Taylor (1969).
60. See, for example, Lee (1981) p. 181.
61. See Sorensen (1965) pp. 513–4; Macmillan (1972) pp. 74–5; and Kahler (1979).
62. See Gooch (1981) ch. 2.
63. See Thomas (1966) and the Sunday Times Insight Team (1982).
64. See, for example, W. Churchill, *HCJ* 906/262–7, 24 February 1976 and 'A day when the few were just too few', *Now*, 16 May 1980.
65. See, for example, J. Amery, *HCJ* 932/535, 18 May 1977 and E. Griffiths, *HCJ* 977/761, 24 January 1980.
66. Macmillan's statement is quoted in Nixon (1980) p. 307.
67. See, for example, 'SALT 2 just like appeasing Hitler, says Senator', *Daily Telegraph*, 14 June 1979.
68. See 'Where the Second World War seems like only yesterday', *The Times*, 29 November 1979.

69. 'Operation Barbarossa' was the code name for the German invasion of Russia in 1941.
70. See 'Schmidt warning of world drifting into war', *The Times*, 21 April 1980 and 'West Germans fear Armageddon', *The Times*, 23 April 1980.
71. See F. Johnson, 'Oh what a lovely war', *Now*, 16 May 1980.
72. See May (1973).

6 THE IMPACT OF THE SCARE

1. See, for example, Zuckerman (1982).
2. At the dates shown below, Gallup asked, 'Would you approve or disapprove if American-made neutron bombs were stored in Britain?'

	Approve	Disapprove	Don't know	Not heard of
April 1978	16%	56%	5%	22%
August 1981	18%	58%	6%	19%

3. In January 1983, Gallup asked, 'Do you think that Britain should or should not allow the new American-controlled Cruise nuclear missiles to be based here?'

   Should 32%; *Should not* 54%; *Don't know* 13%

   At the same time, Gallup asked, 'Do you think Britain should or should not allow existing American nuclear bases in Britain to remain here?'

   Should 55%; *Should not* 36%; *Don't know* 9%

4. In April 1981, Marplan asked, 'Should Britain abandon nuclear weapons altogether no matter what other countries do, maintain our current nuclear capability, or improve it by spending more money on nuclear weapons?'

Abandon nuclear weapons	23%
Maintain current weapons	56%
Improve nuclear weapons	18%
Don't know	3%

5. See, for example, Carver (1982).
6. In January 1983, Gallup asked, 'Taking everything into account, including the cost, which of these comes closest to your view of what armed forces Britain should have to reduce the chances of a war?'

Britain should have only a few or no weapons of any kind	8%
Britain should be strong in conventional, non-nuclear weapons, but no nuclear weapons	22%
Britain should rely on nuclear weapons, with only a small conventional, non-nuclear force	9%
Britain should rely on both nuclear weapons and a strong conventional, non-nuclear force	54%
Don't know	6%

7. In November 1981, Gallup asked, 'Do you think that, from an international point of view, Britain should:

Be on the side of the USA	43%
Be on the side of Russia	1%
Become neutral	46%
Don't know	10%

In October 1981, NOP asked, 'If Russia and its allies launched a non-nuclear attack on Western Europe, but not Britain, which of these do you think Britain should do . . .? And if Russia launched a nuclear attack on Western Europe, but not Britain, what should Britain do . . .?

Recommended British action	Soviet non-nuclear attack	Soviet nuclear attack
Nuclear attack	6%	32%
Non-nuclear attack	39%	12%
No attack	41%	38%
Don't know	13%	18%

8. 'Nuclear Weapons and Preventing War', *Statement on the Defence Estimates, 1981*, vol. I Cmnd 8212–I (HMSO).

9. See, for example, E. P. Thompson, 'Europe: the weak link in the Cold War', in *New Left Review* (1982).

10. In October 1983, Marplan asked, 'Are you in favour of or against Britain's continued membership of NATO?'

   In favour 73%; *Against* 8%; *Don't know* 19%

11. See, for example, 'Tory MP urges war threat against Cuba', *The Times*, 17 January 1980.

12. See, for example, 'Britain believes West will not defend Poles if Russia decides to invade', *The Times*, 29 November 1980.

13. In May 1980, NOP asked, 'Thinking now about Afghanistan, which Russia recently invaded, what action (if any) do you think the United States should take against Russia? And what action (if any) do you think that Europe, including Britain, should take against Russia?'

	USA	Europe
Take no action at all	17%	24%
Boycott the Olympics in Moscow	27%	24%
Reduce trade with Russia	30%	27%
Completely stop trade with Russia	26%	20%
Break off diplomatic relations with Russia	18%	13%
Give arms and money to help the Afghans fight Russia	9%	6%
Take direct military action in Afghanistan against Russia	4%	2%
Other	3%	3%
Don't know	9%	11%

14. See A. J. P. Taylor (1965) pp. 427–30 and Howard (1978) ch. V.

15. See 'Don't send the white feathers', *The Times*, 25 May 1981. In November 1983, Gallup asked, 'Some people say that war is now so horrible that it is better to accept Russian domination than to risk war. Others say it would be better to fight in defence of Britain than to accept Russian domination. Which opinion is closer to your own?'

   Better to be dominated 9%; *Better to fight* 77%; *Don't know* 14%.

16. See, for example, Lord Chalfont, 'Worse even than hunger, a life of liberty denied', *The Times*, 5 January 1981.
17. J. Critchley, *HCJ* 912/1765–6, 10 June 1976.
18. In May 1980, NOP asked, 'Some people think that the Russians are deliberately trying to increase the number of countries under their control. Other people disagree. What do you think?'

    Agree 81%; *Disagree* 11%; *Don't know* 8%.
    Those agreeing with the notion of Russian expansionism were then asked, 'Do you think Britain should resist Russia?'

Yes, even if it means a nuclear war	36%
Yes, but not if it means a nuclear war	27%
No, Britain should not resist Russia	11%
Don't know	7%

    In December 1983, MORI asked, 'I am going to read out a list of statements some people have made for or against having nuclear weapons in Britain. Please would you tell me whether you agree or disagree with each one: "If there were a war with Russia, it would be better to surrender to the Russians than to face the consequences of a nuclear attack."

    Agree strongly 12%; *Tend to agree* 21%; *Neither agree nor disagree* 10%; *Tend to disagree* 19%; *Disagree strongly* 34%; *No opinion* 5%.
19. Howard (1983) p. 229.
20. On the exceptions, see Lord Chalfont, 'We dare not give anything away while the Soviet military build-up goes on', *The Times*, 4 April 1977 and A. Wilson, 'The Bomb: how I changed my mind', *Sanity*, December/January 1981/82.
21. At the dates shown, Gallup asked, 'It has been suggested that Britain should give up relying on nuclear weapons for defence whatever other countries decide. Do you think this is a good idea or a bad idea?'

	Good idea	*Bad idea*	*Don't know*
September 1980	21%	67%	11%
November 1981	33%	58%	9%
November 1982	29%	61%	10%
January 1983	28%	65%	6%
April 1983	27%	66%	7%
May 1983	20%	73%	7%

    In May 1968, Gallup asked, 'Do you agree or disagree with people who want Britain to give up nuclear weapons?'

    Agree 38%; *Disagree* 50%; *Don't know* 12%.
22. In March 1980, the BBC asked, 'Within the next ten years, how likely do you think it is that there will be a nuclear war involving Britain?', and 'Which of these statements best describes your views on nuclear weapons?'

	Very likely	*Quite likely*	*Not very likely*	*Not at all likely*	*Don't know*
I object to them and am protesting against them	1%	1%	1%	1%	0%

I object to them but don't think I can do anything about them	6%	9%	17%	7%	3%
I accept them as a 'necessary evil'	3%	7%	14%	11%	2%
I don't think about them at all	1%	2%	4%	5%	3%

23. See I. Crewe, 'Britain: Two and a Half Cheers for the Atlantic Alliance', in Flynn (1985) pp. 36–9.
24. See Coker (1984).
25. See 'The Nott alternative: a decade of defence we can afford', *Times*, June 18th 1981. At the dates shown, Gallup asked, 'Do you think the Government is spending too much, too little, or about the right amount on armaments and defence?'

	Too much	*About right*	*Too little*	*Don't know*
November 1975	36%	27%	19%	18%
March 1976	24%	23%	33%	20%
August 1976	21%	27%	34%	18%
February 1977	24%	25%	31%	20%
July 1978	17%	23%	37%	24%
November 1979	28%	29%	25%	19%
March 1980	19%	31%	29%	21%
August 1980	24%	35%	24%	18%
June 1982	27%	25%	40%	8%
February 1983	49%	31%	13%	8%
July 1983	46%	34%	12%	8%

26. At the dates shown, Gallup asked, 'It is sometimes said that the foreign policy of Britain depends too much on the USA. Do you think that this is true or untrue?'

	True	*Partly true*	*Untrue*	*Don't know*
February 1965	47%	18%	18%	17%
March 1974	35%	10%	30%	24%

27. See, for example, C. Wright, 'The new White House warmongers', *New Statesman*, 13 March 1981.
28. At the dates shown, Gallup asked, 'In the event of a nation being attacked by Communist-backed forces, there are several things Britain could do about it. As I read the name of each country, please tell me what action you would want to see us take if that country was actually attacked:'

West Germany	*May 1975*	*January 1980*
Send British troops	23%	41%
Send military supplies but not troops	19%	15%
Refuse to get involved	34%	24%
Don't know	15%	11%
Sweden		
Send British troops	21%	30%
Send military supplies but not troops	23%	23%
Refuse to get involved	38%	29%
Don't know	18%	18%

Turkey

Send British troops	4%	13%
Send military supplies but not troops	13%	20%
Refuse to get involved	63%	47%
Don't know	19%	20%

29. See Eichenberg (1983) and Howorth (1984).
30. See 'Churches in alarm over atom threat', *The Times*, 25 November 1980 and Salisbury (1982).
31. The different flavour of the two campaigns is captured in Foot (1983) and Driver (1964).
32. See Groom (1974) p. 328.
33. In October 1982, Gallup asked, 'The British Government intends to acquire an American Trident nuclear weapons system. Do you approve or disapprove of this? If the latter, do you disapprove mainly for cost reasons or mainly because you object to nuclear weapons, or for some other reason?

Approve	32%
Disapprove for cost reasons	12%
Dissaprove because of objection to nuclear weapons	32%
Disapprove for both reasons	8%
Disapprove for other reasons	4%
Don't know	12%

34. See note 86 on pp. 154–5.
35. See Pierre (1972).
36. The British defence debate of the 1950s and 1960s is described in Groom (1974).
37. Early theorising about strategy in the nuclear age is detailed in Kaplan (1983).
38. In September 1980, Gallup asked, 'Which of these statements best describes your views about nuclear weapons:'

Worried and willing to join demonstration against them	7%
Worried and willing to write to MP, newspapers	4%
Worried but won't do anything about it	17%
Worried but do not think anything can be done about them	37%
Not worried about them	30%
Don't know	4%

39. See Snyder (1964) pp. 58–61 and I. Crewe, 'Britain: Two and a Half Cheers for the Atlantic Alliance', in Flynn (1985).
40. For an outstanding example of such restrained discussion, see Howard (1983).

7 CONCLUSION

1. Gibbon (ed. 1909) p. 174.
2. L. Martin, 'The Utility of Military Force', in Adelphi Paper 102 (1973) p. 14.

3. See J. Barry, 'How NATO's nuclear planning elite has tied its own hands', *The Times*, 19 August 1981.
4. See H. Young, 'CND and the perils of nuclear secrecy', *The Sunday Times*, 1 November 1981.
5. See, for example, Healey, 'On European Defence' (1969).
6. In December 1984, Gallup asked, 'Do you think another world war is likely during the next ten years?'

   Likely 15%; *Not likely* 74%; *Don't know* 11%.
7. Most Britons support conventional defence, while few are fully behind the Star Wars programme. See, for example, the Alternative Defence Commission (1983) and Howe (1985).
8. See, for example, Adelphi Papers 182–4 (1983).
9. Howard (1983) p. 236.
10. See, for example, Bull (1983); Howard (1983) pp. 230–6; and the European Security Study (1983).
11. This argument is made in much fuller form in my article 'Reassurance, Consensus, and Controversy: The Domestic Dilemmas of European Defence', in S. Flanagan & F. Hampson (eds), *Securing Europe's Future* (London: Croom Helm, 1986).
12. Carrington (1983) p. 149.
13. See, for example, Pym (1982).
14. This argument is made by Freedman (1984).
15. The surprising amount of hard data now available on the Soviet Union is pointed out in L. H. Gelb, 'What we really know about Russia', *New York Times Magazine*, 28 October 1984.
16. For a critique of the more extreme assertions about the perceptual impact of deterrent power, see Kull (1985).

APPENDIX

1. See Moser (1971) pp. 320–30.
2. See D. Freedman (1978) ch. 19.
3. J. Frankel, 'Defence, Public Opinion and Parliament', in Gregory (1974) p. 256.
4. Strachey (1962) p. 311.
5. The psychological complexities of public opinion are discussed at length in Childs (1965) and Oskamp (1977).
6. In November 1983, Gallup asked, 'What do you think about nuclear weapons in a war? Would you approve or disapprove of using it in these cases:'

	Agree	Disagree	Don't know
Against an enemy that does not have it themselves	4%	89%	6%
Against an enemy that does have it but is not using it	12%	77%	11%
Against an enemy that has it and uses it against us	71%	21%	7%

In October 1981, NOP asked, 'If it seemed likely that Russia would attack or invade Britain, do you think that the government should:'

Defend Britain at all costs	60%
Hold out for the best terms	26%
Surrender unconditionally	5%
Don't know	10%

7. Madge (1939) p. 31.
8. Capitanchik (1983) and Flynn (1985).

Bibliography

Very many books and articles were either directly consulted or had an indirect influence in the preparation of this work. Only the more significant and relevant of these are listed here. All books and pamphlets were published in London unless otherwise stated.

ADELPHI PAPER 102 (1973) *Force in Modern Societies: Its place in international politics* (IISS).

ADELPHI PAPERS 160–1 (1980) *The Future of Strategic Deterrence*, parts I & II (IISS).

ADELPHI PAPERS 166–7 (1981) *Third World Conflict and International Security*, parts I & II (IISS).

ADELPHI PAPERS 182–4 (1983) *Defence and Consensus: The domestic aspects of Western security*, parts I, II & III (IISS).

ADLER, K. and WERTMAN, D. (1981) 'Is NATO in trouble? A survey of European attitudes', *Public Opinion*, Aug/Sept.

ALLAUN, F. (1981) *Questions and Answers about Nuclear Weapons* (CND).

ALTERNATIVE DEFENCE COMMISSION (1983) *Defence without the Bomb* (Taylor & Francis).

ARRIAN (1971) *The Campaigns of Alexander*, translated by A. de Selincourt (Harmondsworth: Penguin).

BAKER, D. (1982) *The Shape of Wars to Come* (Hamlyn).

BARCLAY, C. N. (1969) 'Home Defence: A survey of the defence problems of the United Kingdom', *Brassey's Annual*.

BARNABY, C. F. (1980) *Prospects for Peace* (Oxford: Pergamon).

BARNABY, C. F. and THOMAS, G. P. (eds) (1982) *The Nuclear Arms Race: Control or Catastrophe?* (Frances Pinter).

BARNETT, C. (1970) 'The British Armed Forces in Transition', *RUSI Journal*, June.

BARTLETT, C. J. (1972) *The Long Retreat: A short history of British defence policy, 1945–70* (Macmillan).

BAYLIS, J. (ed.) (1977) *British Defence Policy in a Changing World* (Croom Helm).

BAYLIS, J. (1981) *Anglo-American Defence Relations, 1939–1980: The Special Relationship* (Macmillan).

BAYLIS, J. and SEGAL, G. (eds) (1981) *Soviet Strategy* (Croom Helm).

BAYNES, J. C. M. (1972) *The Soldier in Modern Society* (Methuen).

BAYS, D. (1981) *The Silent Killers: New developments in gas and germ weapons* (Campaign for Nuclear Disarmament).

BEAUMONT, R. A. and EDMONDS, M. (eds) (1975) *War in the Next Decade* (Macmillan).

BECKETT, B. (1982) *Weapons of Tomorrow* (Orbis).

BECKETT, I. and GOOCH, J. (eds) (1981) *Politicians and Defence: Studies in the formulation of British defence policy, 1945–1970* (Manchester University Press).

BELLAMY, C. (1981) 'Space Age Verdun', *RUSI Journal*, March.

BERLITZ, C. (1982) *Doomsday 1999* (Granada).

BERMAN, R. and GUNSTON, B. (1983) *Rockets and Missiles of World War III* (Hamlyn).

BIALER, U. (1980) *The Shadow of the Bomber: The fear of air attack and British politics, 1932-1939* (Royal Historical Society).

BIDWELL, S. (ed) (1978) *World War 3* (Hamlyn).

BISCHOFF, D. (1983) *War Games* (Harmondsworth: Penguin).

BLACKETT, P. M. S. (1956) *Atomic Weapons and East-West Relations* (Cambridge University Press).

BLACKETT, P. M. S. (1962) *Studies of War, Nuclear and Conventional* (Oliver & Boyd).

BLUMENFELD, Y. (1981) *Jenny Ewing – My Diary* (Fontwell: Centaur).

BOLSOVER, P. (1980) *Civil Defence: The cruellest confidence trick* (CND).

BONDS, R. (ed.) (1976) *The Soviet War Machine: An encyclopedia of Russian military equipment and strategy* (Salamander).

BRACKEN, P. (1983) *The Command and Control of Nuclear Forces* (Yale University Press).

BRADLEY, J. (1982) *An Illustrated History of World War III* (Windward).

BRAZIER, J. (1980) *No Easy Answers: A critical examination of British defence policy* (Private publication).

BRIGGS, R. (1982) *When the Wind Blows* (Hamish Hamilton).

BRITISH COUNCIL OF CHURCHES (1959) *Christians and Atomic War: A discussion of the moral aspects of defence and disarmament in the nuclear age* (British Council of Churches).

BRITTEN, S. (1983) *The Invisible Event: An assessment of the risk of accidental or unauthorised detonation of nuclear weapons and of war by miscalculation* (Menard Press).

BRODIE, B. (1962) 'The Possibility of Total War', *Daedalus*, Oct.

BROWN, A. C. (1979) *Operation: World War III – The secret American plan 'Dropshot' for war with the Soviet Union, 1957* (Arms & Armour Press).

BROWN, N. (1964) *Nuclear War: The impending strategic deadlock* (Pall Mall).

BROWN, N. (1969) *British Arms and Strategy, 1970-80* (RUSI).

BROWN, N. (1971) 'Underdevelopment as a threat to World Peace', *International Affairs*, April.

BROWN, N. (1977) *The Future Global Challenge: A predictive study of world security, 1977-90* (RUSI).

BROWN, N. (1981) 'The Delusions of Neutralism', *RUSI Journal*, Sept.

BROWN, N. (1982) *An Unbreakable Nuclear Stalemate* (Windsor: Council for Arms Control).

BROWN, N. (1982) 'The Changing Face of Non-Nuclear War', *Survival*, Sept/Oct.

BROWN, N. (1982) 'The Church and the Bomb: A critical review', *ADIU Report*, Nov/Dec.

BUCHAN, A. (1960) *NATO in the 1960s* (Weidenfeld & Nicolson for ISS).

BUCHAN, A. and WINDSOR, P. (1963) *Arms and Stability in Europe* (Chatto & Windus for the ISS).

BUCHAN, A. (ed.) (1970) *Problems of Modern Strategy* (Chatto & Windus for the IISS).

BUCHAN, A. (1974) *The End of the Post-War Era* (Weidenfeld & Nicolson).
BUCHAN, A. (1974) *Change without War: The shifting structures of world power* (Chatto & Windus).
BULL, H. (1977) *The Anarchical Society: A study of order in world politics* (Macmillan).
BULL, H. (1978) 'Consistency under Pressure', *Foreign Affairs*, (America and the World).
BULL, H. (1983) 'European Self-Reliance and the Reform of NATO', *Foreign Affairs*, Spring.
BURDICK, E. L. and WHEELER, J. H. (1962) *Fail Safe* (New York: McGraw Hill).
BURHOP, E. (1977) *The Neutron Bomb* (CND).
BURROWS, B. and IRWIN, C. (1972) *The Security of Western Europe: Towards a common defence policy* (Charles Knight).
BURTON, J. (1982) *Dear Survivors – Planning after nuclear holocaust: war avoidance* (Frances Pinter).
BUZAN, B. (1983) *People, States and Fear: The national security problem in international relations* (N. Carolina University Press).
CABLE, J. (1983) 'Surprise and the Single Scenario', *RUSI Journal*, March.
CALDER, A. (1969) *The People's War: Britain, 1939–45* (Jonathan Cape).
CALDER, N. (ed.) (1968) *Unless Peace Comes* (Allen Lane).
CALDER, N. (1981) *Nuclear Nightmares* (Harmondsworth: Penguin).
CAMERON, N. (1959) 'In Defence of a Deterrent Strategy', *RUSI Journal*, Nov.
CAMERON, N. (1980) 'Defence and the Changing Scene', *RUSI Journal*, Mar.
CAMERON, N. (1981) 'China, the USSR and Western Defence Policy', *RUSI & Brassey's Defence Yearbook*.
CAMERON, N. (1982) 'Realities of American Power in the 1980s', *RUSI Journal*, Mar.
CAMPAIGN FOR NUCLEAR DISARMAMENT (1982) *Hard Luck/Hard Rock* (CND).
CAMPBELL, D. (1982) *War Plan UK* (Burnett).
CANDLIN, A. H. S. (1971) 'Nuclear Aspects of the Sino-Soviet Confrontation', *RUSI Journal*, Mar.
CAPITANCHIK, D. (1982) *The Changing Attitude to Defence in Britain* (Aberdeen University Centre for Defence Studies).
CAPITANCHIK, D. and EICHENBERG, R. C. (1983) *Defence and Public Opinion*, Chatham House Paper 20 (Routledge & Kegan Paul for RIIA).
CARRINGTON, LORD (1970) 'British Defence Policy', *RUSI Journal*, Dec.
CARRINGTON, LORD (1973) 'British Defence Policy', *RUSI Journal*, Sept.
CARRINGTON, LORD (1983) 'The 1983 Alastair Buchan Memorial Lecture', *Survival*, July/Aug.
CARVER, LORD (1982) *A Policy for Peace* (Faber & Faber).
CHALFONT, LORD (1966) 'The Politics of Disarmament', *Encounter*, Oct.
CHAPLIN, D. (1974) 'The Sino-Soviet Conflict: How Soon?', *RUSI Journal*, Sept.
CHATHAM HOUSE (L. Freedman ed.) (1981) *President Reagan and American Foreign Policy*, (RIIA).
CHICHESTER, M. and WILKINSON, J. (1982) *The Uncertain Ally – British defence policy, 1960–1990* (Aldershot: Gower).

CHILDS, H. L. (1965) *Public Opinion: Nature, formation and role* (Princeton: D. Van Norstrand).

CHURCHILL, W. S. (1977–78) 'Africa: The challenge to the West', *RUSI & Brassey's Defence Yearbook*.

CLARKE, I. F. (1966) *Voices Prophesying War, 1763–1984* (Oxford University Press).

CLARKE, M. (1982) *The Nuclear Destruction of Britain* (Croom Helm).

CLARKE, R. (1968) *We All Fall Down: The prospects of biological and chemical warfare* (Allen Lane).

CLAUSEWITZ, K. VON (1976) *On War*, (M. Howard & P. Paret, eds) (Princeton University Press).

CLOSE, R. (1979) *Europe without Defense?* (New York: Pergamon).

COKER, C. (1984) 'Naked Emperors: The British Labour Party and Defence', *Strategic Review*, Fall.

COKER, C. (1985) 'The Peace Movement and its Impact upon Public Opinion', *Strategic Review*, Winter.

CONQUEST, R. (1979) *Towards a Foreign Policy* (Oxford: Blackwell).

COWLEY, J. (1960) 'Future Trends in Warfare', *RUSI Journal*, Feb.

COX, J. (1977) *Overkill: The story of modern weapons* (Harmondsworth: Penguin).

CRITCHLEY, J. (1977) 'The Military Quandary of the Atlantic Alliance', *Army Quarterly*, July.

CROZIER, B. (1970) *We Will Bury You: Studies in left-wing subversion today* (Tom Stacey).

CROZIER, B. (ed.) (1978) *Strategy of Survival* (Temple Smith).

DANIEL, D. (ed.) (1978) *International Perceptions of the Superpower Military Balance* (New York: Praeger).

DEIGHTON, L. (1978) *SS–GB: Nazi-occupied Britain, 1941* (Jonathan Cape).

DE KADT, E. J. (1964) *British Defence Policy and Nuclear War* (Frank Cass).

DINTER, E. and GRIFFITH, P. (1983) *Not Over by Christmas: NATO's Central Front in World War III* (Chichester: Antony Bird).

DONNELLY, C. N. (1981) 'Civil Defence: A view for 1981', *RUSI & Brassey's Defence Yearbook*.

DONNELLY, C. N. (1983) 'The Military Significance of the Polish Crisis', *RUSI & Brassey's Defence Yearbook*.

DRIVER, C. (1964) *The Disarmers: A study in protest* (Hodder & Stoughton).

ECOLOGY PARTY (ed.) (1980) *How to Survive the Nuclear Age: What the government will not tell you!* (Ecology Party).

EHRLICH, A. (1984) 'Nuclear Winter', *BOAS*, April.

EICHENBERG, R. C. (1983) 'The myth of Hollanditis', *International Security*, Fall.

EILTS, H. F. (1980) 'Security Considerations in the Persian Gulf, *International Security*, Fall.

ELLIS, J. (1980) *The Sharp End of War: The fighting man in World War II* (Newton Abbot: David & Charles).

ENGLAND, B. (1981) *Nuclear Disarmament for Britain: Why we need action not words* (CND).

ENGLISH, R. (1984) 'Eastern Europe's Doves', *Foreign Policy*, Fall.

ERICKSON, J. (1975) 'Soviet Military Capabilities in Europe', *RUSI Journal*, March.

ERICKSON, J. (1976) 'Soviet Ground Forces and the Conventional Mode of Operations, *RUSI Journal*, June.

ERNLE-ERLE-DRAX, R. A. R. P. (1955) 'World War III: Some Pros and Cons', *RUSI Journal*, May.

EUROPEAN SECURITY STUDY (1983) *Strengthening Conventional Deterrence in Europe: Proposals for the 1980s* (Macmillan).

FLYNN, G. (ed.) (1981) *The Internal Fabric of Western Security* (Totowa: Allanheld, Osmun & Co.).

FLYNN, G. and RATTINGER, H. (eds) (1985) *The Public and Atlantic Defense* (Croom Helm for the Atlantic Institute for International Affairs).

FOOT, P. (1983) *The Protesters* (Aberdeen University Centre for Defence Studies).

FORD, D. (1985) *The Button* (New York: Simon & Schuster).

FRANK, J. D. (1968) *Sanity and Survival* (Barrie & Rockcliff).

FRANKEL, J. (1975) *British Foreign Policy, 1945–1973* (Oxford University Press for RIIA).

FREEDMAN, D., PISANI, R. and PURVES, R. (1978) *Statistics* (New York: Norton).

FREEDMAN, L. (1978) 'European Security: The prospect of change', *RUSI Journal*, Mar.

FREEDMAN, L. (1980) *Britain and Nuclear Weapons* (Macmillan for RIIA).

FREEDMAN, L. (1981) 'Strategic Weapons in the 1980s' *RUSI & Brassey's Defence Yearbook*.

FREEDMAN, L. (1981/2) 'NATO Myths', *Foreign Policy*, Winter.

FREEDMAN, L. (1982) 'Limited War, Unlimited Protest', *Orbis*, Spring.

FREEDMAN, L. (1982) *The Evolution of Nuclear Strategy* (Macmillan for IISS).

FREEDMAN, L. (1984) 'Weapons, Doctrines and Arms Control', *Washington Quarterly*, Spring.

GASKELL. R. (1981) *Nuclear Weapons: The way ahead* (Menard Press).

GIBBON, E. (J. B. Bury ed.) (1909) *The History of the Decline and Fall of the Roman Empire*, (Methuen).

GINSBURGS, G. and RUBINSTEIN, A. Z. (eds) *Soviet Foreign Policy towards Western Europe* (New York: Praeger).

GOETZ, W. (1982) *Apocalypse Next* (Eastbourne: Kingsway).

GOLDMANN, K. (1974) *Tension and Detente in Bipolar Europe* (Stockholm: Swedish Institute of International Affairs).

GOLDMANN, K. and LAGERKRANZ, J. (1977) *East/West Tension in Europe, 1971–1975* (Stockholm: Swedish Institute of International Affairs).

GOOCH, J. (1974) *The Plans of War – The General Staff and British military strategy, c.1900–1916* (Routledge & Kegan Paul).

GOOCH, J. (1981) *The Prospect of War – Studies in British defence policy* (Frank Cass).

GOODWIN, P. (1982) *Nuclear War: The Facts* (Papermac).

GRAHAM, D. (1979) *Down to a Sunless Sea* (Robert Hale).

GRAY, C. S. and PAYNE, K. (1980) 'Victory is Possible', *Foreign Policy*, Summer.

GREENE, O. *et al.* (1982) *London after the Bomb – What a nuclear attack really means* (Oxford University Press).

GREENWOOD, D. (1972) *Budgeting for Defence* (RUSI).

GREER, H. (1964) *Mud Pie – The CND Story* (Max Parrish).

GREGORY, F., IMBER, M. and SIMPSON, J. (eds) (1975) *Perspectives upon British Defence Policy, 1945–70* (Southampton University).

GREY, LORD (1925) *Twenty-five Years, 1892–1916* (New York: Frederick & Stokes).

GRIFFITHS, F. and POLANYI, J. C. (1979) *The Dangers of Nuclear War* (Toronto University Press).

GROOM, A. J. R. (1974) *British Thinking about Nuclear Weapons* (Frances Pinter).

GUTTERIDGE, W. (ed.) (1982) *European Security, Nuclear Weapons and Public Confidence* (Macmillan).

GWYNNE-JONES, A. (1958) 'The Nature of the Communist Threat', *RUSI Journal*, Nov.

HACKETT, J. (1963) 'The Profession of Arms', *Survival*, Jan/Feb.

HACKETT, J. *et al.* (1978) *The Third World War: August 1985. A future history* (Sidgwick & Jackson).

HACKETT, J. *et al.* (1982) *The Third World War: The Untold Story* (Sidgwick & Jackson).

HALLE, L. J. (1967) *The Cold War as History* (Chatto & Windus).

HANNING, H. (1970) 'Defence and British Public Opinion', *Brassey's Annual*.

HARBOTTLE, M. (1981) 'Reactions from Europe to the Neutron Bomb', *BOAS*, Oct.

HARDY, T. (1919) *The Dynasts* (Macmillan).

HARRIES-JENKINS, G. (ed.) (1982) *Armed Forces and the Welfare Societies: Challenges in the 1980s* (Macmillan for IISS).

HARRIS, R. and PAXMAN, J. (1982) *A Higher Form of Killing – The secret story of gas and germ warfare* (Chatto & Windus).

HEALEY, D. (1958) 'The Sputnik and Western Defence', *International Affairs*, Apr.

HEALEY, D. (1962) 'The Crisis in Europe', *International Affairs*, Apr.

HEALEY, D. (1969) 'On European Defence', *Survival*, Apr.

HEALEY, D. (1969) 'British Defence Policy', *RUSI Journal*, Dec.

HEATH, E. (1980) 'The Role of Western Military Power in the World Today', *RUSI Journal*, June.

HEATH, E. (1980) 'The 1980 Alastair Buchan Memorial Lecture', *Survival*, Sept/Oct.

HILL, C. (1982) *The Day Comes – A prophetic view of the contemporary world* (Fount paperbacks).

HILL-NORTON, P. (1978) *No Soft Options: The politico-military realities of NATO* (Hurst & Co.).

HILL-NORTON, LORD (1982) 'An Anatomy of Defence Policy', *RUSI & Brassey's Defence Yearbook*.

HINSLEY, F. H. (1963) *Power and the Pursuit of Peace* (Cambridge University Press).

HOLLOWAY, D. (1984) *The Soviet Union and the Arms Race*, 2nd edn. (Yale University Press).

HOLM, H. H. and PETERSEN, N. (eds) (1983) *The European Missiles Crisis: Nuclear weapons and security policy* (New York: St Martin's Press).

HOLST, J. J. and NEHRLICH, U. (eds) (1977) *Beyond Nuclear Deterrence: New aims, new arms* (New York: Crane, Russack & Co.).

HOME, LORD (1976) *The Way the Wind Blows* (Collins).

HOME OFFICE (1974) *Nuclear Weapons* (HMSO).
HOME OFFICE (1980) *Protect and Survive* (HMSO).
HOME OFFICE (1981) *Domestic Nuclear Shelters* (HMSO).
HOWARD, M. (1957) 'Strategy in the Nuclear Age', *RUSI Journal*, Nov.
HOWARD, M. (1958) *Disengagement in Europe* (Harmondsworth: Penguin).
HOWARD, M. (ed.) (1965) *The Theory and Practice of War* (Cassell).
HOWARD, M. (1970) *Studies of War and Peace* (Temple Smith).
HOWARD, M. (1972) 'The Transformation of Strategy', *Brassey's Annual*.
HOWARD, M. (1973) 'The Relevance of Traditional Strategy', *Foreign Affairs*, Jan.
HOWARD, M. (1974) 'Military Science in an Age of Peace', *RUSI Journal*, Mar.
HOWARD, M. (1976) *War in European History* (Oxford University Press).
HOWARD, M. (1978) *War and the Liberal Conscience* (Temple Smith).
HOWARD, M. (ed.) (1979) *Restraints on War: Studies in the limitation of armed conflict* (Oxford University Press).
HOWARD, M. (1980) 'Return to the Cold War?', *Foreign Affairs, America and the World*.
HOWARD, M. (1983) *The Causes of Wars, and other essays* (Temple Smith).
HOWE, G. (1985) 'Defence and Security in the Nuclear Age', *RUSI Journal*, June.
HOWE, R. W. (1981) *Weapons: The international game of arms, money and diplomacy* (Sphere).
HOWORTH, J. and CHILTON, P. (eds) (1984) *Defence and Dissent in Contemporary France* (Croom Helm).
HUNTINGTON, S. P. (1983/4) 'Conventional Deterrence and Conventional Retaliation in Europe', *International Security*, Winter.
IKLE, F. C. (1971) *Every War Must End* (New York: Columbia University Press).
JOHNSON, R. H. (1983) 'Periods of Peril: The Window of Vulnerability and other Myths', *International Security*, Spring.
JOYCE, J. A. (1981) *The War Machine – The case against the arms race* (Hamlyn Paperbacks).
KAHLER, M. (1979/80) 'Rumors of War: The 1914 analogy', *Foreign Affairs*, Winter.
KAHN, H. (1960) *On Thermo-Nuclear War* (Princeton University Press).
KAHN, H. (1962) *Thinking about the Unthinkable* (Weidenfeld & Nicolson).
KALDOR, M. (1978) *The Disintegrating West* (New York: Hill & Wang).
KALDOR, M., SMITH, D. and VINES, S. (eds) (1979) *Democratic Socialism and the Cost of Defence – The report and papers of the Labour Party defence study group* (Croom Helm).
KALDOR, M. (1981) 'END can be a beginning', *BOAS*, Dec.
KALDOR, M. and SMITH, D. (eds) (1982) *Disarming Europe* (Merlin Press).
KAPLAN, F. (1983) *The Wizards of Armageddon* (New York: Simon & Schuster).
KENNEDY, R. F. (1968) *Thirteen Days* (Macmillan).
KERMODE, F. (1967) *The Sense of an Ending* (New York: Oxford University Press).
KIDRON, M. and SMITH, D. (1983) *The War Atlas: Armed conflict – Armed Peace* (Pan).
KING-HALL, S. (1958) *Defence in the Nuclear Age* (Gollancz).

KINGSTON-McCLOUGHRY, E. J. (1957) *Global Strategy* (Jonathan Cape).
KINGSTON-McCLOUGHRY, E. J. (1960) *Defence – Policy and Strategy* (Stevens & Sons).
KINGSTON-McCLOUGHRY, E. J. (1964) *The Spectrum of Strategy: A study of policy and strategy in modern war* (Jonathan Cape).
KISSINGER, H. (1979) *The White House Years* (Weidenfeld & Nicolson and Michael Joseph).
KOENIG, W. J. (1981) *Weapons of World War 3* (Hamlyn).
KULL, S. (1985) 'Nuclear Nonsense', *Foreign Policy*, Spring.
LABOUR PARTY DEFENCE STUDY GROUP (1977) *Sense about Defence* (Quartet).
LANGFORD, D. (1979) *War in 2080: The future of military technology* (Newton Abbot: Westbridge).
LAURIE, P. (1979) *Beneath the City Streets* (Granada).
LE BAILLY, L. (1976–77) 'The Need for NATO Maritime Forces', *RUSI & Brassey's Defence Yearbook*.
LEBOW, R. N. (1984) 'Windows of Opportunity: Do states jump through them?' *International Security*, Summer.
LE CHEMINANT, P. (1959) 'Soviet Military Doctrine: A possible pattern of war', *Brassey's Annual*.
LE CHEMINANT, P. (1960) 'War in the next Ten Years?' *Brassey's Annual*.
LE CHEMINANT, P. (1962) 'Some Pitfalls of Conventional Rearmament', *Brassey's Annual*.
LEE, C. (1981) *The Final Decade – Will we survive the 1980s?* (Hamish Hamilton).
LEEBAERT, D. (ed.) (1979) *European Security: Prospects for the 1980s* (Lexington: Lexington Books).
LEE WILLIAMS, G. and LEE WILLIAMS, A. (1974) *Crisis in European Defence: The next ten years* (Charles Knight).
LIDDELL HART, B. H. (1937) *Europe in Arms* (Faber & Faber).
LIDDELL HART, B. H. (1960) *Deterrent or Defence* (Stevens).
LONGMATE, N. (1975) *If Britain had fallen* (Arrow).
LUKACS, J. (1976) *The Last European War: September 1939/December 1941* (Routledge & Kegan Paul).
LUTTWAK, E. N. (1976) *The Grand Strategy of the Roman Empire from the First Century AD to the Third* (Baltimore: Johns Hopkins University Press).
McALLISTER, G. (ed.) (1955) *The Bomb: Challenge and Answer* (B. T. Batsford).
MACDONALD, I. O. (1981) *Faslane: Facts and Feelings* (Edinburgh: Church of Scotland).
MACKINTOSH, J. M. (1960) 'Soviet Strategy in World War III', *Survival*, July/Aug.
MACKINTOSH, J. M. (1972) *Strategy and Tactics of Soviet Foreign Policy* (Oxford University Press).
MACMILLAN, H. (1971) *Riding the Storm, 1956–59* (Macmillan).
MACMILLAN, H. (1972) *Pointing the Way, 1959–61* (Macmillan).
MACMILLAN, H. (1973) *At the End of the Day, 1961–63* (Macmillan).
MADDOX, J. (1972) *The Doomsday Syndrome* (Macmillan).
MADGE, C. and HARRISON, T. (eds) (1939) *Britain by Mass Observation* (Harmondsworth: Penguin).

MADGE, C. and HARRISON, T. (eds) (1940) *Mass Observation: War Begins at Home* (Chatto & Windus).

MANDELBAUM, M. (1981) *The Nuclear Revolution* (Cambridge University Press).

MARSHALL, A. and RENWICK, D. (1982) *Whoops Apocalypse* (Unwin).

MARTIN, L. (1969) *British Defence Policy: The long recessional*, Adelphi Paper 61 (IISS).

MARTIN, L. (ed.) (1979) *Strategic Thought in the Nuclear Age* (Heinemann).

MARTIN, L. (1982) *The Two-Edged Sword: Armed Force in the Modern World* (Weidenfeld & Nicolson).

MAY, E. R. (1973) *Lessons of the Past: The use and misuse of history in American foreign policy* (New York: Oxford University Press).

MEARSHEIMER, J. J. (1982) 'Why the Soviets can't win quickly in Central Europe', *International Security*, Summer.

MEDICAL CAMPAIGN AGAINST NUCLEAR WEAPONS (1981) *The Medical Consequences of Nuclear Weapons* (Medical Campaign against Nuclear Weapons & Medical Association for the Prevention of War).

MERRITT, R. L. and PUCHALA, D. J. (eds) (1968) *Western European Perspectives on International Affairs* (New York: Praeger).

MIKSCHE, F. O. (1952) *Unconditional Surrender: The roots of a World War III* (Faber & Faber).

MINISTRY OF DEFENCE (1980) *The Future United Kingdon Strategic Nuclear Deterrent Force*, Defence Open Government Document 80/23 (MOD).

MINNION, J. and BOLSOVER, P. (1983) *The CND Story* (Allison & Busby).

MONCKTON, LORD (1968) 'Forward Strategy in Germany', *RUSI Journal*, Feb.

MONTGOMERY, LORD (1954) 'A Look through a Window at World War III', *RUSI Journal*, Nov.

MONTGOMERY, LORD (1956) 'The Panorama of Warfare in a Nuclear Age', *RUSI Journal*, Nov.

MONTGOMERY, LORD (1959) *An Approach to Sanity* (Collins).

MORGAN, C. (1980) *The Shape of Futures Past: The story of prediction* (Exeter: Webb & Bower).

MOSER, C. A. and KALTON, G. (1971) *Survey Methods in Social Investigation*, 2nd edn (Heinemann).

MOSS, N. (1968) *Men who play God: The story of the hydrogen bomb* (Gollancz).

MOULTON, J. L. (1964) *Defence in a Changing World* (Eyre & Spotiswoode).

MOULTON, J. L. (1970) 'Convulsive War and Prolonged Confrontation', *Brassey's Annual*.

MOUNTBATTEN, LORD, ZUCKERMAN, LORD, and NOEL-BAKER, LORD (1980) *Apocalypse Now?* (Nottingham: Spokesman).

MULLEY, F. W. (1962) *The Politics of Western Defence* (Thames & Hudson).

MYERS, K. A. (ed.) (1980) *NATO: The next thirty years* (Boulder, Col.: Westview Press).

NAILOR, P. and ALFORD, J. (1980) *The Future of Britain's Deterrent Force*, Adelphi Paper 156 (IISS).

NEILD, R. (1981) *How to make up your mind about the Bomb* (Andre Deutsch).

NEW LEFT REVIEW (ed.) (1982) *Exterminism and Cold War* (Verso).

NEWMAN, B. and DANDO, M. (eds) (1982) *Nuclear Deterrence: Implications and Policy Options for the 1980s* (Tunbridge Wells: Castle House).

NIXON, R. (1980) *The Real War* (Sidgwick & Jackson).

NOEL-BAKER, P. (1958) *The Arms Race* (Atlantic).

NOEL-BAKER, P. (1978) 'A message for all nations', *BOAS*, May.

NORTHEDGE, F. S. (ed.) (1974) *The Use of Force in International Relations* (Faber & Faber).

OPENSHAW, S., STEADMAN, P. and GREENE, O. (1983) *Doomsday: Britain after nuclear attack* (Oxford: Blackwell).

OSGOOD, R. E. (1979) *Limited War Revisited* (Boulder, Col.: Westview Press).

OSKAMP, S. (1977) *Attitudes and Opinions* (New Jersey: Prentice-Hall).

OWEN, D. (1972) *The Politics of Defence* (Jonathan Cape).

OWEN, D. (1980) *Negotiate and Survive* (Campaign for Labour Victory).

PALME, O. (1982) (Chairman) *Common Security – A programme for Disarmament*, The report of the Independent Commission on Disarmament and Security Issues (Pan).

PEETERS, P. (1979) *Can we avoid a Third World War around 2010?* (Macmillan).

PENTZ, M. (1976) *The Nuclear Arms Race* (British Peace Committee).

PENTZ, M. (1980) *Towards the Final Abyss?* (J.D. Bernal Peace Library).

PERLMUTTER, A. and GOOCH, J. (eds) (1981) *Strategy and the Social Sciences: Issues in defence policy* (Frank Cass).

PERRY ROBINSON, J. P. (1983) 'Recent Developments in the field of Chemical Warfare', *RUSI & Brassey's Defence Yearbook*.

PIERRE, A. J. (1972) *Nuclear Politics: The British experience with an independent strategic force, 1939–1970* (Oxford University Press).

PIERRE, A. J. (ed.) (1984) *Nuclear Weapons in Europe* (New York: Council on Foreign Relations).

POCOCK, T. (1973) *Fighting General: The public and private campaigns of General Sir Walter Walker* (Collins).

PONOMAREV, B. (1981) *The War Danger: Its source and how to stop it* (Moscow: Novosti Press Agency).

POPKESS, B. (1980) *The Nuclear Survival Handbook – Living through and after a nuclear attack* (Arrow).

POSEN, B. R. (1982) 'Escalation and NATO's Northern Flank', *International Security*, Fall.

POWELL, E. (1967) 'An Army in Being', *RUSI Journal*, Aug.

PRIESTLAND, G. (1974) *The Future of Violence* (Hamish Hamilton).

PRINGLE, P. and ARKIN, W. (1983) *SIOP: Nuclear war from the inside* (Sphere).

PRINS, G. (ed.) (1983) *Defended to Death – a study of the nuclear arms race* (Harmondsworth: Penguin).

PYM, F. (1981) 'The Nuclear Element for British Defence Policy', *RUSI Journal*, June.

PYM, F. (1982) 'Defence in Democracies: The public dimension', *International Security*, Summer.

REED, B. and WILLIAMS, G. (1971) *Denis Healey and the Policies of Power* (Sidgwick & Jackson).

REPINGTON, C. (1920) *The First World War, 1914–18: Personal Experiences*, vol. II (Constable & Co.).

RICHARDSON, F. M. (1981) *The Public and the Bomb* (Edinburgh: William Blackwood).

RICHARDSON, L. F. (ed. Q. Wright and C. C. Lienau) (1960) *The Statistics of Deadly Quarrels*, (Stevens & Sons).

RIPPON, G. (1981) 'The Global Threat to the West', *RUSI & Brassey's Defence Yearbook*.

ROBERTSON, E. M. (ed.) (1971) *The origins of the Second World War: Historical Interpretations* (Macmillan).

ROBINSON, A. (1983) *Aircraft of World War 3* (Hamlyn).

RODGERS, W. (1981) 'Yes to Cruise, No to Trident', *RUSI Journal*, March.

ROGERS, B. W. (1982) 'The Atlantic Alliance: Prescriptions for a difficult decade', *Foreign Affairs*, Summer.

ROGERS, P., DANDO, M. and VAN DEN DUNGEN, P. (1981) *As Lambs to the Slaughter: The facts about nuclear war* (Arrow).

ROSECRANCE, R. N. (1968) *Defense of the Realm: British Strategy in the Nuclear Epoch* (Columbia University Press).

ROSHWALD, M. (1959) *Level 7* (Heinemann).

ROTBLAT, J. (1981) 'The Threat Today', *BOAS*, Jan.

ROUCH, J. (1980) *The Zone*, several vols, (New English Library).

ROYAL UNITED SERVICES INSTITUTE (1982) *Nuclear Attack: Civil Defence* (Oxford: Brassey's Publishers).

RUSSELL, B. (1959) *Common Sense and Nuclear Warfare* (George Allen & Unwin).

RUSSELL, B. (1962) 'The Case for British Nuclear Disarmament', *BOAS*, Mar.

RUSSELL, B. (1963) *Unarmed Victory* (George Allen & Unwin).

RUSSELL, B. (1969) *Autobiography*, vol. III (George Allen & Unwin).

RUSSETT, B. (1981/82) 'Security and the Resources Scramble: will 1984 be like 1914?', *International Affairs*, Winter.

SAGAN, C. (1981) *Cosmos* (Macdonald).

SAGAN, C. (1983/84) 'Nuclear War and Climatic Catastrophe: Some policy implications', *Foreign Affairs*, Winter.

SALISBURY, BISHOP OF (Chairman) (1982) *The Church and the Bomb: Nuclear weapons and Christian conscience* (Hodder & Stoughton).

SANDERS, J. W. (1983) *Peddlers of Crisis: The Committee on the Present Danger and the politics of containment* (Boston: South End Press).

SAUNDBY, R. (1958) 'The Royal Air Force in the Atomic Age', *Brassey's Annual*.

SCHELL, J. (1982) *The Fate of the Earth* (Pan).

SCHLESINGER, A. M. (1965) *A Thousand Days: John F. Kennedy in the White House* (Andre Deutsch).

SEGAL, G. *et al.* (1983) *Nuclear War and Nuclear Peace* (Macmillan).

SHUTE, N. (1957) *On the Beach* (Heinemann).

SIBLEY, C. B. (1977) *Surviving Doomsday* (Shaw & Sons).

SKAGGS, D. C. (1983) *Michael Howard: Military Historian and Strategic Analyst* (US Army War College, Carlisle Barracks, Pennsylvania).

SKED, A. and COOK, C. (eds) (1976) *Crisis and Controversy: Essays in Honour of A. J. P. Taylor* (Macmillan).

SLESSOR, J. (1954) *Strategy for the West* (Cassell).

SLESSOR, J. (1957) *The Great Deterrent* (Cassell).

SLESSOR, J. (1962) *What Price Coexistence?* (Cassell).

SLUSSER, R. M. (1973) *The Berlin Crisis of 1961* (Baltimore: Johns Hopkins University Press).

SMART, I. (1975) 'The Great Engines: The rise and decline of a nuclear age', *International Affairs*, Oct.

SMITH, D. (1980) *The Defence of the Realm in the 1980s* (Croom Helm).

SNYDER, W. P. (1964) *The Politics of British Defence Policy, 1945–62* (Ohio State University Press).

SOCIALIST PARTY OF GREAT BRITAIN (1982) *Is a Third World War Inevitable?* (Socialist Party of Great Britain).

SOLZHENITSYN, A. (1978) *Warning to the Western World* (Bodley Head).

SOLZHENITSYN, A. (1978) *Alexander Solzhenitsyn speaks to the West* (Bodley Head).

SORENSEN, T. C. (1965) *Kennedy* (Hodder & Stoughton).

STEINBERG, J. (1965) *Yesterday's Deterrent: Tirpitz and the birth of the German battle fleet* (Macdonald).

STOCKHOLM INTERNATIONAL PEACE RESEARCH INSTITUTE (1977) *World Armaments: The nuclear threat* (Stockholm: SIPRI).

STRACHEY, J. (1962) *On the Prevention of War* (Macmillan).

SUNDAY TIMES INSIGHT TEAM (1974) *Insight on the Middle East War* (André Deutsch).

SUNDAY TIMES INSIGHT TEAM (1982) *The Falklands War* (Sphere).

SZABO, S. (ed.) (1983) *The Successor Generation: International perspectives of post-war Europeans* (Butterworth).

TAYLOR, A. J. P. (1961) *The Origins of the Second World War* (Hamish Hamilton).

TAYLOR, A. J. P. (1965) *English History, 1914–1945* (Oxford University Press).

TAYLOR, A. J. P. (1969) *War by Time-Table: How the First World War began* (Macdonald).

TAYLOR, A. J. P. (1979) *How Wars Begin* (Hamish Hamilton).

TAYLOR, R. and PRITCHARD, C. (1980) *The Protest Makers: The British nuclear disarmament movement of 1958–1965, twenty years on* (Oxford: Pergamon).

THATCHER, M. (1977) *Let Our Children Grow Tall* (Centre for Policy Studies).

THATCHER, M. (1980) 'British Foreign Policy', *Survival*, Mar/Apr.

THOMAS, H. (1966) *The Suez Affair* (Weidenfeld & Nicolson).

THOMPSON, E. P. and SMITH, D. (eds) *Protest and Survive* (Harmondsworth: Penguin).

THOMPSON, E. P. (1982) *Beyond the Cold War* (END & Merlin Press).

THOMPSON, R. (1974) *Peace is Not at Hand* (Chatto & Windus).

THOMPSON, R. (ed.) (1981) *War in Peace: An analysis of warfare since 1945* (Orbis).

THOMPSON, W. K. F. (1971) 'Britain's Strategic Reserves', *Brassey's Annual*.

THOMPSON, W. S. (1982) 'The Persian Gulf and the Correlation of Forces', *International Security*, Summer.

TOWLE, P. (1981) 'The Strategy of War by Proxy', *RUSI Journal*, March.

TREVOR-ROPER, H. R. (1961) 'A. J. P. Taylor, Hitler and the War, *Encounter*, July.

TROMP, H. W. and LA ROCQUE, G. R. (eds) (1982) *Nuclear War in Europe* (Groningen University Press).

TUCHMAN, B. (1962) *The Guns of August* (New York: Macmillan).

TUCKER, A. and GLEISNER, J. (1982) *Crucible of Despair: the effects of nuclear war* (Menard Press).

VEGETIUS (1767) translated by J. Clarke *Military Institutions*, (Private publication).

VERRIER, A. (1966) *An Army for the Sixties: A study in national policy, contract and obligation* (Secker & Warburg).

VIGOR, P. H. (1975) *The Soviet View of War, Peace and Neutrality* (Routledge & Kegan Paul).

VIGOR, P. H. (1980) 'Doubts and Difficulties confronting a would-be Soviet attacker', *RUSI Journal*, June.

VIGOR, P. H. (1983) *Soviet Blitzkrieg Theory* (Macmillan).

WALKER, P. (1975) 'The Opposition's View of British Defence Policy', *RUSI Journal*, June.

WALL, P. (ed.) (1977) *The Southern Oceans and the Security of the Free World* (Stacey International).

WALTZ, K. (1981) *The Spread of Nuclear Weapons: More may be Better*, Adelphi Paper 171 (IISS).

WARGAMES RESEARCH GROUP (1979) *Wargames Rules for Armoured Warfare at Company or Battalion Battle Group Level, 1950–1985* (Worthing: WRG).

WARNER, P. (1980) *Invasion Road* (Cassell).

WASSERMAN, S. L. (1983) *The Neutron Bomb Controversy: A study in alliance politics* (New York: Praeger).

WAY, P. (1979) *Sunrise* (Gollancz).

WILSON, D. (1974) 'Anglo-Soviet Relations: The effect of ideas on reality', *International Affairs*, June.

WILSON, H. (1971) *The Labour Government, 1964–1970: A Personal Record* (Weidenfeld & Nicolson).

WILSON, H. (1979) *Final Term: The Labour Government, 1974–76* (Weidenfeld & Nicolson).

WINGFIELD-STRATFORD, E. (1932) *They that Take the Sword* (Routledge & Sons).

WOLFE, J. N. and ERICKSON, J. (1970) *The Armed Services and Society: Alienation, Management and Integration* (Edinburgh University Press).

WOOD, D. (1976) *Attack Warning Red: The Royal Observer Corps and the Defence of Britain, 1925 to 1975* (Macdonald & Jane's).

ZUCKERMAN, LORD (1982) *Nuclear Illusion and Reality* (Collins).

Reference was also made to the following journals and periodicals:

Daily

Daily Mirror	*Sun*
Daily Telegraph	*The Times*
Guardian	

Weekly

The Listener	*Observer*
New Society	*Sunday Mirror*
New Statesman	*Sunday Telegraph*
Now	*Sunday Times*

Monthly

Bulletin of the Atomic Scientists   *Sanity*
Protect and Survive Monthly

Bimonthly/Quarterly

ADIU Report   *International Security*
Army Quarterly   *Orbis*
Council for Arms Control Bulletin   *RUSI Journal*
Foreign Affairs   *Strategic Review*
Foreign Policy   *Survival*
International Affairs   *Washington Quarterly*

Annual

Brassey's Annual   *The Military Balance*
RUSI & Brassey's Defence Yearbook   *Strategic Survey*

The following official publications were also examined:

Statement on the Defence Estimates
House of Commons Journal
House of Lords Journal
Fifth Report from the Foreign Affairs Committee
Sixth Report from the Expenditure Committee

Finally, opinion poll data was consulted through the files of the following
organisations:

Gallup, 202 Finchley Road, London NW3.
Marplan Limited, Bridgewater House, Great Suffolk Street, London SE1.
NOP Market Research Limited, Tower House, Southampton Street, London
    WC2.
Market & Opinion Research International, 32 Old Queen Street, London SW1.
BBC Broadcasting Research, 254 The Langham, London W1.

Name Index

Acheson, Dean, 91

Baynes, Sir John, 40–1 n7
Bidwell, Shelford, 14, 20, 26
Briggs, Raymond, 38
Brockway, Lord, 51
Brodie, Bernard, 51
Brown, Neville, 8, 25, 76, 99
Buchan, Alastair, 40
Butt, Ronald, 61 n122

Cable, James, 90 n6
Calder, Nigel, 35, 46 n44, 73–4, 79 n77
Callaghan, James, 44, 72
Cameron, Sir Neil, 13 n8, 45
Campbell, Duncan, 37, 91
Carlton, David, 48 n59
Carrington, Lord, 40 n6, 133
Carter, Jimmy, 44, 67
Carver, Lord, 36
Chalfont, Lord, 42–3, 115
Chamberlain, Neville, 36, 55
Chichester, Michael, 30 n99
Clausewitz, Karl von, 14
Conquest, Robert, 75–6 n65
Crozier, Brian, 5, 18–19

Dowding, Sir Hugh, 30
Driver, Christopher, 59

Eden, Sir Anthony, 108
Erickson, John, 95

Feld, Bernard, 50 n66
Foot, Michael, 116
Foxley-Norris, Christopher, 12 n7, 93 n15
Frankel, Joseph, 139–40
Freedman, Lawrence, 5, 35, 71, 80, 84–5

Garnett, John, 32
Gibbon, Edward, 126
Gooch, John, 102 n42
Goodwin, Peter, 85 n98
Gorbachev, Mikhail, 47
Graham, David, 99 n36
Grey, Sir Edward, 107
Greenwood, David, 5

Hackett, Sir John, 2, 14, 26, 29, 34, 42, 81, 102

Haig, Alexander, 33
Hanning, Hugh, 106 n54
Harbottle, Michael, 23
Hardy, Thomas, 81
Healey, Denis, 36 n144, 84 n92
Hepburn, Neil, 38–9
Hill-Norton, Lord, 34 n131, 78 n74
Home, Alex Douglas, 119
Howard, Michael, 5, 16, 40, 42, 70, 83, 87–8, 90, 101–3, 115, 131
Humphrey, Nick, 50, 58–9, 98–9

Joyce, James Avery, 76 n66

Kahn, Herman, 11
Kaldor, Mary, 73 n58
Kennedy, John, 50, 107
Khruschev, Nikita, 53

La Rocque, Gene, 68 n32
Laurie, Peter, 15 n20, 79 n77
Lee, Christopher, 45 n38
Liddell Hart, Basil, 11
Lynn, Vera, 103

Macmillan, Harold, 59, 107–8, 119
Martin, Laurence, 32, 66, 84–5, 126
Maudling, Reginald, 44 n29
May, Ernest, 109
Moulton, James, 18
Mountbatten, Lord, 36–7, 77 n73
Mulley, Fred, 43 n28

Neild, Robert, 60 n119
Nixon, Richard, 4, 20, 40
Nostradamus, 98
Nott, John, 31 n106, 36 n142

Oram, Lord, 106 n55
Owen, David, 41

Pentz, Michael, 8, 69 n36, 76 n65
Pink, Ralph Bonner, 30 n102
Powell, Enoch, 53–4
Pym, Francis, 13 n8

Reagan, Ronald, 45, 47, 67, 98, 116, 119, 131
Rippon, Geoffrey, 53 n88
Robertson, John 33 n123

Subject Index